D0590359

THE COMPLETE BOOK OF

HOME
BAKING

THE COMPLETE BOOK OF
HOME
BAKING
MARY NORWAK

TREASURE PRESS

First published in Great Britain by Ward Lock Ltd

This edition published by Treasure Press
59 Grosvenor Street
London W1
Reprinted 1984

© 1979 Ward Lock Ltd

ISBN 0 907407 79 X

All rights reserved. No part of this publication may be reproduced,
stored in a retrieval system, or transmitted, in any form or by
any means, electronic, mechanical, photocopying or otherwise,
without the prior permission of the Copyright owners.

Printed in Czechoslovakia

50531

Contents

WEIGHTS AND MEASURES

Imperial	US
2½ oz Allbran	1 cup
1 lb apples (diced)	4 cups
2 oz bacon, streaky	3 slices fatty bacon
2 oz bean sprouts	1 cup
4 oz black or redcurrants, blueberries	1 cup
4 oz breadcrumbs (fine dried)	1 cup
2 oz breadcrumbs (fresh soft), cake crumbs	1 cup
8 oz butter, margarine, lard, dripping	1 cup butter, margarine, shortening, drippings
3-4 oz button mushrooms	1 cup
8 oz cabbage (finely chopped)	3 cups
12 oz clear honey, golden syrup, molasses, black treacle	1 cup (1 lb =1⅓ cups) honey, maple syrup, molasses, black treacle
1 oz cooking chocolate	1 square baking chocolate
4½ oz cornflour	1 cup cornstarch
8 oz cottage, cream cheese	1 cup
¼ pint single, double cream	½ cup + 2 tablespoons (⅔ cup) light, heavy cream
2 oz curry powder	½ cup
3 oz desiccated coconut	1 cup shredded coconut
4 oz digestive biscuits (8 biscuits)	1 cup Graham crackers
7 oz dried chick peas, haricot beans	1 cup garbanzos, navy beans
4 oz flour, plain or self-raising	2 tablespoons all-purpose or self-rising flour
½ oz gelatine (1 tablespoon sets 2 cups liquid)	2 envelopes
3 oz preserved ginger (chopped)	⅓ cup
8 oz glacé cherries	1 cup candied cherries
3½ lbs gooseberries	9 cups
4 oz grated cheese, Cheddar type, Parmesan	1 cup
4 oz ground almonds	1 cup
7 oz long-grain rice	1 cup
4 oz macaroni, raw	1 cup
8 oz mashed potato	1 cup
8 oz minced raw meat	1 cup ground raw meat, firmly packed
4 oz nuts (chopped)	1 cup
2 oz onion (chopped)	½ cup
2 oz parsley (chopped)	1½ cups
6 oz pickled beetroot (chopped)	1 cup
6 oz peeled prawns	1 cup peeled shrimp
5-6 oz raisins, currants, sultanas (chopped), candied peel	1 cup (1 lb =3 cups)
5 oz raspberries	1 cup
3½ oz rolled oats	1 cup
8 oz sausagemeat	1 cup
5 oz strawberries, whole	1 cup
8 oz sugar, castor or granulated	1 cup, firmly packed
4 oz sugar, icing (sieved)	1 cup sifted confectioner's sugar
8 oz tomatoes (chopped)	1 cup
2¾ oz (smallest can) tomato purée	¼ cup
4 teaspoons dried yeast	4 teaspoons active dry yeast
¼ pint yoghurt	½ cup + 2 tablespoons (⅔ cup)

Liquid Measurements

20 fluid oz =1 Imperial pint   16 fluid oz =1 American pint

10 fluid oz =½ Imperial pint   8 fluid oz =1 American cup

Introduction

The first bread was baked well over 12,000 years ago, made of coarsely crushed grain mixed with water and baked on a flat heated stone by the fire – the grain was a mixture of whole grains and ground wheat, barley, oats with the seeds of grasses. The ancient Egyptians allowed wheat dough to ferment so that gas formed and the bread was lighter; they also developed baking ovens and many kinds of bread were baked on large estates, the workers being paid in bread and beer.

In Britain, flat bread was baked for centuries, for few houses had ovens attached to their open fireplaces, until late in the eighteenth century. The flat baking stone was improved upon by the use of the girdle or griddle, a flat iron plate which was suspended over the open fire. Something nearer our own method of baking developed with the use of a covered cauldron which contained the dough, and on which heated ashes or turves were placed to give all-round heat. This primitive type of oven is still sometimes used in Ireland and is known as a 'Bastable'.

In medieval times, people took their bread seriously – bread, hard cheese, fat bacon and beer formed the staple diet of the poor, while the rich could enjoy many varieties of fine breads to accompany their meat meals, and used thick slices of four-day old bread as plates. In 1552, at Ingatestone Hall in Essex, more than 20,000 loaves were baked, but in towns and cities, bread was produced by professional bakers. In thirteenth-century London, there were guilds for brown breadmakers and white breadmakers who worked from secret recipes, and in towns most people bought their bread, or took their own bread and pies to the professional baker for finishing.

The earliest cakes derived from simple bread mixtures, and many a housewife made a treat for the children by adding a little extra fat or fruit to surplus bread dough (as in Lardy Cake) or by making simple mixtures of flour and fat with a little precious dried

7

fruit or spice which could be cooked in small portions on the griddle over the fire (such as scones and griddlecakes). In farmhouses and other large houses with ovens, yeast-raised cakes were baked which were like heavily spiced, sweetened and fruited breads, but gradually well-beaten eggs were used to produce lighter cakes. Eighteenth-century recipes often specify three hours' beating to get the right texture for a cake! Other raising agents such as baking powder were not developed until the nineteenth century, and finally halfway through the century, self-raising flour appeared. At last the way was opened to whisking up feather-light cakes with the minimum of effort, and now today's cooks can also enjoy the benefits of mechanical aids to beating.

These developments were obviously employed by the professional baker, and many people found it tiresome or unnecessary to bake at home, but today the wheel has turned full circle, and people are again taking pride in home-baking. This has largely been brought about by the dullness of commercial products, for the individual professional bakers in towns and villages have largely been replaced by factories. The recipes are prepared to give a standard quality and value for money, with a resulting overall blandness so that a product may possibly appeal to the maximum number of people. Those who enjoy crusty loaves, nutty-textured biscuits, feathery sponges, solid fruit cakes and creamy confections have therefore returned to the kitchen stove, and found an astonishing amount of enjoyment in home-baking.

Many people find baking bread or cakes is therapeutic and relaxing, and the results are undoubtedly satisfying for both cook and consumer. Baking is a happy combination of science and art – no other kind of cooking needs such careful attention to detail in measuring, mixing and baking, yet the results are often an edible work of art, sadly ephemeral. The recipes in this book have been tested and eaten by my family for many years with great satisfaction, and I hope you will enjoy making them as much as we do. Not long ago, a cookery student said to me 'I don't see how your recipes can possibly work – they're too easy', but she found that she could get beautiful results with amazing ease, and that is how I hope you find them. Just follow each simple instruction carefully, and you will really enjoy baking – I must confess it is my favourite kind of cooking.

1 Breadmaking Methods

Before starting the recipes, it is a good idea to study the ingredients for breadmaking, and the methods of using them. It is then possible even for the beginner to achieve success right from the start.

Apart from the food ingredients, little equipment is necessary. A large mixing bowl is important to allow for the expansion of the dough. An old china washing bowl, or a polythene washing-up bowl are ideal, and help to keep the dough warm. A large wooden spoon or spatula is useful for stirring in and mixing before kneading, but a dough hook on an electric mixer will serve to both mix and knead. Large baking sheets are useful for hand-made loaves, rolls and buns, but loaf tins and cake tins are needed for some recipes. These are best if really thick, solid and old-fashioned (they are often found at jumble sales), and should not be washed, but only wiped dry and clean. Lard or oil can be used for greasing them.

INGREDIENTS

Yeast

Yeast is a traditional raising agent which was universally used until about 100 years ago, when chemical raising agents became common. Yeast cookery has many advantages. The yeast adds B vitamins (essential for energy) to the baked goods. Yeast cookery opens up a new range of recipes not only for bread but cakes, puddings and batters. It is economical because smaller quantities of fat and sugar are used and it gives a big yield. Use fresh or dried but not brewer's yeast, autolysed or tonic yeast.

Fresh yeast is quick and easy to use but it is becoming much more difficult to buy. It should be creamy in colour, cool to touch and easy to break. To keep it fresh, store in a loosely tied polythene bag in a cold place. It will keep 4–5 days. Fresh yeast can be stored in a refrigerator for up to a month or a freezer for six months.

Dried yeast is a great convenience because it will keep up to six months if stored in a tightly lidded tin in a cool place. If there is much air space in the tin it will not keep so well. It is available in 100g/4oz tins or 25g/1oz packets from many grocers, chemists and health food stores.

Remember:

(25g/1oz fresh yeast or 15g/½oz dried yeast)

Yeast quantities vary according to the type of dough: allow 25g/1oz fresh yeast or 15g/½oz dried yeast to 1.5kg/3lb strong plain white flour; 50g/2oz fresh yeast or 25g/1oz dried yeast to 1.5kg/3lb wholemeal flour is an average quantity.

In enriched recipes which contain extra fat, sugar, eggs or fruit, the growth of yeast is retarded and additional yeast should be used.

Flour

Flours vary in composition and broadly speaking, are defined according to their rate of extraction. Extraction rate of flour means the percentage of the whole grain that remains in the flour after milling. *Wholemeal flours* contain the whole of the cleaned wheatgrain – nothing must be added or taken away. *Brown or wheatmeal flours* usually contain 80–90% of the cleaned wheatgrain.

White flours usually contain 70–72% of the cleaned wheatgrain although lower extraction flour can be produced. 'Patent' flours for example, are top grade white flours containing only 40–50% of the wholegrain and therefore only a trace of bran so that they are very white in colour. Patent flours give the best cooking results and are more expensive to buy; only a small proportion of the total flour produced is Patent grade.

The bran and germ which give wholemeal/brown flour its

colour are removed when white flour is milled (although sometimes a little remains). These products normally go into 'wheatfeed', the by-product of flour milling used for animal food, but occasionally they may be used for proprietary bran or wheatgerm products.

Wholemeal or brown flours give variety in colour and flavour to cooking. Because they contain all, or a high proportion of, the bran and germ in the wheatgrain, baked goods made with these flours have a limited rise and closer texture than those made with white flours.

White Flour

For best results choose a strong plain flour called bread flour by bakers. Strong flour absorbs more liquid and develops quickly with kneading into a firm elastic dough giving a larger volume and a lighter texture when baked into bread. A soft flour absorbs less liquid, gives a smaller volume and a closer, shorter texture.

Brown Flour

The types of bread made with brown flour vary in name:
Wholemeal A true wholemeal is made from flour from the whole wheatgrain. It has a close texture and a good nutty flavour. The loaves are often sprinkled with cracked wheat and may be shaped as cobs, pots and batons.
Stoneground Wholemeal Bread The flour for this type of loaf is ground between stones instead of metal rollers. It has the same nutritive value as wholemeal bread.
Wheatgerm Bread Tin shape, made from white or brown flour with wheatgerm added. It is usually sold under proprietary names.

Rye, Barley and Oats

These were traditional ingredients in British breads, but are now seldom used. Barley and oats are not suitable for yeast-raised breads, but are used for some griddle breads raised with baking powder or bicarbonate of soda. Rye can be used with yeast and produces a slightly tough, sour-tasting bread which provides a good basis for sandwiches and gives a delicious contrast of texture and flavour when used with meat, fish and cheese. Rye bread can be neatly sliced and the slight toughness encourages chewing and thus helps keep the teeth in good trim. A few recipes using these different flours (obtainable from health food shops) are given, mainly in the chapter on foreign breads.

Salt

This gives flavour to yeasted goods, and prevents the yeast from fermenting too quickly. Too much salt kills the yeast.

Sugar

This is a food for yeast and used to be used to cream yeast. A high concentration of sugar tends to kill some of the yeast cells which in turn causes the very yeasty flavour sometimes associated with home-made bread. Natural brown sugar gives an excellent flavour. It is now considered better to cream yeast with liquid.

Fat

This enriches doughs, increases loaf volume, improves the softness and colour of the crumb and delays staling. When fat is melted before using, it should be cooled before adding to other ingredients.

Liquid

This may be milk, water or a mixture of both. Quantity varies depending on the flour, and the recipe. Slightly less than 300ml/½ pint liquid to 450g/1lb strong flour is a useful guide. Soft flour will take less. Add all the liquid at once. Extra flour can be added if the dough is too soft to handle easily. Milk adds extra food value and strengthens doughs, improving the keeping quality and crust colour. Lukewarm liquid keeps the yeast working.

Eggs, Soya Flour, Dried Fruits, Malt

These can be added to doughs to increase food value and make richer and varied goods. Malt is an improver but too much makes doughs very sticky.

BASIC BREADMAKING METHODS

Method of Adding Yeast to the Flour

For all yeast recipes you have a choice of ways of adding the yeast:

1) *Dissolved Yeast Method (or Straight Dough Method)*
For all yeast recipes.
Fresh Yeast Blend the fresh yeast in the liquid and add to the flour to make a dough.
Dried Yeast Dissolve a teaspoon of sugar in the warm liquid (110°F/44°C). Sprinkle dried yeast on top. Leave in a warm place for 10 minutes or until frothy, then add to the dry ingredients to make a dough. A higher temperature is needed to start dried yeast than fresh yeast.

2) *Sponge Batter Method*
Especially good for rich yeast recipes and for dried yeast.
Make a batter with: a third of the flour in the recipe; all the yeast – fresh or dried; all the liquid – warm; and a teaspoon of sugar. No salt should be added at this stage.
Leave until the mixture froths up like a sponge (about 20 minutes).
Then add the rest of the flour, salt and other ingredients such as fruit, and mix to a firm dough.

3) *Rubbing-in Method for Fresh Yeast*
This is the easiest method and is suitable for soft doughs, quick breads and sweet doughs. Rub the yeast into the flour, it is not necessary to break it up completely, add liquid and make a soft dough. Beat well to distribute the yeast evenly.

Kneading Dough

All doughs must be kneaded after mixing. Kneading is necessary to get a good rise and even crumb texture.

To knead by hand Keeping fingers together fold dough towards you then push down and away from you with palm of hand. Give dough a quarter turn and repeat kneading, developing a rocking rhythm. Continue until dough feels elastic, firm and is no longer sticky. It takes about 10 minutes to develop most doughs. *Quick Wheatmeal Bread* takes only 2 minutes.

To knead by mixer Follow manufacturer's instructions for using the dough hook. Place yeast liquid or yeast batter in the mixer bowl, add dry ingredients, turn to lowest speed and mix for 1–2 minutes to form the dough. Increase speed slightly and mix for a further 2 minutes to knead the dough.

Rising Dough

All yeast dough must be risen at least once before baking to allow time for the yeast to work. The dough must be covered during rising to prevent a skin forming on the surface.

Rise dough in a large, lightly oiled polythene bag (tied loosely at the top, allowing enough space for dough to rise), or a large lightly oiled plastic storage container with a lid, or a large bowl inside a large lightly oiled polythene bag. Leave to rise until double in size and dough springs back when pressed gently with a floured finger. The rising time varies with temperature and type of dough and can be chosen to fit in with the day's plans. A warm place gives a quick rise and a refrigerator a slow one. Richer doughs take longer to rise than plain ones, are easier to handle, and give best results when given a slow rise. Always remember to return refrigerator-risen dough to room temperature before shaping. Rolls should not be risen overnight in a refrigerator unless the cabinet temperature is 40°F/5°C or under. Use a temperature to suit your convenience. When time allows, a slow rise gives better results because it controls yeast growth, and the dough rises gradually, giving a better loaf.

It may take 45–60 minutes in a warm place, 1½–2 hours at room temperature (65°–70°F/18°–21°C), 8–12 hours in a cold room or larder, or up to 24 hours in a refrigerator depending on the temperature.

Proving (Second Rising)

Risen dough must be knocked back by flattening firmly with the knuckles to remove the air bubbles and ensure a better rise and more even texture. Knead quickly to make dough firm and ready for shaping. When kneading or shaping dough use only a little flour when necessary. Too much flour spoils the colour of the crust. After shaping rise again, or prove, by placing tins or baking trays inside a large, lightly oiled polythene bag, tied loosely at the top or with the ends tucked under tins. Leave until dough doubles in size or fills the tins. Remove from polythene and bake.

Baking

Bake in the centre of a hot oven.

Plain white bread and wholemeal bread should be baked at a temperature of 450°F/230°C/Gas Mark 8.

Enriched bread should be baked at a temperature of 375°–425°F/190°–220°C/Gas Mark 5–7.

Cooked loaves shrink slightly from sides of the tin and sound hollow when tapped underneath with the knuckles. The crust should be golden brown.

Attractive Finishes

A container of water in the oven during baking gives a crisp crust. Bread is baked when it sounds hollow if tapped underneath with the knuckles. If it is not quite cooked, it should be returned to the oven without the tins and cooked for a further 5 minutes.

Plain loaves painted with rich milk or cream before baking have a gleaming brown crust; beaten eggs give a dark crust; melted butter or margarine a crisp, crunchy crust. Thick milk and sugar syrup (15ml/1 tablespoon milk to 2 tablespoons sugar) painted on after baking gives loaves and buns a sweet sticky finish.

Wholemeal loaves look good if brushed with a solution of salt and water before baking, then scattered with cracked wheat (from a health food shop), porridge oats or cornflakes. White loaves are more often finished with poppy seeds or sesame seeds.

SHORT-TIME DOUGHS

A modern method of breadmaking known as the short-time dough method enables bread to be made in approximately 1¾ hours. This method, by the addition of a small amount of ascorbic acid (vitamin C) reduces, and almost cuts out, the first rising period, thereby reducing the overall time of breadmaking considerably. A slight readjustment of the basic recipe for bread is necessary when using the short-time dough method.

The quantity of yeast is increased and a little sugar added to those recipes without sugar. Fresh yeast is recommended for use with this method. Dried yeast may be used but it will take approximately one hour longer to rise. 25g/1oz fresh yeast and 25mg ascorbic acid to 675g/1½lb fresh flour for plain white and wholemeal bread and 25g/1oz fresh yeast and 25mg ascorbic acid to 450g/1lb flour for enriched doughs is recommended.

Ascorbic acid tablets are obtainable from all chemists in 25mg, 50mg and 100mg sizes. The ascorbic acid is dissolved in the yeast liquid before adding the other ingredients.

Short-time Dough Temperatures

In order to complete the rising in the given time a dough temperature of 78°–82°F/26°–28°C is recommended.

To obtain this temperature use liquid at a temperature of 90°–100°F/32°–38°C when kitchen is cool or 80°–90°F/27°–32°C when kitchen is warm.

The first rising for short-time dough ed to 5 minutes resting for plain doughs and 10 minu ig for enriched doughs. The second rising or proving aft ig will take 45–50 minutes at room temperature (70°F/21°C).

Baking temperatures and times are the same as for standard doughs.

STORAGE

How to Keep Flour

The best way to store flour is to keep it in its bag on a cool, dry airy shelf. If the kitchen is rather damp or steamy, put the bag into a container such as a tin with a lid or a stoppered storage jar. The container should, of course, be washed and thoroughly dried before refilling with fresh supplies. Don't add new flour to old. Under these conditions plain flour keeps well for 4–6 months; self-raising flour for 2–3 months.

Wholemeal flour may go rancid if stored incorrectly or kept for too long. It is best bought in small quantities and stored in a cool dry place away from other flours. Wholemeal or wheatmeal flours can be kept for up to 2 months.

How to Keep Bread

Some breads keep fresh better than others. Loaves, such as French, Vienna and other very crusty breads, are best eaten on the same day they are baked. Others, such as the enriched breads, sliced white bread and starch-reduced breads, keep fresh for several days. How long a loaf keeps fresh depends on the ingredients used to make the dough and how long it was baked, as well as its storage.

To keep bread at its best (soft, moist and free from mould), it should be stored at normal room temperature in a clean, well-ventilated, dry container such as a bread bin or crock. Free circulation of air around the loaf is necessary to keep the crust crisp and this means that the container should not be airtight. To discourage mould growth, the container must be kept perfectly dry and free from crumbs. It should be washed out each week with hot soapy water. A little vinegar in the rinsing water is an extra precaution against mould.

Wrapped bread should be kept in its wrapper, and a clean polythene bag makes a good container for uncut loaves. The end of the wrapper or bag should be folded loosely under the loaf to allow air to circulate. Wrapped in their own paper or in polythene, loaves can be put into the bread bin, or left on a dry airy shelf.

The refrigerator is not the best place to store bread, chiefly because the temperature of the domestic refrigerator is the temperature at which bread stales most rapidly. A loaf kept for one day in the refrigerator is similar to three-day-old bread. On the other hand, if the kitchen or pantry is damp, bread is better wrapped and stored in the refrigerator, especially in warm weather. This reduces mould growth. Bread stored in the freezer keeps well for a little over a month, though very crusty breads do not keep well. Wrap the bread in a polythene bag and seal tightly before putting in the freezer (for further details, see Chapter 18).

Why Bread Goes Stale

After baking, moisture escapes from a loaf and changes take place within the crumb causing it to stale. Staling leaves the crumb dry and the crust leathery. Dough can be enriched with fat (lard, butter, margarine, oil or vegetable shortening) and in some recipes with milk and eggs, too. These additions help to soften the crumb. This is why enriched breads, such as milk bread, appear to stay fresh longer than loaves made from plainer mixtures. Malt breads and sweet breads with treacle or fruit also keep moist. A lightly baked loaf has a moister crumb and a thinner crust and usually stays fresh longer than a well-baked, crusty loaf. Newly baked bread is quite free from mould, but if mould spores fall in the cut surface of the bread the mould will grow and flourish. Spores are always in the atmosphere and can lodge and develop in the corners of a bread bin, particularly if stale crumbs are left from the previous loaves.

Freshening Bread

Bread that has become a little stale can be freshened by placing the loaf or rolls in a covered tin, which must not be airtight, or in a cake tin well covered with baking foil or by wrapping the loaf tightly in foil. Place the tin or foil-wrapped bread in a hot oven at 450 °F/230 °C/Gas Mark 8 for 5–10 minutes. The bread should be allowed to cool in the tin or foil when it is taken from the oven. Bread freshened in this way will taste and smell like newly baked bread again. There is no need to moisten the bread with water before freshening. Crusty breads tend to lose their crispness soon after baking. If they are not too stale, they can be crisped-up by putting the loaf uncovered into a hot oven for 5–10 minutes. Bread and rolls reheated in this way are best served and eaten while still warm. The service of hot rolls at any type of meal is much appreciated. Prepare these in the same way by heating, un-covered, in a hot oven for a few minutes.

BASIC RULES FOR HOME-MADE BREAD

1) Do follow recipe quantities for flour, yeast and liquid.

2) Do warm both basin and flour to avoid chilling the dough, which slows up the working of the yeast.

3) Do make the dough rather on the soft side for a light loaf. If the dough is too stiff it cannot expand under the influence of the yeast.

4) Do work the dough thoroughly to ensure an even distribution of yeast through the dough. If this is not done, the yeast will not work properly and the dough will not rise enough.

5) Cover during rising with a lightly greased polythene bag or a wet tea cloth (which must not be allowed to dry out).

6) Do keep the dough warm, and warm the tins.

7) Don't make the dough too hot or it will produce a very coarse, breakable crumb or irregular texture.

8) Don't try to shorten the rising time of the dough. Under-proving or under-fermentation will give a heavy soggy loaf with a crust that may break away from the top.

9) Don't let the dough rise for too long. Over-proving or over-fermentation results in a loss of strength, colour, scent and flavour.

10) Don't bake the bread at too low a temperature or it will be pale, moist and flavourless. The oven must be pre-heated and at the correct temperature.

POSSIBLE FAULTS

Poor volume, pale crust and flat top. Dough too wet or too dry. Too little salt or yeast. Flour too soft or self-raising. Proving temperature too high and/or too long. Insufficiently kneaded. Under-fermented.

'Flying top' or cracked crust. Flour too soft. Dough too tight. Fermentation time not long enough. Too much dough for size of tin.

Heavy close texture. Flour too soft. Too much salt. Insufficient kneading or fermentation time. Yeast killed by rising in too hot a place. Oven too cool, therefore over-long baking time.

Uneven texture and holes. Too much liquid/salt. Too long or too short fermentation. Not sufficiently kneaded after first rising. Over-proved. Dough left uncovered during first rising, therefore forming a hard skin which will give streaks when kneaded.

Coarse crumb and poor crumb colour. Flour too soft. Insufficient salt. Dough too tight. Under- or over-proving.

Sour acid and yeasty flavour. Too much yeast, stale yeast or yeast creamed with sugar. Too long fermentation.

Bread stales quickly and is crumbly. Too much yeast. Flour too soft. Rising too quickly in too warm a place – over-fermentation.

2 Basic Breads

These bread recipes will give a variety of loaves and rolls, but also form the basis of many fancy breads, both sweet and savoury (see Chapters 3 and 5).

Basic White Bread

This method for making white bread can be used as a basis for all types of yeast cookery. The dough may be used for Dough Cake, Lardy Cake, Pizza and Yeast Pastry.

Mix dry ingredients with yeast liquid and water. Work to a firm dough, adding extra flour if needed, until the dough leaves the bowl clean. You may need a little more flour or water to make the dough depending on the type of flour used. Turn the dough on to a lightly floured board, knead and stretch the dough, by folding towards you, then pushing down and away from you with palm of hand. Give dough a quarter turn and repeat kneading, developing a rocking rhythm until it feels firm and elastic and no longer sticky (about 10 minutes). Shape the kneaded dough into a round ball, place in a large lightly greased polythene bag, loosely tied, or 20cm/8in saucepan with lid. Stand the dough to rise until it doubles in size and springs back when lightly pressed with a floured finger. Rising times can be varied: 45–60 minutes in a warm place; 2 hours at room temperature (65–70 °F); 12 hours in cold rooms; 24 hours in refrigerator (refrigerated dough must be allowed to return to room temperature before shaping).

Turn the dough on to a lightly floured board, divide into four, flatten each piece firmly with the knuckles to knock out the air bubbles, and knead to make a firm dough. When kneading and moulding bread it is important not to use too much flour in dusting as this will spoil the colour of the loaf.

Dry Mix
1.5kg/3lb strong plain flour
25g/1oz salt

Yeast Liquid
Blend 25g/1oz fresh yeast in
300ml/½ pint water or
Dissolve 1 teaspoon sugar in
300ml/½ pint warm
(110°F/44°C) water,
then sprinkle on 15g/1
level tablespoon dried
yeast, and leave until
frothy (about 10 minutes).

Additional ingredients
25g/1oz lard rubbed into dry
mix
600ml/1 pint water

21

To make a tin loaf, shape each piece by either folding in three or rolling up like a Swiss roll; tuck the ends under. The finally moulded dough should exactly fit the tin.

Place each dough piece in a greased 450g/1lb loaf tin. Put inside a greased polythene bag and put aside until the dough rises to the tops of the tins (1–1½ hours at room temperature, longer in a refrigerator). Remove the polythene cover.

Bake the loaves in the centre of a hot oven, 450°F/230°C/Gas Mark 8 for 30–40 minutes or until the loaves shrink slightly from the sides of the tin and the crust is a deep golden brown.

For a crustier loaf, turn the loaves out on to a baking sheet and bake for a further 5–10 minutes.

When sufficiently baked, the loaves should sound hollow when tapped on the base. Cool on a wire rack.

Cob or Bap

Divide dough into 4 or more pieces and shape each piece to a round ball. Flatten and place on a floured baking sheet. Dust with flour. Cover, prove and bake at 450°F/230°C/Gas Mark 8 for about 40 minutes or less depending on size.

Rolls

The total quantity of dough is sufficient to make about 36 round rolls. If you wish to make only a few, divide some of the dough into equal pieces weighing about 50g/2oz. Roll each piece into a ball using the palm of the hand. Press down hard at first and then ease up. This is best done on an unfloured board with a little flour on the palm of the hand only. Place rolls on a floured tray. Cover, prove and bake at 450°F/230°C/Gas Mark 8 for about 20 minutes.

Crown Loaf

Divide part of the dough into six 50g/2oz pieces. Work each piece to form a smooth ball. Place five to form a ring in a greased 15cm/6in sandwich tin and place the sixth in the centre. Brush with egg wash and sprinkle with poppy seeds. Cover, prove and bake at 450°F/230°C/Gas Mark 8 for about 25 minutes.

Plaits

The total quantity of dough is sufficient to make 4 plait loaves. Divide each piece of dough into three. Roll each of the three pieces into a long thin roll, gather ends together and plait. Place on a lightly floured baking sheet, brush with egg wash and sprinkle with poppy seeds. Cover, prove and bake at 450°F/230°C/Gas Mark 8 for 30–40 minutes.

Alternative Finishes
The loaves may be brushed before baking with any of the following: water; milk; beaten egg and water or milk and a pinch of sugar; egg white. For a change, sprinkle a few poppy seeds on top.

Enriched White Bread

This bread dough is made by the sponge batter method. Any yeast recipe may be made this way by making a batter of one-third of the flour, all the liquid, sugar and yeast, but not the salt. Allow this batter to froth before adding the rest of the ingredients.

It is especially good when using dried yeast, as the yeast does not need reconstituting first, or for getting a 'lively brew' for recipes which are rich in sugar or fat. The texture will be shorter than that of plain white bread because of these additional ingredients.

The following recipe is for a basic dough using 450g/1lb flour and is suitable for making 2 small plaits, a crown loaf or a variety of fancy rolls. It can also be used as a base for a fruited dough or to make a selection of fancy breads using the risen dough.

Batter ingredients
150g/5oz strong plain flour
1 teaspoon sugar
15g/½oz fresh yeast or 8g/¼oz dried yeast
250ml/8fl.oz warm milk

Dough ingredients
325g/11oz plain flour
1 teaspoon salt
50g/2oz butter
1 beaten egg

Egg Wash
Beaten egg
1 teaspoon sugar
15ml/1 tablespoon water

To make the batter, blend the batter ingredients together in a large bowl.

Set aside until frothy (20 minutes in a warm place, longer in a cool one). To make dough, mix the remaining flour with the salt and rub in the butter. Add the egg and flour mixture to the batter and mix well to give a fairly soft dough that leaves the sides of the bowl clean. Turn the dough on to a lightly floured surface and knead until it is smooth and no longer sticky (about 10 minutes). No extra flour should be necessary.

Place the dough in a lightly greased polythene bag, loosely tied, or a 20cm/8in saucepan with lid, and allow to rise until double in size and the dough springs back when pressed gently with a floured finger. Rising times can be varied to suit your convenience: 45–60 minutes in a warm place for a quick rise; 2 hours at average room temperature for a slower rise; up to 12 hours in a cold room, larder or refrigerator for an overnight rise (refrigerated dough must be returned to room temperature before shaping).

Turn the dough on to a floured surface and knead lightly. It is important not to use too much flour for dusting when kneading and moulding the dough as this spoils the colour and texture of the loaf. Form into a variety of shapes.

Plaits

Divide the dough into 2 equal pieces. For three-strand plaits, divide each piece into three, and roll each of the three sections into a long thin strand. Gather the three ends together and plait, or for two-strand plaits divide each piece into two and roll into two strands 30–35cm/12–14in long. Arrange the two strands in a cross on the board. Take the two opposite ends of the bottom strand and cross them over in the centre. Repeat this with the other strand. Cross each strand separately until all the dough is used up, building the plait vertically. Finally gather the short ends together and lay the plait on its side.

Place the plaits on a lightly greased tin, brush with egg wash, and sprinkle with poppy seeds. Put inside a lightly greased polythene bag and rise again until double in size.

Bake in a moderate oven at 375°F/190°C/Gas Mark 5 on the middle shelf for 45–50 minutes or until the loaf sounds hollow when tapped underneath and is slightly browned.

Crown Loaf

Use half of the dough and divide it into six equal pieces. Work each piece to form a smooth ball, place five to form a ring in a greased 15cm/6in sandwich tin and the sixth in the centre. Rise and bake as above.

Fancy Rolls

A variety of fancy rolls – twists, cottage, clover etc. may be made using 50g/2oz dough for each roll. Rise and bake as above. For shaping instructions, see Shaped Morning Rolls (p. 36).

RIGHT A selection of tea-time favourites, including scones, sponge cake, gingerbread and fruit cake

OVERLEAF A variety of brown loaves and rolls, including Irish brown soda bread, wholemeal loaves and flowerpot bread

Basic Wholemeal Bread

To make dough with fresh yeast, mix the flour, salt and sugar together in a bowl. Blend yeast into the water and add all at once. Mix to soft scone-like dough (adding more flour if necessary) that leaves the bowl clean.

To make dough with dried yeast, dissolve a teaspoon of the sugar in a cupful of water used in the recipe (to get the best result this water should be warmed to 110°F/44°C or hand hot) then sprinkle dried yeast on top. Leave until frothy (about 10 minutes). Add with rest of liquid to flour, salt and remaining sugar. Mix to a soft scone-like dough. Knead the dough thoroughly until it feels firm and elastic and no longer sticky (5–10 minutes).

Shape the dough into a round ball and place in a closed container, such as a large greased polythene bag, lightly tied, or a 20cm/8in greased saucepan with lid, to keep it moist and prevent skinning. Stand the dough to rise until it doubles in size and springs back when pressed lightly with a floured finger.

Rising times can be varied to suit your convenience: about 1 hour in a warm place; 2 hours at room temperature; overnight in a cold room or larder; 24 hours in a refrigerator.

Cool rising makes a stronger dough and therefore better bread. Surplus dough can be kept in a refrigerator in a loosely tied polythene bag or plastic pot for use next day or the day after. To use refrigerated dough, soften by standing in a warm place for 15–20 minutes then shape rolls or loaves from cold dough.

When risen, turn the dough on to a board and knead again until firm. Divide into 2 or 4, flatten each piece firmly with the knuckles to knock out air bubbles.

To Make a Tin Loaf

Stretch dough into an oblong the same width as the tin. Fold into three or roll up like a Swiss roll and turn over so the seam is underneath. Tuck in the ends and place in tin. Brush the tops with salted water and put each tin inside a greased polythene bag. Leave to rise until the dough comes to the top of the tin and springs back when pressed with a floured finger (about 1 hour at room temperature).

LEFT Rolls can be made into various shapes. These are knotted rolls

1.5kg/3lb wholemeal flour
2 tablespoons salt
2 tablespoons sugar
25g/1oz lard, rubbed into
    flour
50g/2oz fresh yeast or
    25g/1oz dried yeast
900ml/1½ pints water

Variations

1) Divide each loaf into 4 small pieces, shape into rolls and fit into the tin.

2) Shape each piece of dough into a round cob, dust with flour and put on to floured baking sheet, rise and bake.

3) Shape all the dough into a round cob, place on a large floured baking sheet. Cut with a cross to make four sections, scatter with cracked wheat or flour, cover with greased polythene and rise. Mark in four sections again, if necessary, before baking at 450°F/230°C/Gas Mark 8 for 40–45 minutes.

Quick Wheatmeal Bread

225g/8oz each brown and white strong plain flours (or in any proportion)
8g/¼oz lard, rubbed in
2 teaspoons salt
2 teaspoons sugar
15g/½oz fresh yeast or 8g/¼oz dried yeast
300ml/½ pint lukewarm water

This easy recipe makes about 675g/1½lb dough and takes 5 minutes to mix, 30 minutes to rise in a warm place, and 30 minutes to bake the risen dough into a loaf or rolls. The dough can also be used to make a selection of tea breads and as a base for Pizza.

To make dough with fresh yeast, mix the flours, salt and sugar together in a bowl. Blend yeast in the water and add all at once. Mix to a soft scone-like dough (adding more flour if necessary) that leaves the bowl clean.

To make dough with dried yeast, dissolve a teaspoon of the sugar in a cupful of water used in the recipe (to get the best result this water should be warmed to 110°F/44°C or hand hot), then sprinkle dried yeast on top. Leave until frothy (about 10 minutes). Add with rest of liquid to flours, salt and remaining sugar. Mix to a soft scone-like dough.

Knead the dough thoroughly on a lightly floured surface.

This quantity makes two small loaves. Divide the dough into two pieces.

Shape each piece to half-fill a well-greased 450g/1lb loaf tin or a 10–12.5cm/4–5in flower pot. Brush the tops with salt and water and sprinkle with cornflakes or cracked wheat. Put to rise inside a large greased polythene bag, loosely tied, until the dough has doubled in size and springs back when lightly pressed with a floured finger. Remove bag. Bake on middle shelf of hot oven at 450°F/230°C/Gas Mark 8 for 30–40 minutes.

To Make Rolls

This quantity makes 12 rolls. Flatten the dough to 1.25cm/½in thickness on a floured board. Cut into rounds with a 6.75cm/2½in cutter or divide dough in 12 pieces and roll into rounds using palm of one hand. Press down hard at first and then ease up. This is best done on an unfloured board with a little flour on the palm of the hand only. Place on a floured baking sheet.

Soft-sided Rolls
Shape and pack 2cm/¾in apart and dust with flour. Bake and pull apart while still warm.

Crusty Rolls
Leave 2.5cm/1in space all round, brush tops with salt and water and sprinkle with cracked wheat or cornflakes.

Cover rolls with greased polythene. Rise to double size and bake at top of hot oven at 450°F/230°C/Gas Mark 8 for 20–25 minutes.

SHORT-TIME METHOD OF BREADMAKING

The short-time method of breadmaking enables bread to be made in approximately 1¼ hours.
1) The addition of a small amount of ascorbic acid (vitamin C) reduces the first rising period to a five-minute resting period for plain doughs and ten minutes for enriched doughs. Ascorbic acid (vitamin C) tablets are obtainable from chemists in 25mg, 50mg and 100mg sizes. The ascorbic acid is dissolved in the yeast liquid.
2) Fresh yeast is recommended for use with this method. Dried yeast may be used but it will take approximately 1 hour to rise. N.B. 25g/1oz fresh yeast is equivalent to 15g/½oz dried yeast.
3) In order to complete the rising in the given time a dough temperature of 78°F–82°F/26°C–28°C is recommended. To obtain this temperature use liquid at a temperature of: 90°–100°F/32°–38°C when kitchen is cool; 80°–90°F/27°–32°C when kitchen is warm.
4) The second rising (proving) after shaping will take approximately 45–50 minutes at room temperature (70°F/21°C). If the temperature is below 70°F/21°C, the proving time will be greater than 45–50 minutes, thus increasing the overall time of making bread.

Plain White Bread (Short-Time Method)

Yeast liquid
Blend 25g/1oz fresh yeast in 425ml/14fl.oz water
Dissolve 25mg ascorbic acid in the yeast liquid

Additional ingredients
675g/1½lb strong plain flour
15g/½oz salt
8g/¼oz sugar
15g/½oz lard

This quantity of flour makes about 1kg 150g/2½lb dough, sufficient to make one large or two small loaves or approximately 18 rolls. This dough may also be used to make a lardy cake, dough cake, herb cake or yeast pastry.

Prepare the yeast liquid. Put flour, salt and sugar in a large bowl and rub in the lard. Mix the dry ingredients with the yeast liquid using a wooden fork or spoon. Work to a firm dough, adding extra flour if needed, until the sides of the bowl are clean. Turn the dough on to a lightly floured board or table, and knead thoroughly until dough feels smooth and elastic (about 10 minutes). To do this, fold dough towards you and then push down and away with the heel of your hand. Shape dough into a ball and place in the lightly greased polythene bag and leave to stand for 5 minutes. For a large loaf, grease 1kg/2lb loaf tin. Remove dough from polythene bag and flatten into an oblong the same width as the tin. Fold into three and turn over so that the seam is underneath. Smooth over top, tuck in ends and place in tin.

For two small loaves, grease two 450g/1lb loaf tins. Divide dough into two and shape as above.

Rolls
Divide dough in 18 equal pieces of 50g/2oz each. Roll each piece into a ball. To form a ball, use an unfloured board and a little flour on the palm of the hand. Press down on the piece of dough with the palm of the hand, hard at first, roll the dough around, gradually easing up the palm of the hand. Place rolls on a lightly greased baking sheet, about 2.5cm/1in apart.

To rise, place tins inside a lightly greased polythene bag and leave to rise at room temperature for 45–50 minutes. Less time is required for rolls (approximately 30 minutes at room temperature). When risen, the dough should spring back when lightly pressed with a floured finger. Remove the polythene bag. Bake the loaves in the centre of a hot oven at 450°F/230°C/Gas Mark 8 for 30–35 minutes and rolls near the top for 15–20 minutes until golden brown. Remove loaf from tins or rolls from baking sheet and cool on a wire rack. Cooked loaves shrink slightly from the sides of the tin and sound hollow when tapped underneath with the knuckles.

Wholemeal Bread (Short-Time Method)

Make in the same way as Plain White Bread (Short-time method).

Yeast liquid
Blend 25g/1oz fresh yeast in 450ml/¾ pint water
Dissolve 25mg ascorbic acid in the yeast liquid

Additional ingredients
675g/1½lb wholemeal flour
15g/½oz salt
8g/¼oz sugar
15g/½oz lard

Enriched White Bread (Short-Time Method)

This quantity of flour makes approximately 800g/1¾lb dough, sufficient to make one crown loaf and one small plait or 14 rolls. This dough may also be used to make fruit loaves, stollen, Swedish tea-ring, Hungarian coffee cake and Bannock.

Prepare the yeast liquid. Put flour, sugar and salt into a large bowl and rub in butter or margarine. Mix the dry ingredients with yeast liquid and beaten egg using a wooden fork or spoon. Work to a firm dough, adding extra flour if needed, until the sides of the bowl are clean. Follow method for Plain White Bread (short-time method) but leave to stand for 10 minutes. Remove dough from polythene bag. Knead for 1–2 minutes to knock out air bubbles. Shape into loaves or rolls.

Yeast liquid
Blend 25g/1oz fresh yeast in 250ml/8fl.oz milk
Dissolve 25mg ascorbic acid in the yeast liquid

Additional ingredients
450g/1lb strong plain flour
1 teaspoon sugar
1 teaspoon salt
50g/2oz butter or margarine
1 beaten egg

Crown Loaf
Grease a 15cm/6in sandwich tin. Cut off 6×50g/2oz pieces of dough. Work each piece to form a smooth ball, place five to form a ring in the tin and the sixth in the centre.

Plait
Grease a baking tray. Divide the remainder of the dough (about 450g/1lb) into two equal pieces. Roll each piece to a strip 30×35cm/12×14in long. Arrange the two strips in a cross on the table. Then take each end of the bottom strip and cross them over

in the centre. Cross each strip alternately 2 or 3 times, building the plait vertically. Finally gather the short ends together and lay the plait on its side. Place the plait on the baking tray.

Rolls

Grease a baking sheet. Divide the dough into 50g/2oz pieces. Shape into plain or fancy rolls – cottage, plaits, knots and coils.

Place baking tray inside a lightly greased polythene bag and leave to rise at room temperature. Loaves will take about 30–40 minutes. Rolls will take less time. The dough should spring back when lightly pressed with a floured finger. Remove polythene. Brush with egg wash, made by beating together 1 egg, 15ml/1 tablespoon water and a pinch of sugar and sprinkle with poppy seeds if wished.

Bake the crown loaf and plait on the middle shelf of a moderately hot oven, 375°F/190°C/Gas Mark 5 for 45 minutes; the rolls on top shelf for 20 minutes or until golden brown. Cool loaves and rolls on a wire rack.

Vienna Bread

Yeast liquid

40g/1½oz fresh yeast blended with 450ml/¾ pint water and milk mixed or dissolve 1 teaspoon sugar in 450ml/¾ pint warm (110°F/44°C) water and milk mixed and sprinkle on 20g/¾oz of dried yeast and leave until frothy (about 10 minutes)

Other ingredients

25g/1oz lard
675g/1½lb strong plain flour
2 teaspoons salt
1 teaspoon sugar

Prepare the yeast liquid. Rub lard into dry ingredients. Add yeast liquid to dry ingredients, work to a firm dough, adding extra flour if needed, until dough leaves bowl clean. Turn dough out on to a lightly floured surface and knead thoroughly until firm, elastic and no longer sticky (about 10 minutes). Shape the kneaded dough into a ball and place in a large oiled polythene bag, loosely tied at the top. Leave to rise at room temperature until dough doubles in size and springs back when lightly pressed with a floured finger (1½–2 hours).

Turn risen dough on to a lightly floured surface, flatten with the knuckles to knock out the air bubbles and knead until smooth. Divide the dough into five equal pieces, about 225g/8oz in weight. Roll out each piece to an oval about 22.5cm/9in in length. If the skin starts to break, stop rolling and allow the piece to recover. Roll each piece up from the long side to form a tight roll. Place on a lightly greased baking tray with the seam underneath. Cover with a lightly oiled polythene bag. Rise until double in size and the dough springs back when lightly pressed with a floured finger.

Remove polythene and make 3 or 4 diagonal cuts across the loaf with a sharp knife. Place in a hot oven at 450°F/230°C/Gas Mark 8 in which two pans or tins of water have been placed in the bottom to produce a steamy atmosphere. Bake for 15 minutes, open the oven door, remove the pans and let the steam escape. Bake for a further 15 minutes without the steam to give the desired crispy crust. Cool on a wire rack.

Rolls may also be prepared from this dough using 50g/2oz dough per roll.

Scotch Bap and Soft Morning Rolls

Prepare the yeast liquid. Mix flour and salt together and rub in lard. Add yeast liquid and work to a firm dough until sides of bowl are clean. Turn dough on to a lightly floured surface and knead thoroughly until firm and elastic and no longer sticky. It will take about 10 minutes. Shape dough into a ball and place in a large lightly greased polythene bag, loosely tied at the top. Leave to rise until doubled in size and dough springs back when pressed with a floured finger. It takes about 45–60 minutes in a warm place, 2 hours at average room temperature, or up to 24 hours in a refrigerator. (Dough risen in a refrigerator must be returned to room temperature before shaping.)

Turn risen dough on to a lightly floured surface, flatten with the knuckles to knock out air bubbles, and knead until dough is firm (about 2 minutes).

Scotch Bap
Cut off two-thirds of the dough to make a large bap. Shape into a ball and roll out with a floured rolling pin to about 2cm/¾in thick. Place on a well-floured baking tray and dredge top with flour.

Soft Morning Rolls
Divide remaining dough into four equal-sized pieces, shape each into a ball and roll out to an oval, about 1.25cm/½in thick. Place on a floured baking tray and dredge tops with flour.

Cover bap and morning rolls with greased polythene and allow to rise until double in size (about 45 minutes at room temperature). Press bap and each roll gently in centre with three fingers to prevent blisters. Bake in oven at 400°F/200°C/Gas Mark 6 for 20–30 minutes for the bap and 15–20 minutes for the morning rolls. Cool on a wire rack covered with a cloth to keep the bread soft.

Yeast liquid
15g/½oz fresh yeast blended with 300ml/½ pint warm milk and water mixed

Other ingredients
450g/1lb strong plain flour
1 teaspoon salt
50g/2oz lard

Shaped Morning Rolls

Batter ingredients
150g/5oz strong plain flour
1 teaspoon sugar
15g/½oz fresh yeast
250ml/8fl. oz warm milk

Dough ingredients
325g/11oz strong plain flour
1 teaspoon salt
50g/2oz margarine
1 beaten egg

Egg wash
Beaten egg
1 teaspoon sugar
15ml/1 tablespoon water

To make batter, blend the batter ingredients together in a large bowl. Set aside until frothy (20 minutes in a warm place; longer in a cool one). To make dough, mix remaining flour with salt and rub in margarine. Add egg and flour mixture to the batter and mix well to give a fairly soft dough that leaves sides of bowl clean. Turn dough on to a lightly floured surface and knead until it is smooth and no longer sticky (about 10 minutes). No extra flour should be necessary. Place dough in a lightly greased polythene bag, loosely tied, and allow to rise until double in size and dough springs back when pressed gently with a floured finger.

Turn dough on to a floured surface and knead lightly. Divide into 50g/2oz pieces and make into following shapes:

Cottage Rolls
Cut off one-quarter of the dough piece. Use three-quarters of the dough to make a round roll for the base and place on a greased baking sheet. Form the remaining quarter into a small round roll and place on top of the larger roll. Push floured handle of a wooden spoon through the top roll until it touches the baking sheet.

Bloomer Rolls
Roll each piece of dough into an oval shape 7.5–10cm/3–4in long. With a sharp knife, make three diagonal slashes across the top of each roll. Place the rolls on a greased baking sheet.

Knot
Roll each dough piece out to a strand 10–12.5cm/4–5in long. Take the two ends of the strand and form a knot. Place on a greased baking tray. Brush all the rolls with egg wash and cover the trays with lightly greased polythene sheets or bags. Leave to rise until double in size (approximately 20–30 minutes). Remove polythene bag and bake at 375°F/190°C/Gas Mark 5 for 20–25 minutes.

Coil
Roll each dough piece out to a strand 10–12.5cm/4–5in long. Coil up dough from one end.

Plait
Divide each dough piece into three. Roll each piece out to a strand 10cm/4in long. Pinch the three ends together at one end and plait the strands. Pinch the remaining ends together.

Place all the rolls on a greased baking tray. Brush the rolls well with egg wash and sprinkle with poppy seeds. Cover with a lightly greased polythene bag and rise at room temperature until the rolls are double in size and dough springs back when gently pressed with a lightly floured finger (approximately 20–30 minutes). Remove polythene bag and bake at 375°F/190°C/Gas Mark 5 for 20–25 minutes.

Wholemeal Farmhouse Bread

Grease 4×450g/1lb bread tins. Place flour and salt into a mixing bowl and rub in the fat. Add yeast to the water and mix until well dissolved. Make a well in the centre of the flour and add the yeast liquid. Mix well to form a soft dough, turn out on to a lightly floured surface and knead for 5 minutes. Cover with tea towel and leave in a warm place for approximately 30 minutes or until doubled in size. Turn on to floured surface and re-knead. Divide dough into 4 equal portions and shape to fit the greased bread tins. Cover and leave in a warm place until dough has risen 1.25cm/½in above rim of tins. Bake in a hot oven at 450°F/230°C/Gas Mark 8 for 20 minutes. Reduce heat to 425°F/220°C/Gas Mark 7 for a further 15 minutes.

1.5kg/3lb 100% stoneground wholemeal flour
20g/¾oz salt
25g/1oz butter
25g/1oz fresh yeast
900ml/1½ pints lukewarm water

Flowerpot Bread*

Mix flours and salt in a bowl and rub in lard. Mix sugar into flour. Blend yeast into water and add to flour, all at once. Mix to a soft scone-like dough, which leaves the bowl clean, adding a little more flour if necessary. Knead dough on a lightly floured surface until smooth (about 2 minutes). Divide dough in half and place in two well-greased 12.5cm/5in flowerpots. Put inside a large, lightly oiled polythene bag, loosely tied at the top, and allow to rise till double in size and dough springs back when pressed with a floured finger. Rising times vary with temperature. For a quick rise allow ½ hour in warm place; a slower rise takes 1–1½ hours at average room temperature and a cold rise takes 12–24 hours in a refrigerator. Remove bag. Bake, standing upright, on middle shelf of hot oven at 450°F/230°C/Gas Mark 8 for 30–40 minutes.

175g/6oz strong plain flour
225g/8oz wholemeal flour
2 teaspoons salt
15g/½oz lard
2 teaspoons sugar
15g/½oz fresh yeast
300ml/½ pint water

*NOTE: When first using a flowerpot this way, grease it well and bake it empty once or twice in a hot oven. This is essential to prevent breaking. Keep the flowerpots clean and dry for re-use.

Berkshire Wholemeal Bread

1.7kg/3½lb wholemeal flour
450g/1lb strong plain white flour
1 tablespoon salt
50g/2oz lard
40g/1½oz fresh yeast
1 teaspoon sugar
1.5 litres/2½ pints water

Stir together the wholemeal and white flour and the salt in a warm basin. Rub in the lard. Crumble the yeast into a small basin with the sugar and add 300ml/½ pint warm water. Leave until frothy. Make a well in the centre of the flour and add the yeast liquid and the remaining warm water. Knead thoroughly until smooth. Cover with a clean tea towel and leave to rise in a warm place for 1 hour. Divide into four or five pieces and knead and shape. Put into warm greased bread tins (this will make four 675g/1½lb or five 450g/1lb loaves), and leave in a warm place for 20 minutes. Bake at 425°F/220°C/Gas Mark 7 for 45 minutes.

Potato Bread

450g/1lb potatoes
900g/2lb strong plain flour
15g/½oz salt
15g/½oz fresh yeast
300ml/½ pint water

Boil the potatoes and sieve them. While hot, mix with the flour, salt, yeast and water. Mix and knead well together, shape and divide mixture between three 675g/1½lb tins. Leave in a warm place for 2 hours, and bake at 450°F/230°C/Gas Mark 8 for 45 minutes. This gives a loaf which is light both in colour and texture.

Bridge Rolls

450g/1lb strong plain flour
1 teaspoon salt
2 teaspoons sugar
25g/1oz butter
300ml/½ pint milk
25g/1oz fresh yeast
2 eggs
Beaten egg

Put the flour, salt and sugar into a warm bowl. Melt the butter. Warm the milk and blend a little with the yeast. Add the butter, milk and eggs to the flour and then work together thoroughly to make a soft dough. Cover with a cloth and put in a warm place for about 45 minutes to rise. Knead again and roll out 1.25cm/½in thick. Cut into finger lengths and shape rounded ends. Put on a greased baking sheet so that the rolls just touch. Leave in a warm place for 10 minutes. Brush with a little beaten egg and bake at 450°F/230°C/Gas Mark 8 for 15 minutes. A few poppy seeds can be scattered on top of the rolls before baking.

Country Dinner Rolls

Stir the flour and salt together in a warm basin and rub in the butter. Cream the yeast and sugar. Warm the milk and add it to the beaten egg. Mix with the yeast and add to the flour. Mix and knead until smooth. Cover with a cloth and leave in a warm place for 1 hour. Knead the dough lightly and form into rolls. Put on a greased tray and leave in a warm place for 15 minutes. Brush over with beaten egg and bake at 450°F/230°C/Gas Mark 8 for 20 minutes.

450g/1lb strong plain flour
1 teaspoon salt
25g/1oz butter
1 egg
15g/½oz fresh yeast
1 teaspoon sugar
300ml/½ pint milk

Aberdeen Buttery Rowies

Sieve the flour and salt into a warm bowl. Cream the yeast and the sugar together and add to the flour with the warm water. Knead together to form a smooth dough. Cover and leave in a warm place until the dough has doubled in size. Put the lard and butter into a basin and beat together until thoroughly blended. Divide the fat into three portions and divide each portion into small pieces. Roll out the dough to a rectangle on a floured board. Dot the first portion of fat all over it. Fold over the top third of the dough, and fold the bottom third over it. Press down, give the pastry a half-turn and roll out again. Repeat the process with the remaining two portions of fat. Divide into 24 pieces and form each one into an oval shape. Put on a greased and floured baking sheet, cover and leave in a warm place for 30 minutes. Bake at 400°F/200°C/Gas Mark 6 for 20 minutes.

450g/1lb strong plain flour
1 teaspoon salt
25g/1oz fresh yeast
15g/½oz caster sugar
450ml/¾ pint warm water
175g/6oz lard
175g/6oz butter

Kent Huffkins

Warm the mixing bowl, sift in the flour and salt, and rub in the lard. Cream the yeast and sugar together, add the milk and water and mix with the flour to make a light dough. Put in a warm place for 1 hour to rise. Knead well, then divide into 8 cakes and roll out flat to about 2.5cm/1in thick. Leave to prove till well risen, press each one in the centre with a floured thumb, then bake at 450°F/230°C/Gas Mark 8 for 20 minutes, turning the loaves over halfway through the baking. Take them out of the oven and wrap in a warm cloth until cool to keep the crust soft and tender.

675g/1½lb strong plain flour
1½ teaspoons salt
50g/2oz lard
15g/½oz fresh yeast
1 teaspoon sugar
450ml/¾ pint warm milk and
  water

Simple Harvest Loaf

450g/1lb strong plain flour
2 teaspoons salt
15g/½oz lard
Beaten egg

Yeast liquid
Blend 15g/½oz fresh yeast in
270ml/9fl.oz warm water

Mix the flour and salt in a bowl and rub in lard. Add yeast liquid all at once and mix to a firm dough, adding extra flour if needed until dough leaves sides of bowl clean. Turn on to a lightly floured board and knead until dough is smooth (about 10 minutes). Leave to rise in a bowl covered with a lid or lightly greased polythene bag in a warm place until double in size (about 45–60 minutes). Punch dough well to knock out any air bubbles, divide into four pieces. Roll three of the pieces into 50cm/20in-long strands and join together at one end. Place on a lightly greased baking sheet and plait loosely together and tuck ends underneath. Brush with egg wash. Divide fourth piece into two and roll each to a 50cm/20in-long strand. Join together at one end and twist strands loosely. Lay twist along centre of plait and tuck ends underneath. Brush twist with egg wash. Leave to rise at room temperature, covered with greased polythene until dough springs back when pressed lightly (about 30 minutes). Bake in a hot oven at 450°F/230°C/Gas Mark 8 for 30–40 minutes.

Shaped Harvest Bread

1.5kg/3lb strong plain flour
20g/¾oz salt
25g/1oz fresh yeast
A little beaten egg
A few drops of gravy
  browning
Currants

Sift flour and salt. Mix warm water with yeast, pour into dry ingredients and work well together with the hands to make an elastic dough. Knead well until smooth, then prove the dough in a warm place until double in bulk, which will take about 1–1½ hours. The dough can then be formed into shape and baked immediately. It will lose its crisp outline if left to rise again.

For a large design it is best to model the dough directly on to baking trays, upside down, so that the finished loaf will slide off easily. For a large piece of bread, model it on two baking sheets laid side by side, and place on the oven rack on a table before beginning to form a shape.

'Loaves and Fishes'
Take half the dough, form into an oval shape, and roll about 2.5cm/1in thick, then place on to a baking sheet. Take half the remaining dough, roll with the hands into a long sausage shape, then twist to form a rope. Brush the edge of the 'platter' with beaten egg, and place rope edging in position. With remaining dough, form small flat fishes and tiny cottage loaves. Arrange on the base, and brush the whole design with beaten egg. Bake just

above the centre of a hot oven at 425°F/220°C/Gas Mark 7 until it is set and golden brown (about 20 minutes) then lower the heat to 325°F/170°C/Gas Mark 3 for 20 minutes.

'Wheatsheaf and Mouse'

Take about 225g/8oz dough and form into a sausage shape about 30cm/12in long. Place on centre of baking trays and flatten the sausage slightly. This is the base on which the design will be modelled. Using 350g/12oz dough, form a crescent shape and put it curving around the top of the stalk, flattening this shape too. Using about half the remainder of the dough, roll with the hands small sticks of dough a little thinner than a pencil and about 30cm/12in long and lay each one along the basic stalk shape to cover it. Make a plait with three of these sticks. Cut a little v-shape out of the sides of the stalks fairly high up, and bind the stalks with the plait, tucking the ends well under the sheaf.

Reserve about 50g/2oz dough for the mouse. With remaining dough, make small sausage shapes of dough, weighing about 25g/1oz each and lay them round the top of the crescent, like the rays of the sun, and cover the crescent. Brush the whole sheaf with beaten egg. Clip each sausage shape with a pair of scissors – these form the ears of corn.

Knead a little gravy browning into the dough for the mouse, and take off a tiny piece for the tail. Mould the dough into a pear-shape, then model the head and nose, and lift up small flaps for the ears. Make a thin tail and curl it round the mouse, and put in currant eyes. Bake as for loaves and fishes.

3 Savoury Breads

Basic bread dough can be flavoured with herbs or cheese, for instance, to make loaves which are good to eat with soups or cold meals. Risen dough is also excellent used as a pastry with savoury fillings, or as a base for such dishes as pizza. The dough can be used with a topping, or wrapped round the savoury filling.

Pizza

8g/¼oz fresh yeast
150ml/¼ pint water
225g/8oz strong plain flour
   (white or white and brown
   mixed)
1 level teaspoon salt
8g/¼oz lard (rubbed into
   flour)

Basic Filling
Olive oil
350g/12oz cheese
450g/1lb sliced or canned
   tomatoes
Pepper
1 teaspoon fresh or dried
   thyme (or oregano,
   marjoram or basil)
Anchovy fillets
Stoned and halved black
   olives

Pizza is a country dish from Italy, and is an open savoury platter of dough with a savoury topping. There are many different shapes, sizes and kinds of pizza. The best known, *Neapolitan Pizza*, is very colourful with its fillings of tomatoes, herbs, cheese and black olives. Other fillings include ham, salami, bacon, eggs, fish. The following basic recipe is enough for four people, but a good time to make pizza is when you are making bread. You will need just under 450g/1lb risen dough (white or brown).

Blend the yeast into the water and leave for 10 minutes. Mix into dry ingredients. Work to a firm dough, adding extra flour if needed, until the dough leaves the bowl clean. Turn the dough on to a lightly floured board and knead, by pulling it up and pressing it down, until it feels smooth and elastic. Put the dough to rise inside a lightly greased polythene bag, lightly tied, until it doubles in size and springs back when pressed with a floured finger.

Turn the risen dough on to a board. Flatten with the knuckles or a rolling pin to a long strip. Brush with oil and roll up like a Swiss roll. Repeat this three times in all. Divide the dough into four, if making individual pizzas, and roll each piece into a flat circle to fit 17.5cm/7in sponge tins, or roll out the dough to fit an oiled baking sheet. Brush the dough with olive oil and cover with alternate layers of cheese, tomato and seasoning and finish with a layer of

42

cheese. Decorate with a lattice of anchovy fillets and black olives. Bake on top shelf of oven at 450 °F/230 °C/Gas Mark 8 for 25–30 minutes.

It is not necessary to rise the pizza before baking but it is improved by standing in a cool place for half an hour. The cheese looks better if very thinly sliced, rather than grated. Mozzarella should be used, but is not always obtainable, so any cheese which melts smoothly may be used. Mixed dried Italian herbs are sometimes obtainable, which are suitable for pizza.

Filling Variations
1) Use 100–225g/4–8oz sliced salami, chopped streaky bacon, cold ham or tuna fish in addition to the other ingredients.
2) Use fried onions or mushrooms for added flavour.
3) Instead of anchovy fillets, make a lattice of strips of streaky bacon and decorate with pickled walnuts or capers, instead of olives.

Tuna and Green Pepper Pizza

Prepare dough as for basic recipe. Drain and chop the tuna. Sauté the sliced onion, sliced green pepper and sliced tomato in a little oil for 10 minutes while rolling and shaping the dough. Brush the dough with oil and cover with tomato purée, tuna, grated cheese, chopped onion and green pepper. Season and then top with sliced tomato. Bake towards top of oven at 450°F/230°C/Gas Mark 8 for 20 minutes.

200g/7oz can tuna
1 small onion
1 small green pepper
1 tomato
50g/2oz concentrated tomato purée
225g/8oz grated Cheddar cheese

Pizza Francescana

Place cheese on flattened dough, cover with the ham and mushrooms and finally the tomatoes. Season with pepper and salt. Bake as basic Pizza.

100g/4oz Bel Paese cheese
225g/8oz cooked ham (cut into strips)
100g/4oz sliced mushrooms
225g/8oz sliced tomatoes
Salt and pepper

Pizza San Remo

450g/1lb onions
50g/2oz butter
Salt and pepper
Sardines
Stoned black olives to
    decorate

Slice the onions finely. Melt the butter and sauté the onions by cooking with the butter over a low heat in a covered pan for 10 minutes. Season to taste. Spread over the flattened dough and place sardines on top. Garnish with black olives. Bake as basic Pizza.

Calzone

15g/½oz fresh yeast
300ml/½ pint warm water
450g/1lb strong plain flour
1½ teaspoons salt
25g/1oz lard

Filling
225g/8oz cooked ham (cut
    into 8 slices)
225g/8oz Bel Paese cheese
    (cut into 8 slices)
Olive oil
Salt
Freshly ground black pepper

Prepare yeast liquid by dissolving yeast in water and leaving to stand for 10 minutes. Mix flour and salt and rub in lard. Add yeast liquid and work to a firm dough until sides of bowl are clean. Turn dough on to a lightly floured surface and knead thoroughly until firm and elastic and no longer sticky. This will take about 10 minutes. Shape into a ball and place in large, lightly oiled polythene bag, loosely tied at the top. Leave to rise until dough is double in size and springs back when gently pressed with a floured finger (about 1 hour in a warm place).

Turn risen dough on to a lightly floured surface, flatten with knuckles to knock out air bubbles and knead until firm, about 2 minutes. Divide into 8 equal pieces. Roll out each piece into a 15cm/6in circle on a lightly floured surface. Place a folded slice of ham and a slice of cheese on half of each circle. Sprinkle with a little olive oil and season well. Fold over other half of circle and press edges together, making a semi-circular shape. Place on a greased baking sheet and cover with a sheet of lightly oiled polythene. Leave to prove for 15 minutes in a warm place. Bake at 425°F/220°C/Gas Mark 7 for 20 minutes. Serve warm if possible. This is good with a tomato sauce flavoured with some grated Parmesan cheese.

Hungarian Bacon Rolls

Dissolve the yeast in the warm water. Mix together the salt, sugar, pepper, eggs, cream and flour and add the yeast liquid. Knead until smooth and shiny. Cover with a cloth and leave in a warm place for 1 hour. Grill the bacon until crisp and crumble the rashers into small pieces. Roll out 1.25cm/½in thick and cut into 5cm/2in rounds. Put on a greased baking sheet and leave in a warm place for 30 minutes. Slash the surface of each roll with 3 diagonal cuts. Beat the egg yolk and milk together and use to brush the tops of the rolls. Bake at 350°F/180°C/Gas Mark 4 for 20 minutes and serve hot.

25g/1oz fresh yeast
50ml/2fl.oz warm water
½ teaspoon salt
½ teaspoon sugar
½ teaspoon black pepper
2 eggs
150ml/¼ pint sour cream
275g/10oz strong plain flour
450g/1lb lean bacon
1 egg yolk
15ml/1 tablespoon milk

Lahm Ajoun

Break off pieces of dough about 5cm/2in diameter and roll them into balls. Roll out on a lightly floured board into thin pieces about 15cm/6in across. Put on baking sheets. Make the filling by mincing together the lamb, onion, garlic and green pepper. Stir in the parsley, salt, allspice, pepper and chopped tomatoes. Put about 3 tablespoons of the filling on the centre of each piece of dough and spread it so that it comes to the edge of the dough. Bake at 425°F/220°C/Gas Mark 7 for 20 minutes until the meat is cooked. This 'bread' comes from the Middle East and can be eaten as a main dish, or in place of sandwiches.

675g/1½lb risen white bread
dough
450g/1lb lean lamb
1 large onion
2 garlic cloves
1 green pepper
4 tablespoons chopped fresh
parsley
½ teaspoon salt
¼ teaspoon ground allspice
Pinch of black pepper
225g/8oz drained canned
tomatoes

Onion Kuchen (1)

Put the milk and half the butter in a saucepan. Bring to the boil, stirring until the butter melts. Take off the heat and leave for 10 minutes. Cream the yeast with the water and leave for 10 minutes. Mix together the flour, half the salt and the sugar together and stir in the yeast and milk mixtures. Mix thoroughly, cover and leave in a warm place for 1½ hours to rise until double in bulk. Melt the remaining butter and add the onions cut into thin slices. Cook gently for 10 minutes, stirring often. Cool. Beat the egg, cream and remaining salt together. Knead the dough and break off pieces to form 5cm/2in balls. Put on to a baking sheet and flatten slightly. Press onions into tops of balls. Spread with the cream mixture and sprinkle with poppy seeds. Leave in a warm place for 45 minutes. Bake at 375°F/190°C/Gas Mark 5 for 25 minutes.

250ml/8fl.oz milk
100g/4oz butter
25g/1oz fresh yeast
50g/2fl.oz lukewarm water
350g/12oz strong plain flour
½ teaspoon salt
1 teaspoon sugar
4 medium onions
1 egg
50ml/2fl.oz sour cream
2 tablespoons poppy seeds

Onion Kuchen (2)

225g/8oz risen white bread
    dough
225g/8oz onions
50g/2oz butter
15g/½oz plain flour
150ml/¼ pint milk
¼ teaspoon salt
Pinch of pepper
¼ teaspoon garlic salt
1 teaspoon poppy seeds

Grease and flour a 20cm/8in sandwich tin. Roll out the dough on a lightly floured board to fit the tin. Place the dough in the tin, cover with a lightly greased polythene bag and allow to rise until double in size (30–45 minutes at room temperature). Cook the sliced onions in the butter in the saucepan until just tender. Stir in the flour and cook for 1 minute. Add the milk and bring to the boil. Stir and boil for 1 minute. Stir in the salt, pepper and garlic salt. Spoon the onion mixture on the risen dough base and sprinkle with poppy seeds. Bake on middle shelf of oven at 375°F/190°C/Gas Mark 5 for 30 minutes.

Cheese Loaf

15g/½oz fresh yeast
300ml/½ pint water
450g/1lb strong plain flour
2 teaspoons salt
1 teaspoon mustard powder
1 teaspoon pepper
100–175g/4–6oz finely
    grated Cheddar cheese

Mix yeast in water and leave 10 minutes. Mix with dry ingredients, reserving a little cheese for top of loaves. Leave dough in a warm place for 1 hour. Shape dough into two 450g/1lb greased loaf tins and leave for 1 hour. Sprinkle grated cheese on top and bake the loaves on middle shelf of oven at 375°F/190°C/Gas Mark 5 for 45 minutes. Care should be taken not to overbake. Cool on wire rack.

Cheese and Celery Loaf
Sprinkle 25g/1oz grated cheese mixed with 1 teaspoon celery salt on top of the loaves before baking.

Cheese Braid
Divide half-risen dough into two equal pieces and roll each piece to a strip 30cm/12in long. Arrange the two strips in a cross on the board. Then take the opposite ends of each strip and cross them over in the centre. Cross each strip alternately two or three times. Finally, gather the short ends together and put the braid on its side inside a large greased polythene bag to prove, then put on a floured baking sheet, and bake on the middle shelf of oven at 375°F/190°C/Gas Mark 5 for 30–40 minutes until golden brown. Cool on wire rack.

4 Foreign Breads

There must be thousands of different breads made regularly all over the world, depending on the raw materials available, a variety of cooking utensils and different types of fires and ovens. Many of these are very difficult to reproduce away from their countries of origin, so the breads in this chapter are those which can most easily be made at home with everyday ingredients. One or two different types of flour are used and these can generally be obtained from wholefood shops.

French Flutes

Put half the flour into a bowl. Cream the yeast with a little of the water which should be lukewarm. Gradually add more water to make up 300ml/½ pint. Mix into the bread and knead until the water has been absorbed. Cover with a dry cloth and leave for 3 hours in a warm place. Warm the remaining water and add the salt. Pour this over the dough, which will have a crusty skin on it,. and mix well until the skin disappears. Gradually add the remaining flour and knead for 15 minutes. Lift the dough and slap it down in the bowl and keep repeating this process for 5 minutes. Cover with a damp cloth and leave in a warm place for 2 hours. Divide into 4 portions and roll into balls. Leave on a floured board, covered with a dry cloth for 15 minutes. Roll and pull each ball into a long sausage which will fit the baking sheet. Put the loaves on a cloth and pull the cloth tightly up at the sides and between the loaves so that they do not expand sideways. Cover with another cloth and leave in a warm place for 1 hour. Lift carefully on to baking sheets. Slash each loaf three times with a sharp razor or knife and bake at 450°F/230°C/Gas Mark 8 for 45 minutes. After the first 30 minutes, turn the loaves and brush the crusts with melted butter or milk.

900g/2lb strong plain flour
25g/1oz fresh yeast
600ml/1 pint water
15g/½oz salt

Brioche

15g/½oz fresh yeast
30ml/2 tablespoons water
225g/8oz strong plain flour
½ level teaspoon salt
15g/½oz caster sugar
2 beaten eggs
50g/2oz melted and cooled
    butter

Egg wash
1 beaten egg
15ml/1 tablespoon water
Pinch of sugar

Prepare yeast liquid by blending yeast with 30ml/2 tablespoons water. Sift together flour, salt and sugar in a large bowl. Add yeast liquid, eggs and butter and work to a soft dough. Turn on to a lightly floured surface and knead well for about 5 minutes. Place dough in a lightly greased large polythene bag and allow to rise at room temperature for 1–1½ hours. Grease twelve 7.5cm/3in brioche tins or deep bun tins with melted lard. Divide risen dough into 4 equal pieces and then each of them into 3 equal pieces. Shape about three-quarters of each piece into a ball and put in tin. Firmly press a hole in the centre and place remaining piece of dough, shaped as a ball, in the centre. Repeat with remaining pieces and place all the tins on a baking tray. Put inside a large greased polythene bag and leave to rise until double in size, about 1 hour in a warm place. Blend together all ingredients for egg wash. Brush with egg wash and bake in the middle of the oven at 450°F/230°C/Gas Mark 8 for 10 minutes. Serve warm.

Grand Brioche
Place all the dough in a greased 20cm/8in brioche mould. Rise, brush with egg wash and bake in a hot oven, 450°F/230°C/Gas Mark 8 for 15–20 minutes.

Ring Brioche
Roll brioche dough into a ring shape and place on a greased baking sheet. Join the ends together and snip round the top at intervals with scissors. Rise, egg wash and bake as above.

Brioche Pies
Roll out the dough and cut into 7.5cm/3in circles. Fill half with a mixture of fruit, sugar and chopped candied peel in a sweet rum sauce or about 175g/6oz diced Gruyère cheese, seasoning and mixed herbs. Top with another circle of dough and press the edges well together. Place the pies in a circle in a greased 20cm/8in sandwich tin. Cover and rise for about 40 minutes. Brush with egg wash and bake in a very hot oven, 450°F/230°C/Gas Mark 8 for 15–20 minutes.

Fruit Brioche
Line a greased flan ring or 17.5cm/7in sandwich tin with a quarter of the brioche dough. Cover with a layer of frangipane (50g/2oz butter beaten with 50g/2oz caster sugar, gradually beat in 1 egg,

followed by 50g/2oz ground almonds and 2 teaspoons flour). Top with sliced fruit and cover with another quarter of the dough. Rise, egg wash and bake as above. Serve sprinkled with icing sugar.

Filled Brioche

Scoop out the centres of small cooked brioche and fill with mixture of fruit, purées or mousses.

Vienna Fritters

Roll out quarters of the brioche dough to 30mm/⅛in thickness. Put teaspoonfuls of filling, cream, custard, mixed fruits, mincemeat or savoury filling at regular intervals. Moisten round each spoon of filling, put another layer of dough on top and press well together between each filling. Cut into squares or rounds, cover and leave to rise. Fry in deep fat at 350°F/180°C until golden brown.

Croissants

Croissants are the classic crisp, flaky rolls of the Continental breakfast, but are also delicious for lunch or dinner.

The secret of making good croissants is to have firm dough and an equally firm fat so that they form definite layers. The pastry is light because it is made by a combination of two methods of aeration: the yeast fermentation of a rich dough; the trapping of air with the fat as in flaky pastry.

The pastry is kept cold throughout its preparation and only risen at a warmer temperature after shaping.

The following points will help towards the success of your croissants:

1) Use a strong plain flour to make a strong dough.
2) Good layering of fat is important, so roll the dough thin and use margarine or butter that is hard and at room temperature.
3) While standing, the pastry must always be put in a polythene bag to prevent skinning and cracking.
4) To keep the fat in definite layers, keep the pastry chilled while standing. This makes the pastry firm to roll and keeps its shape.
5) Care must be taken during rolling to keep the edges of the pastry straight and the corners square.
6) Work quickly when handling the dough so that it does not become too warm and soft.

450g/1lb strong plain flour
2 level teaspoons salt
25g/1oz lard – rubbed in
1 beaten egg
25g/1oz fresh yeast
250ml/8fl.oz water
100–175g/4–6oz hard
  margarine or butter

Egg Wash
1 egg
A little water
½ teaspoon sugar

Make a dough with flour, salt, lard, egg and yeast creamed in water. Knead on a lightly floured board, until the dough is smooth, about 10–15 minutes. Roll the dough into a long strip approximately 50×20cm/20×8in and 60mm/¼in thick, taking care to keep the dough piece rectangular. Soften margarine or butter with knife, then divide into three. Use one part to dot the dough, covering the top two-thirds of the dough and leaving a small border clear. Fold in three, by bringing up the plain part of the dough first, then bringing the top part over. Turn the dough so that the fold is on the right-hand side. Seal the edges by pressing with the rolling pin. Re-shape to a long strip by gently pressing the dough at intervals with the rolling pin. Again, take care to keep the dough piece rectangular. Repeat with the other two portions of fat. Place in a greased polythene bag and allow to rest in the refrigerator for 30 minutes. Roll out, as before, to a rectangular strip. Repeat folding and rolling three times more. Place in the refrigerator for at least 30 minutes. The dough can be stored overnight in the refrigerator at this stage for up to three days, ready to make croissants at any time. Roll the dough to a rectangle about 55×32.5cm/22×13in. Cover with greased polythene and leave 10 minutes. Trim edges with a sharp knife to leave rectangle 53.5×30cm/21×12in and divide lengthwise. Cut each strip into six triangles 15cm/6in high with a 15cm/6in base. Brush with egg wash. Roll up each triangle loosely, towards point, finishing with the tip underneath. Curve into crescent shape.

Alternative Shaping
Roll the dough into a rectangle about 65×27.5cm/26×11in. Cover and rest for 10 minutes. Trim edges to leave rectangle 62.5×25cm/25×10in and divide in half lengthwise. Cut each strip into nine triangles 12.5cm/5in high with a 12.5cm/5in base. Brush with egg wash and roll into croissant shapes as before. After shaping, put croissants on ungreased baking sheet, or Bakewell paper. Brush tops with egg wash, cover with greased polythene and leave at room temperature for about 30 minutes until light and puffy. Brush again with egg wash before baking. Bake on middle shelf of oven at 425°F/220°C/Gas Mark 7 for 15–20 minutes. Croissants are best served warm.

French Chocolate Croissants

Cream the yeast and sugar until liquid, and add most of the warm milk. Sieve the flour with a pinch of salt into a warm mixing bowl, make a well in the centre, add the yeast liquid and 25g/1oz melted butter. Bind to a soft dough, using a little more liquid if necessary. Knead lightly on a floured board and leave to rise in a warm place until doubled in size, about 30 minutes. Knead again then roll into an oblong three times as long as it is wide. Soften remaining butter, divide into three and make the croissants as in previous recipe. Dot one portion of butter in small pieces over the top two-thirds of the dough. Fold the bottom third up and the top third down over the butter, seal the edges and turn so that the folded edges are at the sides. Roll into an oblong again and repeat the process twice. Between rolling, cover dough and leave in a cool place for a short time to relax it. Finally roll out thinly and cut into triangles with 22.5cm/9in long sides and 15cm/6in base. Place a few pieces of chocolate at the base of each and roll up covering the chocolate. Curl the ends round to form a crescent. Place on baking trays and leave in a warm place for 15–20 minutes until well risen. Brush with beaten egg and bake near the top of the oven at 450°F/230°C/Gas Mark 8 for 10–15 minutes until golden brown. Eat the croissants on the day they are made. Chocolate croissants used to be a special treat for French children.

15g/½oz fresh yeast
1 teaspoon caster sugar
150ml/¼ pint and 60ml/4
*   tablespoons warm milk*
275g/10oz strong plain flour
Pinch of salt
150g/5oz butter
100g/4oz plain chopped
*   chocolate*
Beaten egg to glaze

Challah

Mix the yeast and saffron in the water and leave to stand for 5 minutes. Sift the flour, salt and sugar. Mix the yeast liquid with 175g/6oz flour mixture, stirring until smooth. Cover with a cloth and leave in a warm place for 30 minutes until double in size. Add the beaten eggs and mix well. Add the remaining flour and knead until smooth and elastic. Put into a bowl, dust with a little flour and cover with a cloth. Leave for about 2 hours in a warm place until double in bulk. Knead for 5 minutes and divide into three pieces. Roll with the hands into long round strips and plait them together, tucking in the ends. Put on a greased baking sheet, cover and leave to rise for 1 hour. Brush well with egg yolk and bake at 400°F/200°C/Gas Mark 6 for 10 minutes. Reduce to 375°F/190°C/Gas Mark 5 and bake for 35 minutes.

25g/1oz fresh yeast
⅛ teaspoon saffron
250ml/8fl.oz lukewarm
*   water*
450g/1lb strong plain flour
½ teaspoon salt
1 teaspoon sugar
2 eggs
1 egg yolk

51

Pitta

675g/1½lb risen dough (white or brown)
Flour

Knock back the risen dough and divide it into six even-sized pieces. On a lightly floured board, knead each piece into a ball and then roll each piece to an oval shape approximately 20×10cm/8×4in. Dust lightly with flour and fold in half by bringing the top over the bottom. Press the edges together lightly to seal. Put on to a well-greased baking sheet, but do not leave to prove again. Bake at 425°F/220°C/Gas Mark 7 for 20 minutes. Remove from the baking sheet and wrap the bread loosely in foil so that it will remain soft as it cools. This bread makes a convenient 'pocket' to hold kebabs slipped from their skewers, or salads, eggs or cold meats.

Chapattis

225g/8oz wholemeal flour
Large pinch of salt
25g/1oz butter
165ml/5½ fl.oz and 1 tablespoon water
15ml/1 tablespoon corn oil

Put the flour into a bowl with the salt. Rub in the butter until the mixture is like fine breadcrumbs. Mix in the water to give a stiff dough. Knead on a lightly floured board for 15 minutes. Leave the dough on the board and cover with the bowl. Leave to rest for 30 minutes. Divide the dough into eight pieces and roll out each piece to a 15cm/6in round. Heat the oil in a frying pan. Fry each piece for 3 minutes, turning often. Serve warm with curry.

Naan Bread

½ teaspoon dried yeast
30ml/2 tablespoons warm water
675g/1½lb self-raising flour
450ml/¾ pint natural yogurt
Large pinch of salt
50g/2oz melted butter

Stir the yeast into the water and leave for 5 minutes until it starts to bubble and work. Put the flour into a bowl and work in the yogurt, salt and yeast liquid. Mix well and knead lightly. Cover with a damp cloth and leave to stand in a warm place for 24 hours. Divide the dough into 12 pieces. On a lightly floured board, roll each piece into an oval about 60mm/¼in thick. Put the pieces on a greased baking sheet. Brush each one with melted butter and grill for 2 minutes on each side under high heat until brown. Serve warm. This is a traditional accompaniment to Indian tandoori food. The bread should be flat and soft, moist inside and slightly scorched outside.

5 Fruit Breads and Yeastcakes

Many delicious fruit breads and cakes can be made from white, brown or enriched white bread doughs. Many of these originated as 'special occasion' cakes in country districts to use up odd pieces of plain dough, and they are particularly associated with harvest time.

Russian Easter Bread

Warm the milk and dissolve the yeast. Add 25g/1oz flour and leave in a warm place for 30 minutes. Beat the egg yolks, salt, butter and sugar together. Mix together the yeast and egg mixtures and work in the flour to give a soft, smooth dough. Add the peel. Cover with a cloth and leave to rise for 1½ hours. Divide the mixture into three pieces and plait them loosely. Put on a floured baking sheet and leave for 30 minutes. Brush with a little egg and milk beaten together and bake at 400°F/200°C/Gas Mark 6 for 40 minutes.

150ml/¼ pint milk
25g/1oz fresh yeast
225g/8oz strong plain flour
3 egg yolks
Pinch of salt
75g/3oz melted butter
75g/3oz sugar
100g/4oz chopped mixed peel

Caraway Seed Bread

Mix the flour, salt and caraway seeds in a warm basin. Mix the yeast with the sugar and 150ml/¼ pint water and leave until frothy. Add the lard to the remaining water. Add the yeast mixture and the lard mixture to the flour and beat well. Leave in a warm place covered with a cloth for 1 hour to rise. Knead well and then form into two round loaves. Put on a greased baking sheet and leave for about 45 minutes in a warm place until double in size. Bake at 400°F/200°C/Gas Mark 6 for 40 minutes. This bread is good served with cheese.

900g/2lb strong plain flour
1½ teaspoons salt
3 teaspoons caraway seeds
25g/1oz fresh yeast
1 teaspoon brown sugar
600ml/1 pint lukewarm
  water
50g/2oz lard

Fruit Tea Bread

40g/1½oz fresh yeast
150ml/¼ pint water
450g/1lb strong plain flour
2 teaspoons salt
25g/1oz lard
15ml/1 tablespoon honey
    made up to 150ml/¼ pint
    liquid with warm milk
100g/4oz seedless raisins
100g/4oz currants
100g/4oz mixed peel

Cream yeast in lukewarm water. Mix flour and salt, rub in lard, add and blend in yeast liquid and honey and milk. Work to a dough by squeezing with fingers until it leaves the bowl clean. Turn on to a lightly floured board and knead until dough feels smooth and elastic (about 5 minutes). Put dough in a lightly greased polythene bag, lightly tied, or a saucepan with lid and rise until dough doubles its size and springs back when lightly pressed with a floured finger. Turn the dough on to board and work in the fruit. Divide the dough into two, flatten each piece and roll up like a Swiss roll to fit the greased 450g/1lb tins. Place tins in lightly greased polythene bags and leave to rise until dough doubles in size and springs back when lightly pressed with a floured finger. Remove polythene. Bake on middle shelf of oven at 375°F/190°C/Gas Mark 5 for 30–40 minutes. Brush tops of hot loaves with wet brush dipped in honey. Cool on a wire tray.

Iced Twist

225g/8oz strong plain flour
Pinch of salt
25g/1oz butter
15g/½oz fresh yeast
1 teaspoon sugar
120ml/4fl.oz milk
1 egg
50g/2oz sugar
Glacé cherries, angelica and
    nuts

Icing
Icing sugar
Lemon juice or water

Put the flour and salt into a warm basin. Melt the butter. Cream the yeast with the sugar. Add the butter, yeast, warm milk, egg and sugar to the flour and mix well. Knead thoroughly, cover with a cloth and leave for about 45 minutes until the dough has doubled in size. Knead again and form into a long strip. Divide into three pieces and plait them together, tucking the ends under. If liked, the plait can be formed to a circle. Cover and leave in a warm place for 15 minutes. Brush with a little beaten egg or some milk and bake at 450°F/230°C/Gas Mark 8 for 25 minutes. When cold, coat with a thin layer of icing made by mixing the icing sugar and liquid until smooth. Sprinkle with cherries, angelica and nuts.

Gooseberry Bread

Simmer the gooseberries in very little water until soft enough to sieve. Put flour and salt into a warm bowl. Cream the yeast with the sugar and add to the flour, together with the gooseberry purée. Knead well and leave in a warm place for 6 hours. Shape into two 450g/1lb loaf tins and leave to rise for 2 hours. Bake at 425°F/220°C/Gas Mark 7 for 15 minutes, then reduce heat to 375°F/190°C/Gas Mark 5 for 45 minutes.

225g/8oz gooseberries
675g/1½lb strong plain flour
½ teaspoon salt
15g/½oz fresh yeast
1 teaspoon sugar

Swedish Christmas Bread

Melt the butter and add the stout, heating until lukewarm. Put into a large bowl and add the treacle, half the flour, salt, grated peel and aniseed or fennel. Dissolve the yeast in a little warm water and work it into the mixture. Retain about 100g/4oz white flour, and work the remainder into the dough and mix well, beating until the dough is smooth and firm. Cover with a cloth and leave in a warm place until the dough has doubled in bulk. Knead with the remaining flour until firm and glossy. Divide into three pieces and shape into long loaves. Put on to greased baking sheets, cover with a cloth and leave for 1 hour. Prick the surfaces of the loaves with a cocktail stick or thin skewer. Bake at 300°F/150°C/Gas Mark 2 for 1 hour. Halfway through baking, brush the tops of the loaves with a little black treacle mixed in water. Brush with the same mixture when the loaves are baked, and wrap them in clean tea towels to keep soft.

50g/2oz butter
900ml/1½ pints stout
225g/8oz black treacle
800g/1lb 12oz rye flour
350g/12oz strong plain flour
1 teaspoon salt
Peel of 2 oranges
1 tablespoon ground aniseed or fennel seed
75g/3oz fresh yeast

Yule Bread

Put the flour into a warm basin and rub in the butter. Keep a pinch of sugar, and put the remaining sugar and salt into the flour. Cream the yeast with the pinch of sugar and a little lukewarm milk and leave until frothy. Pour yeast into the flour and leave to rise for 15 minutes. Stir in beaten eggs and as much warm milk as will make a light dough. Beat well and leave to rise for 1 hour. Add the dried fruit, peel and spices and leave to rise for 1 hour. Put into three 1kg/2lb loaf tins lined with greased paper, and leave to rise for 45 minutes. Bake at 425°F/220°C/Gas Mark 7 for 20 minutes, then reduce heat to 375°F/190°C/Gas Mark 5 for 1 hour.

900g/2lb strong plain flour
350g/12oz butter
350g/12oz sugar
1 teaspoon salt
40g/1½oz fresh yeast
Milk
3 eggs
450g/1lb currants
225g/8oz sultanas
100g/4oz chopped mixed peel
½ teaspoon ground nutmeg
1 teaspoon ground cinnamon

Orange Bread

25g/1oz fresh yeast
150ml/¼ pint water
450g/1lb strong plain flour
2 teaspoons salt
25g/1oz sugar
1 large orange
1 egg
175g/6oz mixed dried fruit

Mix yeast in water and leave for 10 minutes. Mix in flour, salt and sugar. Squeeze juice from the orange, and chop the flesh and skin very finely. Add orange rind and juice, egg and fruit and 45–60ml/3–4 tablespoons extra water if required, but the dough should not be too soft. Leave in a warm place for 1 hour. Shape into two 450g/1lb loaf tins and leave for 15 minutes. Bake at 400°F/200°C/Gas Mark 6 on the middle shelf of oven for 30–45 minutes. Brush the baked bread with a wet brush dipped in honey or syrup. Cool on a wire tray.

Orange Treacle Bread

450g/1lb risen orange dough
   (½ previous recipe)
60ml/4 tablespoons black
   treacle

Prepare and rise dough as in the previous recipe. Add the treacle and work in very well with one hand until the mixture is evenly brown in colour and no longer streaky. Put into greased 450g/1lb loaf tin, rise and continue as for Orange Bread.

Ginger and Orange Fruited Bap

350g/12oz risen white bread
   dough
15g/½oz caster sugar
25g/1oz finely chopped
   crystallised ginger
50g/2oz currants
Grated rind of 1 orange

Work all ingredients together in a basin by squeezing with one hand until thoroughly mixed. Shape into a round 15cm/6in across and 6.25cm/2in deep and put on a greased baking sheet. Place in a lightly greased polythene bag and allow to rise until double in size and dough springs back when pressed with a lightly floured finger. Bake on the middle shelf of oven at 425°F/220°C/Gas Mark 7 for 30 minutes. Brush top of hot bap with a wet brush dipped in honey.

Dough Cake

450g/1lb risen white bread
   dough
50g/2oz butter
50g/2oz caster sugar
100g/4oz mixed dried fruit
1 teaspoon ground mixed
   spice

Work all ingredients together in a basin by squeezing with one hand until thoroughly mixed. Put dough into greased 900g/2lb loaf tin. Place in lightly greased polythene bag and allow to rise to the top of the tin. Bake on middle shelf of oven at 400°F/200°C/Gas Mark 6 for about 40 minutes. Brush top of hot loaf with a wet brush dipped in honey to give a glaze.

Lardy Cake

Lardy Cake can be served hot as a pudding, with jam, or as a cake for tea. Leftover Lardy Cake is good toasted too, or it can be refreshed by wrapping tightly in foil and placing in a hot oven, 450°F/230°C/Gas Mark 8 for 10 minutes. Cool in the foil.

Turn the dough on to a lightly floured board and roll firmly to 60mm/¼in thick strip with a rolling pin. Spread one-third of the fat in little pats on the dough. Sprinkle with one-third of the sugar and spice and sultanas and fold into three. Roll out to a strip again, and repeat the procedure with fat and sugar twice more. Put the rolled dough in a baking tin 20×25cm/8×10in and press down firmly to fill up the corners. Criss-cross the top by lightly scoring with a very sharp knife. Place in a lightly greased polythene bag and allow to rise to double in size. Bake on middle shelf of oven at 425°F/220°C/Gas Mark 7 for about 30 minutes. Remove from the tin and spoon any syrup remaining in the tin over the surface of the cake.

675g/1½lb risen white bread dough
100g/4oz lard or butter
100g/4oz caster sugar
1 teaspoon ground mixed spice
100g/4oz sultanas

Wiltshire Lardy Cake

Put the flour, salt and spice into a warm bowl. Cream the yeast and sugar and add to the flour with the warm milk to make a soft dough. Beat thoroughly, cover and leave to stand in a warm place for about 45 minutes until double in size. Roll out to 60mm/¼in thick on a well-floured board. Spread on half the lard, sugar and fruit. Fold in three, turn to left and roll again. Repeat with the remaining lard, sugar and fruit. Roll out to an oblong 2.5cm/1in thick and put into a deep tin the same size as the cake. Leave in a warm place for 1 hour until well risen. Score the top with a knife, brush with a little sugar dissolved in water and bake at 450°F/230°C/Gas Mark 8 for 30 minutes.

225g/8oz strong plain flour
¼ teaspoon salt
¼ teaspoon ground mixed spice
8g/¼oz fresh yeast
1 teaspoon sugar
150ml/¼ pint warm milk
50g/2oz lard
50g/2oz sugar
50g/2oz mixed dried fruit

Sultana Dough Cake

450g/1lb bread dough
75g/3oz caster sugar
75g/3oz butter
200g/7oz sultanas
1 egg

Put the dough to rise in a warm place to double in size. While the dough is rising, put the sugar, butter and sultanas into a warm bowl and leave to stand in a warm place. See that the egg is also kept warm. When the dough has risen, break it into small pieces and put into the bowl with the sugar mixture. Add the egg and work all the mixture together until thoroughly blended. The mixture will be soft and can almost be poured. Put it into a 17.5cm/7in tin lined with greaseproof paper. Cover and leave in a warm place for 30 minutes. Bake at 400°F/200°C/Gas Mark 6 for $1\frac{1}{4}$ hours.

ENRICHED WHITE BREAD DOUGH AND VARIATIONS

This bread dough is made by the sponge batter method. Any yeast recipe may be made this way by making a batter of one-third of the flour, all the liquid, sugar and yeast, but not the salt. Allow this batter to froth before adding the rest of the ingredients. It is especially good when using dried yeast.

Basic Recipe

Batter ingredients
150g/5oz strong plain flour
1 teaspoon sugar
15g/½oz fresh yeast or 8g/¼oz dried yeast
250ml/8fl.oz warm milk

Dough ingredients
300g/11oz strong plain flour
1 teaspoon salt
50g/2oz butter
1 egg

Egg Wash
Beaten egg
1 teaspoon sugar
15ml/1 tablespoon water

Blend the batter ingredients together in a large bowl. Set aside until frothy, 20 minutes in a warm place, but longer in a cool one. Mix the remaining flour with the salt, and rub in the butter. Add the egg and the flour mixture to the batter and mix well to give a fairly soft dough that leaves the sides of the bowl clean. Turn the dough on to a lightly floured surface and knead until it is smooth and no longer sticky – about 10 minutes. No extra flour should be necessary. Place the dough in a lightly greased polythene bag, loosely tied, and allow to rise until double in size and the dough springs back when pressed gently with a lightly floured finger. Rising times can be varied to suit your convenience: 45–60 minutes in a warm place for a quick rise; 2 hours at average room temperature for a slower rise; up to 12 hours in a cold room, larder or refrigerator for an overnight rise.

Refrigerated dough must be returned to room temperature before shaping.

Fruited Enriched Dough

To the basic recipe add the following with the dough ingredients:

100g/4oz currants
100g/4oz sultanas
25g/1oz chopped mixed peel
25g/1oz chopped nuts
Grated rind of 1 lemon

Fruit Twists

Divide half the risen dough into 8 equal pieces and shape these into long thin rolls. Twist the ends in opposite directions. Place side by side in a lightly greased 20cm/8in square tin and cover with a polythene bag. Prove for 40 minutes and brush with egg wash. Bake at 375°F/190°C/Gas Mark 5 for 30 minutes.

Stollen

Mould half the risen dough to an oval shape 30×20cm/12×8in. Brush with melted butter and spread 50g/2oz chopped glacé cherries over one half. Fold one half over the other and press lightly together. Place on a floured baking sheet and cover with greased polythene. Leave to prove until double in size. Brush with melted butter. Bake at 350°F/180°C/Gas Mark 4 for 40–45 minutes. While still hot brush with sugar glaze.

Bun Loaf

Knock back half the risen dough. Press dough out into a rectangle the same width as the tin. Then fold into three and fit into a greased 450g/1lb loaf tin. Cover with lightly greased polythene and prove until dough has doubled in size. Bake at 425°F/220°C/Gas Mark 7 for 35–40 minutes. Brush the hot loaf with a sugar glaze.

RECIPES USING ENRICHED BREAD DOUGH

French Fruit Bread

Peel and core the apples and dice the flesh finely. Put all filling ingredients together in a pan and heat for 1 minute. Roll dough to a rectangle 22.5×30cm/9×12in long. Place on a greased baking sheet. Spread filling down centre of the dough. Make diagonal cuts 5cm/2in apart down remaining dough on both sides. Cross alternate strips over filling to make a braid. Cover and rise for about 30 minutes. Bake at 375°F/190°C/Gas Mark 5 for 30–35 minutes. Decorate with water icing, made from icing sugar, lemon juice and water.

1 basic recipe enriched bread dough

Filling
2 eating apples
50g/2oz soft brown sugar
¼ teaspoon salt
½ teaspoon ground cinnamon

Swedish Tea Ring

1 basic recipe enriched bread dough
15g/½oz melted butter
50g/2oz soft brown sugar
2 teaspoons ground cinnamon

Roll dough to a rectangle 22.5×30cm/9×12in. Brush with melted butter, and sprinkle the sugar and cinnamon over the dough. Roll up tightly from the long edge and seal the ends together to form a ring. Place on a greased baking sheet and with scissors cut slashes at an angle 2.5cm/1in apart to within 1.25cm/½in of the centre. Turn the cut sections on their sides. Cover with a lightly greased polythene bag and rise for about 30 minutes. Bake at 375°F/190°C/Gas Mark 5 for 30–35 minutes. Decorate with water icing, and some chopped cherries and nuts.

Hungarian Coffee Cake

1 basic recipe enriched bread dough

Filling
50g/2oz melted butter

Coating ingredients
75g/3oz caster sugar
1 teaspoon ground cinnamon
25g/1oz chopped walnuts
Few raisins

Divide the dough into 24 equal pieces and roll into balls the size of a walnut. Roll each ball in the melted butter. Mix the coating ingredients together and roll each ball in this. Arrange a double row round a large greased tin mould leaving room for rising. Sprinkle with a few raisins. Cover with a lightly greased polythene bag and rise for about 30 minutes. Bake at 400°F/200°C/Gas Mark 6 for 25–30 minutes.

Bannock

1 basic recipe enriched bread dough

Filling
25g/1oz sultanas
25g/1oz currants
15g/½oz chopped mixed peel
Milk for brushing

Work fruit into risen dough. Knead well and shape into a round and then flatten to approximately 20cm/8in across and 1.25cm/½in thick. Put on a greased and floured tray and slash with a sharp knife into 8 equal sections. Brush top with milk. Cover with lightly greased polythene bag and rise for about 30 minutes. Brush again with milk. Bake at 400°F/200°C/Gas Mark 6 for 20 minutes. Cool on a wire tray.

Cinnamon Orange Swirl

Squeeze the orange juice and chop or mince the flesh and peel finely. Work the juice and minced flesh and peel into the risen dough. Roll dough to a rectangle 15×32.5cm/6×12in long. Brush lightly with water and sprinkle with cinnamon and sugar. Roll up tightly from the short edge and place in a greased 450g/1lb loaf tin. Cover with a lightly greased polythene bag and rise for about 45–50 minutes. Bake at 400°F/200°C/Gas Mark 6 for 30–35 minutes. When cold, ice with water icing.

1 basic recipe enriched bread dough

Filling
½ orange
1 tablespoon ground cinnamon
25g/1oz soft brown sugar

Apple Kuchen

Roll risen dough to fit a 20cm/8in sandwich tin. Place dough in greased tin. Peel and core the apples and cut in thin slices. Arrange the slices of apple on the top and sprinkle over the brown sugar and cinnamon. Cover with a greased polythene bag and rise for about 30 minutes. Bake on the middle shelf of oven at 425°F/220°C/Gas Mark 7 for 35–40 minutes.

225g/8oz basic recipe enriched bread dough

Filling
450g/1lb cooking apples
25g/1oz soft brown sugar
1 teaspoon ground cinnamon

Wheatmeal Fruit Breads

Mix the flours, lard, salt and sugar together in a bowl. Blend yeast in the water and add all at once. Mix to a soft scone-like dough (adding more flour if necessary) that leaves the bowl clean. Knead the dough thoroughly on a lightly floured surface. Put the dough into a lightly greased polythene bag lightly tied, and allow to rise to double in size before using. Choose the variety of loaf and topping from the following recipes. The method of making is the same for each.

Basic Dough
225g/8oz each strong brown and white plain flours (or in any proportion you like)
8g/¼oz lard
2 teaspoons sugar
2 teaspoons salt
15g/½oz fresh yeast
300ml/½ pint water

Fig and Treacle Bread
675g/1½lb risen wheatmeal dough (all basic recipe)
225g/8oz black treacle
225g/8oz chopped dried figs
100g/4oz soft brown sugar
50g/2oz butter

Ginger Loaf
450g/1lb risen wheatmeal dough (⅔ basic recipe)
50g/2oz black treacle
25g/1oz butter or 30ml/2 tablespoons oil
1½–2 teaspoons ground ginger
50g/2oz sultanas

Apricot and Walnut Loaf
350g/12oz risen wheatmeal dough (½ basic recipe)
100g/4oz chopped dried apricots
50g/2oz chopped walnuts
25g/1oz sugar
25g/1oz butter

To Make the Loaves
Squeeze and work all the ingredients together in a basin, with one hand until the mixture is no longer streaky. Two-thirds fill the prepared tins (bottom-lined and greased) and put inside a polythene bag until dough rises to within 1.25cm/½in of the top of the tins (1 hour in a warm place, longer in a cooler one). Cover with one of the toppings above and bake on middle shelf of oven at 400°F/200°C/Gas Mark 6. Fig and Treacle Bread (45–50 minutes); Ginger Loaf (30–40 minutes); Apricot and Walnut Bread (40–45 minutes). Cool in tin 10 minutes and then on wire tray.

Toppings
1) Sprinkle with a crumble of 25g/1oz butter, 25g/1oz sugar, 40g/1½oz plain flour rubbed together until it looks like coarse breadcrumbs
2) Sprinkle crushed cornflakes on top of the dough
After baking, brush the hot loaf with a wet brush dipped in honey or syrup.

Continental Family Cake

Rub fresh yeast into dry mix. If using dried yeast dissolve sugar in warm milk and sprinkle dried yeast on top. Leave until frothy (about 10 minutes). Add eggs, milk and orange pulp and mix thoroughly with a wooden spoon to a very soft dough. Half fill a 20cm/8in square greased tin. Spread a layer of red jam on top of mixture and cover with crumble topping. Put to rise until double in size inside a large lightly oiled polythene bag (about 2 hours at room temperature, less in a warm place). Bake on middle shelf of oven at 400°F/200°C/Gas Mark 6 for 30–35 minutes. Cool in tin for 10 minutes then turn out on to a wire rack.

Dry Mix
275g/10oz strong plain flour
50g/2oz caster sugar
1 teaspoon salt
75g/3oz margarine
175g/6oz currants

Additional ingredients
25g/1oz fresh yeast or
    15g/½oz dried yeast and ½
    level teaspoon sugar
2 eggs
75ml/3fl.oz milk
Minced rind and juice of ½
    orange

Crumble topping
Red jam
25g/1oz butter
40g/1½oz plain flour
25g/1oz sugar
1 teaspoon ground cinnamon

Gugelhupf

This cake should be baked in a fluted tin ring, but a plain ring tin can be used. Warm the milk and dissolve the yeast in it. Add 50g/2oz flour and leave the mixture in a warm place for 30 minutes. Beat in the melted butter, sugar, eggs, grated orange rind, and juice. Add the raisins which have been soaked in the rum. Beat in the remaining flour to make a very soft dough. Grease the tin and dust it thoroughly with breadcrumbs or semolina. Fill the tin with the dough which should come about halfway up the tin. Leave in a warm place for 1 hour until the dough reaches the top of the tin. Bake at 400°F/200°C/Gas Mark 6 for 40 minutes. Cool on a wire rack and dust with icing sugar.

65ml/2½fl.oz milk
25g/1oz fresh yeast
225g/8oz strong plain flour
50g/2oz melted butter
50g/2oz sugar
2 eggs
1 orange
50g/2oz raisins
15ml/1 tablespoon rum
Fine breadcrumbs or semolina

6 Teacakes, Buns and Yeast Pastries

Home-made crumpets, and muffins, teacakes, fruit buns and yeast pastries bear no resemblance to the shop-bought varieties because the ones you make yourself are a hundred times better. You can indulge in richer doughs, more dried fruit, stickier glazes and more jam in the doughnuts. Here are the traditional favourites which are delicious fresh from the oven or griddle, and just as good next day if toasted and buttered.

Crumpets

350g/12oz strong plain flour
15g/½oz fresh yeast
375ml/12½fl.oz warm water
½ teaspoon bicarbonate of
   soda
2 teaspoons salt
150ml/¼ pint milk

Blend flour, yeast and water in a large bowl and mix well. Cover with a polythene bag and leave until very light and fluffy, and about to collapse. Stir bicarbonate of soda and salt into milk and stir briskly into the batter adding a little extra milk if necessary so the batter is runny. Very lightly grease a hot griddle, heavy frying pan or hotplate. Pour one or two tablespoons of mixture into pre-greased poaching rings, lower heat and cook gently for 10 minutes or until crumpet is well set. Turn crumpet and cook top for 2–3 minutes until golden brown. Once mixture has set, poaching rings can be removed, re-greased and re-used while first crumpets finish cooking. To serve crumpets, toast under a hot grill and top with butter.

Traditional Muffins

15g/½oz fresh yeast
300ml/½ pint warm water
450g/1lb strong plain flour
1 teaspoon salt
Fine semolina

Make yeast liquid with yeast and water. Add yeast liquid to flour and salt and knead until dough is smooth. Place in greased polythene bag and leave to rise for about 1 hour at room temperature. The dough is ready when it springs back if pressed with a lightly floured finger. Knead lightly again and roll out on floured board to 1.25cm/½in thickness. Leave to rest for 5 minutes, covered and cut into 7.5cm/3in rounds. Re-roll and cut until all dough is used up. Place on well-floured baking sheet and dust tops with fine semolina. Place in large polythene bag and leave for 30–40 minutes at room temperature. Test with floured finger again. Cook on hot, greased griddle, frying pan or hotplate for about 6 minutes each side, until golden brown. Alternatively, cook in oven at 450°F/230°C/Gas Mark 8 for about 10 minutes, turning after 5 minutes. To serve, pull muffins open all the way round with the fingers, leaving the two halves joined in the middle, and toast slowly on both sides. Pull apart, butter each half well, put together again and serve hot. It is possible to make muffins from ordinary risen white bread dough if you have some to spare, or only want to make a small quantity of muffins. Roll out risen dough and proceed as above.

Rich Muffins

Mix yeast liquid as in previous recipe. Place flour, salt, beaten egg, melted butter and yeast liquid in a large bowl. Mix and knead until a smooth dough is formed (about 10 minutes). The dough is intended to be quite soft, so add as little flour as possible. Proceed as for Traditional Muffins.

25g/1oz fresh yeast
270ml/9fl.oz warm milk
450g/1lb strong plain flour
1 teaspoon salt
1 egg
25g/1oz melted butter

Derbyshire Oatcake

Sift together oatmeal and flour with salt. Cream yeast and sugar and add warm water. Stir into dry ingredients and leave in a warm place for 30 minutes. Heat griddle and grease lightly. Pour on a little batter and cook for about 2 minutes. Turn and cook the other side. Serve hot with butter or dripping, or with crisp hot bacon.

225g/8oz fine or medium
  oatmeal
225g/8oz strong plain flour
Pinch of salt
25g/1oz fresh yeast
1 teaspoon sugar
300ml/½ pint warm water

Basic Yeast Buns

Batter ingredients
100g/4oz strong plain flour
1 teaspoon sugar
25g/1oz fresh yeast
150ml/¼ pint warm milk
90ml/3fl.oz warm water

Dough ingredients
350g/12oz strong plain flour
1 teaspoon salt
50g/2oz sugar
50g/2oz butter or margarine rubbed into flour
1 beaten egg

Glaze
50g/2oz sugar
60ml/4 tablespoons water

Blend the batter ingredients together in a large bowl and set aside until the batter froths (20–30 minutes). Mix the dough ingredients with the chosen filling into the batter to give a fairly soft dough that leaves the sides of the bowl clean. Turn the dough on to a lightly floured surface and knead until it is smooth and no longer sticky (about 5 minutes). Put the dough to rise in a lightly greased polythene bag, loosely tied, or in a 20cm/8in saucepan with lid. Leave to rise until double in size (1–1½ hours at room temperature, longer in a refrigerator).*

Turn risen dough on to a floured surface and flatten with the knuckles to knock out air bubbles. Knead to make a firm dough. Divide the dough into 12–14 pieces and shape using palm of one hand, press down hard at first then ease up. Do not overwork the dough. A little oil on the working surface and the palm of the hand helps to give a smooth finish. Place the buns well apart on a lightly floured baking sheet. Put inside a greased polythene bag and leave to rise until the dough feels springy – about 30 minutes. Remove polythene bag and bake, just above centre of oven at 425°F/220°C/Gas Mark 7 for 15–20 minutes. Brush warm buns with glaze and cool on a wire tray or finish as suggested below.

*NOTE: A cooler dough makes the buns easier to shape, but refrigerated dough must be returned to room temperature before shaping.

Cornish Splits
Omit eggs from basic recipe and add 30ml/4 tablespoons water. Divide risen dough into 4 equal pieces. Shape as for buns. Do not glaze. When cold, split and fill with jam and whipped cream.

100g/4oz currants

Currant
Make as basic dough.

100g/4oz stoned dates
50g/2oz walnuts

Date and Walnut
Chop dates and walnuts finely and add to dough.

Red jam
Grated rind of 1 lemon

Jam
Add lemon rind to dough. Place small quantity of stiff jam in centre of risen dough and pinch into shape.

London
Make as basic dough.

Swiss
Use plain dough made with lard and milk. Divide risen dough into 12 pieces and shape into 22.5cm/5in long rolls. Rise and bake. When cool decorate with water icing.

100g/4oz currants
50g/2oz chopped mixed peel
½ teaspoon ground nutmeg

Rich Yeast Buns

Proceed as in previous recipe until shaping stage is reached. Knead dough thoroughly and roll to a rectangle 30×22.5cm/ 12×9in. Brush with melted butter and spread with chosen filling. Roll up from the longest side like a Swiss roll and seal the edge. Cut into 9 equal slices and place these, cut side down, on a lightly greased baking tray well apart or in a 17.5cm/7in square cake tin. Put inside a polythene bag and rise until dough feels springy – about 30 minutes. Remove polythene bag. Finish buns as suggested. Bake just above the middle of the oven at 375°F/190°C/Gas Mark 5 for 20–25 minutes on a baking tray, or 30–35 minutes in a tin.

Batter ingredients
50g/2oz strong plain flour
½ teaspoon sugar
15g/½oz fresh yeast
120ml/4fl.oz warm milk

Dough ingredients
175g/6oz strong plain flour
½ teaspoon salt
15g/½oz butter, margarine or lard
1 beaten egg
Melted butter for brushing dough

Glaze
Combine ingredients in pan over low heat. Spread on dough. After rising, brush with egg or milk and sprinkle with poppy seeds.

1 beaten egg
1 tablespoon poppy seeds

Apricot or Prune
Soak fruit overnight in a little water. Chop fruit and spread with other ingredients over dough. Glaze baked buns with a wet brush dipped in honey.

100g/4oz dried apricots or prunes
25g/1oz chopped almonds
½ teaspoon ground cinnamon
25g/1oz sugar

Butterscotch
Mix butter and sugar and spread on dough.

25g/1oz butter
175g/6oz soft brown sugar

75g/3oz Cheddar cheese
100g–175g/4–6oz bacon,
  lightly fried
Caraway or poppy seeds

Chelsea Cheese

Grate cheese and chop bacon finely. Spread on dough. After rising, brush with beaten egg or milk and sprinkle with a few caraway or poppy seeds.

Jam for filling
50g/2oz caster sugar
½ teaspoon ground cinnamon

Doughnuts

Roll 50g/2oz pieces of dough into a round, cover and leave to rise. Place a small quantity of stiff jam in the centre of risen dough, and pinch into shape. Deep-fat fry at 360°F/190°C for 4 minutes. Drain and roll in sugar and cinnamon.

Hot Cross Buns

Batter
100g/4oz strong plain flour
25g/1oz fresh yeast
1 teaspoon sugar
150ml/¼ pint milk
100ml/3½ fl.oz water

Dough
350g/12oz strong plain flour
1 teaspoon salt
½ teaspoon ground mixed spice
½ teaspoon ground cinnamon
½ teaspoon ground nutmeg
50g/2oz sugar
50g/2oz butter, melted and
  cooled
1 beaten egg
100g/4oz currants
25–50g/1–2oz chopped
  mixed peel

Glaze
30ml/2 tablespoons milk
30ml/2 tablespoons water
40g/1½oz sugar

To make the batter, place flour in a large mixing bowl. Add yeast and sugar. Warm milk and water to about 110°F/44°C (lukewarm), add to flour and mix well. Set aside until frothy. To make the dough, sift together flour, salt, mixed spice, cinnamon, nutmeg and sugar. Stir butter and egg into risen yeast batter, add dry ingredients, fruit and peel; mix together. The dough should be fairly soft. Turn on to a lightly floured board and knead until smooth. For extra light buns, place dough in a lightly greased polythene bag and leave at room temperature until double in size, about 1½ hours. Divide the dough into 12 pieces and shape into buns using palm of one hand. Press down hard at first, then ease up. Arrange buns, well spaced apart, on floured baking sheet and place inside a lightly greased polythene bag and allow to rise at room temperature for about 45 minutes (only 30 minutes if dough has had initial rising). Make quick slashes with a very sharp knife or razor just cutting surface of dough to make a cross. Bake at 425°F/220°C/Gas Mark 7 for 15–20 minutes. To glaze, bring the milk and water to the boil for 2 minutes. Brush hot buns twice with glaze, then leave to cool. If liked, raisins may be used instead of currants. Instead of marking the buns with a knife, you can form crosses with almond paste or shortcrust pastry (about 50g/2oz for this recipe) and put the crosses on the buns before the final proving.

Bath Buns

Put the flour and salt into a warm bowl and rub in the butter. Add the milk, the yeast creamed with 1 teaspoon sugar and the eggs. Knead well, cover with a cloth and leave for about 45 minutes until the dough has doubled in size. Knead in the sugar, lemon peel, sultanas and mixed peel and form into 10 rough balls. Leave for 10 minutes in a warm place to rise. Brush with a little beaten egg or milk and sprinkle with roughly crushed cube sugar. Bake at 450°F/230°C/Gas Mark 8 for 15 minutes.

350g/12oz strong plain flour
Pinch of salt
100g/4oz butter
65ml/2½ fl.oz sour milk
40g/¾oz fresh yeast
1 teaspoon sugar
2 eggs
75g/3oz sugar
Grated peel of 1 lemon
75g/3oz sultanas
25g/1oz chopped mixed peel
Beaten egg or milk
Cube sugar

Chelsea Buns

Put the flour into a warm bowl and add 50g/2oz butter, the yeast creamed with 1 teaspoon sugar, and warm milk. Mix well and knead thoroughly. Cover and leave about 45 minutes until the dough has doubled in size. Re-knead into a rectangle. Brush with the remaining melted butter, sprinkle with the sugar and currants and roll up firmly like a Swiss roll. Cut across in 375cm/1½in thick slices. Put these cut side up on a greased baking sheet, fairly close together but leaving room to swell. Leave in a warm place for 10 minutes, and brush with a little beaten egg. Bake at 450°F/230°C/Gas Mark 8 for 15 minutes. Melt sugar in milk and brush this glaze over the buns as soon as they come from the oven, sprinkling lightly with caster sugar.

350g/12oz strong plain flour
75g/3oz melted butter
15g/½oz yeast
1 teaspoon sugar
200ml/⅓ pint milk
40g/1½oz sugar
40g/1½oz currants
Beaten egg

Glaze
1 teaspoon granulated sugar
30ml/2 tablespoons milk
25g/1oz caster sugar

Wigs

450g/1lb strong plain flour
1 teaspoon ground mixed
   spice
8g/¼oz caraway seeds
50g/2oz sugar
Pinch of salt
300ml/½ pint milk
15g/½oz fresh yeast
50g/2oz melted butter

Put the flour, spice, caraway seeds, sugar and salt into a warm bowl. Warm the milk and add a little to the yeast. Add the yeast and remaining milk to the flour, together with the melted butter. Knead well to make a soft smooth dough. Roll out on a floured board and cut into wedge shapes. Put on a floured baking sheet and leave in a warm place for 30 minutes. Bake at 450°F/ 230°C/Gas Mark 8 for 20 minutes. Wigs are old ceremonial cakes traditionally served with ale or elderberry wine; some versions are made without yeast.

Cream Splits

350g/12oz strong plain flour
¾ teaspoon salt
40g/1½oz sugar
40g/1½oz butter
20g/¾oz fresh yeast
300ml/½ pint warm water
Raspberry or strawberry jam
Double cream
Icing sugar

Put the flour, salt and sugar into a bowl and rub in the butter. Cream the yeast with a little of the warm water. Work into the flour together with the remaining water and mix well to a firm dough. Cover with a cloth and leave in a warm place for about 45 minutes until the dough has doubled in size. Knead well and divide into 18 pieces. Shape into round buns and put on a greased baking sheet. Put in a warm place for 10 minutes and bake at 450°F/230°C/Gas Mark 8 for 15 minutes. Cool and cut tops diagonally. Spread the opening with jam and fill with whipped cream. Dust tops with icing sugar.

Doughnuts

225g/8oz strong plain flour
Pinch of salt
25g/1oz butter
25g/1oz sugar
15g/½oz yeast
1 teaspoon sugar
150ml/¼ pint milk
1 egg
Jam
Caster sugar

Put the flour and salt into a warm basin and rub in the butter. Add the sugar and the yeast creamed with 1 teaspoon sugar. Add warm milk and egg, mix well and knead thoroughly. Cover and leave to rise about 45 minutes until double in size. Knead again and form into 12 balls. Make a hole in each with a finger and put in a little jam. Pinch each hole together and leave the doughnuts in a warm place for 10 minutes to rise. Fry in hot deep fat until golden. Drain and toss in caster sugar, adding a little cinnamon if liked.

Isle of Wight Doughnuts

Work together the lard, flour, sugar and spices. Cream the yeast with a little warm milk and work into the flour. Add enough milk to make a rather firm dough. Knead until smooth and leave to stand for about 1½ hours until risen. Knead again and form into balls the size of a small apple. Hollow the balls with the thumb and put a few currants in the middle. Form the dough round them again. Fry in hot fat until golden, drain and toss in caster sugar.

50g/2oz lard
900g/2lb strong plain flour
100g/4oz sugar
1 teaspoon ground allspice
Pinch of ground cinnamon
Pinch of ground cloves
Pinch of ground mace
25g/1oz fresh yeast
300ml/½ pint milk
25g/1oz currants
Caster sugar

Northumberland Twists

Mix the flour and sugar together until evenly blended. Heat the butter and stir it into the flour. Add a pinch of salt if the butter is not salted. Cream the yeast with a little warm water and add this to the flour mixture. Add enough warm water to make a firm dough. Knead until smooth and leave in a warm place to rise for 2 hours. Roll out on a floured board and cut into strips about 3.75cm/1½in wide and 10cm/4in long. Twist slightly and put on to a greased baking tin. Brush well with sherry and sprinkle with caster sugar. Bake at 375°F/190°C/Gas Mark 5 for 20 minutes.

900g/2lb strong plain flour
225g/8oz caster sugar
225g/8oz butter
Pinch of salt
25g/1oz fresh yeast
A little warm water
A little sherry
Caster sugar

Caraway Cakelets

Dissolve the golden syrup in warm milk. Cream the yeast with a little of the sugar. Mix all the ingredients together and leave to rise for 1 hour. Knead thoroughly and shape into 4 buttered sponge sandwich tins. Leave in warm place for 45 minutes. Bake at 450°F/230°C/Gas Mark 8 for 15 minutes. Remove from the oven, brush the tops with melted butter and return to oven for 15 minutes. Split and butter and eat hot. These teacakes keep moist and soft for about a week and can be toasted, or rebaked after being dipped in warm milk. Caraway tastes best when hot.

75g/3oz golden syrup
300ml/½ pint warm milk
25g/1oz fresh yeast
1 teaspoon sugar
450g/1lb strong plain wholemeal flour
225g/8oz strong plain white flour
1 teaspoon salt
1 tablespoon caraway seeds
Melted butter

Kolaches

45ml/3 tablespoons milk
25g/1oz fresh yeast
½ teaspoon salt
1 tablespoon sugar
100g/4oz soft butter
4 eggs
4 egg yolks
450g/1lb strong plain flour
Plum or apricot jam or
  fillings (see below)
Beaten egg yolk

Warm the milk, add the yeast, and leave until the mixture bubbles. Stir in the salt and sugar. Put the butter in a large bowl and beat in 1 egg and 1 yolk. Beat very hard and then add 1 egg and 1 yolk again. Continue beating hard and adding eggs until they are absorbed. Mix in yeast mixture and flour, beating hard. Cover with a cloth and leave for about 1 hour until double in size. Take off pieces of dough about the size of a large walnut and form into balls. Put 5cm/2in apart on a greased baking sheet, cover and leave to rise in a warm place for 30 minutes. Press a hollow in the centre of each with a thumb and put in jam or filling. If preferred, form dough into squares, put in filling and bring up points, pinching them together but leaving holes along sides. Brush with a little beaten egg yolk and bake at 350°F/180°C/Gas Mark 4 for 20 minutes. Dust generously with icing sugar. These come from Czechoslovakia and are given a variety of fillings:

450g/1lb prunes
2 teaspoons sugar
15g/½oz butter
Pinch of ground cinnamon
Few drops of vanilla essence

Prune Filling
Cook the prunes until soft, remove stones and chop flesh coarsely. Stir in sugar, butter, cinnamon and vanilla. Cool and use.

75g/3oz poppy seeds
Grated rind and juice of 1
  lemon
75g/3oz soft brown sugar or
  honey
50g/2oz raisins or currants
30ml/2 tablespoons milk or
  cream

Poppy Seed Filling
Powder the poppy seeds in a blender. Put into a saucepan with the other ingredients and cook for 3 minutes, stirring well to make a smooth paste. Cool before using.

1250ml/8fl.oz single cream
50g/2oz soft brown sugar
15g/½oz plain flour
2 egg yolks
1 teaspoon vanilla essence

Custard Filling
Heat the cream to lukewarm. Stir the sugar and flour together and beat in egg yolks. Whisk in the warm cream and stir over a gentle heat until thick and smooth. Cool and stir in vanilla essence.

Horseshoe Tea Ring

Sieve the flour with a pinch of salt into a warm mixing bowl, rub in 25g/1oz butter. Cream yeast and sugar together, add beaten egg and warm milk. Make a well in the centre of the flour, pour in liquid and mix to a soft dough, turn on to a floured board. Knead until smooth. Cover and leave in the bowl in a warm place until double in size, about 30 minutes. Chop two-thirds of the chocolate, grate remainder. Mix the chopped chocolate, almonds and raisins together for the filling. Roll the dough into a rectangle 40×20cm/16×8in and brush with melted butter. Sprinkle over the filling then roll up, starting with one long side. Seal the ends carefully. Lift on to a greased baking tray and form into a horseshoe shape, with the join underneath. Leave in a warm place until well risen then bake at 425°F/220°C/Gas Mark 7 for 25–30 minutes until golden brown. Cool on a wire tray. Mix the icing sugar with water, coat the top and sprinkle with grated chocolate.

225g/8oz strong plain flour
Pinch of salt
40g/1½oz butter
15g/½oz fresh yeast
1 teaspoon caster sugar
1 egg
60ml/4 tablespoons warm milk
100g/4oz plain chocolate
50g/2oz flaked almonds
50g/2oz seedless raisins
Melted butter
225g/8oz icing sugar, sieved

Teacakes

Put the flour into a warm bowl and rub in the butter. Add the fruit, warm milk, egg and the yeast creamed with the sugar. Mix thoroughly and knead well. Cover with a cloth and leave in a warm place for about 45 minutes, until the dough has doubled in size. Knead again and divide into three pieces. Shape into flat round cakes and put on a warm greased baking sheet. Leave for 10 minutes. Bake at 450°F/230°C/Gas Mark 8 for 12 minutes. Melt 1 tablespoon sugar in 30ml/2 tablespoons milk and brush this glaze over the teacakes as soon as they are taken out of the oven.

225g/8oz strong plain flour
15g/½oz butter
40g/1½oz mixed dried fruit
150ml/¼ pint warm milk
1 egg
15g/½oz fresh yeast
1 teaspoon sugar

Cumberland Teacakes

Put the yeast into a basin with a pinch of sugar and the liquid and leave until frothy. Stir together the flour and salt, and rub in the lard and butter. Stir in the sugar and currants. Make a well in the centre and add the yeast liquid and the eggs. Mix to a soft dough and leave to rise in a warm place for 1 hour. Divide into 24 pieces and form into round flat cakes. Put on warm greased baking sheets. Leave to rise in a warm place for 10 minutes. Bake at 450°F/230°C/Gas Mark 8 for 15 minutes.

25g/1oz fresh yeast
100g/4oz sugar
600ml/1 pint warm milk and water
1.5kg/3lb strong plain flour
1 teaspoon salt
50g/2oz lard
50g/2oz butter
175g/6oz currants
2 eggs

73

Danish Pastries

Basic Dough
225g/8oz strong plain flour
Pinch of salt
25g/1oz lard
1 teaspoon caster sugar
1 beaten egg
150g/5oz butter

Yeast Liquid
Blend 15g/½oz fresh yeast into 75ml/5 tablespoons cold water or dissolve ½ teaspoon sugar in 75ml/5 tablespoons warm (110°F/44°C) water. Sprinkle 2 level teaspoons dried yeast on top. Leave until frothy (about 10 minutes).

Egg Wash
Beat an egg with a little water and ½ teaspoon sugar

To make the dough, sift flour and salt and rub in the lard. Add sugar, egg and yeast liquid and mix to a soft dough. Turn on to a lightly floured board and knead very lightly until smooth. Place inside a lightly greased polythene bag to rest in a cool place for 10 minutes.

To make the pastry, beat the butter until soft. Roll out the dough to a 25cm/10in square. Spread all the butter in a rectangle in the middle and fold the two unbuttered sides so that they just overlap in the middle. Seal the bottom and top. Roll to an oblong strip about three times as long as it is wide. Fold evenly in three. Place in a polythene bag to rest in a cool place for 10 minutes. Turn out ready to roll in opposite direction. Repeat the rolling, folding and resting twice more. Finally, rest the dough for 10 minutes and roll out for use as required.

To Shape the Pastries

Crescents (half the dough makes 8 pastries). Roll out half the basic dough to a circle 22.5cm/9in across and cut into 8 sections. Cut a small lengthwise slit near the pointed end. Put a piece of almond paste in the middle and roll up towards the point and curl into a crescent shape. Place on a baking sheet about 2.5cm/1in apart and brush with egg wash.

Stars and Envelopes (half the dough makes 4 of each). Roll out half the basic dough into a rectangle about 15×30cm/6×12in and cut into eight 7.5cm/3in squares.

For the *stars*, place a small dot of almond paste in the centre. Snip each corner to within 1.25cm/½in of the centre and draw alternate corners to the centre overlapping each other. Brush with egg wash and place on baking sheet.

For the *envelopes*, put a little almond paste or custard filling in the centre. Fold the four corners to the centre and press down well. Brush with egg wash and place on a baking sheet.

Pinwheels and Twists (half the dough makes 4 of each). Roll out half the basic dough into an oblong about 30×20cm/12×8in. Spread with spice filling (see filling recipes) and scatter with a few currants and finely chopped peel. Cut in half lengthwise.

For the *pinwheels*, roll up one strip from the short end to make a fat roll about 10cm/4in wide. Cut into four 2.5cm/1in slices. Place cut side down on baking sheet and brush with egg wash.

For the *twists*, fold remaining strip of pastry into three. Cut into four strips parallel with the open sides. Twist and put on baking sheet, brush with egg wash.

Brushes and Combs (half the dough makes 4 of each). Roll out half of the basic dough into a rectangle 20×30cm/8×12in. Spread a thin layer of pastry filling along the centre and fold one side over the top of the filling. Brush with egg wash and fold the other side on top of this. Turn pastry over, place on a baking sheet and brush with egg wash. Cut diagonally to give eight pieces. Four of these are the *brushes*. For the *combs*, make 5–6 slashes in the same direction down the long side of the other four pieces. Sprinkle each piece with chopped nuts and sugar.

Pretzel. Roll out half the basic dough to a thin strip about 36×36cm/24×24in. Spread a thin layer of pastry filling down the middle and a layer of custard filling on top. Sprinkle on a few raisins. Fold one side over the top of the filling. Brush with egg wash and fold the other side on top of this. Turn pastry over, place on baking sheet and tie in a knot to form a pretzel shape. Brush with egg wash and sprinkle with chopped nuts and sugar.

Fillings

Custard Filling. Blend together 1 egg yolk, 1 tablespoon each sugar and plain flour and 150ml/¼ pint milk. Thicken over low heat. Remove from heat and mix in a few drops of vanilla essence.

Almond Paste. Work 25g/1oz ground almonds and 25g/1oz caster sugar to a smooth paste with a little egg white. Add 2 drops of almond essence.

Spice Filling. Cream together 25g/1oz butter, 25g/1oz caster sugar or icing sugar and 1 teaspoon ground cinnamon.

Pastry Filling. Cream together 100g/4oz butter, 75g/3oz caster sugar and a few drops of vanilla essence.

Cover the pastries with a lightly greased polythene sheet and allow to rise in a slightly warm place until the dough is puffy and springs back when pressed with a lightly floured finger (about 20 minutes). Bake towards top of oven at 425°F/230°C/Gas Mark 7 for 12–15 minutes. Ice and finish while still hot.

To Finish
Crescents. Brush with a little glacé icing and sprinkle with flaked almonds.

Star. Put a little custard in the centre and top with a spot of red jelly or a bit of glacé cherry.

Envelopes. Fill slits at corners with custard and replace in oven for 1 minute to set. Decorate centre with glacé icing and chopped nuts.

Pinwheels and Twists. Brush with a little glacé icing and sprinkle with chopped nuts.

Yeast Pastry

Flaky Pastry (suitable for Banbury and Eccles Cakes, pastries and sausage rolls)

450g/1lb risen white bread dough
175g/6oz lard and margarine mixed

Roll out the bread dough firmly to a strip 3.75cm/$\frac{3}{4}$in thick on a floured board. Put one-third of the fat, in little pats, on the dough, flour lightly, fold in three, press the edges to seal in the air. Turn the dough through a right angle so that the folded edge is on the right-hand side. Put the pastry in a lightly greased polythene bag in a refrigerator or cold place for 15 minutes. Repeat twice more. Roll out the pastry, as above, fold in three and return to refrigerator or cold place for 2 hours, or preferably overnight, before use. Roll the pastry out to required thickness, and proceed as usual, but rest the finished pastry in a warm place for 20 minutes before baking. Bake on top shelf of oven at 450°F/230°C/Gas Mark 8.

Short Pastry (good for tarts and plate pies)

225g/8oz risen white bread dough
225g/8oz plain flour
225g/8oz lard and margarine mixed

Rub fat into flour. Work fat and flour well into dough. Roll out and use as required. Bake on middle shelf of oven at 400°F/200°C/Gas Mark 6.

RIGHT   A wheatsheaf and mouse shaped harvest loaf

OVERLEAF   Gugelhupf; this yeastcake is very simple to make

7 Breads Without Yeast

Plain, savoury, and sweet breads can be made without yeast, if self-raising flour, bicarbonate of soda or baking powder are used. These breads are more like cake in texture and are best eaten when very fresh. Bread made without yeast should be mixed quickly without kneading. It is best made in small loaves and should be baked as soon as the ingredients are mixed in a moderate to hot oven.

Irish White Soda Bread

Stir dry ingredients into basin and rub in fat. Make a 'well' in the centre and stir in sufficient buttermilk or milk to give a soft spongy dough. Knead lightly on a floured surface. Shape quickly into a round cake approximately 5cm/2in thick. Place on a floured baking sheet and score the top lightly three times with a sharp knife. Bake at 400°F/200°C/Gas Mark 6 for 35 minutes or until well-risen and browned underneath. Cool on a wire rack. Eat very fresh.

450g/1lb plain flour
1 teaspoon salt
1 teaspoon cream of tartar
1 teaspoon bicarbonate of soda
25g/1oz lard
300ml/½ pint buttermilk or milk

LEFT   Plaited fruit loaf

81

Irish Brown Soda Bread

100g/4oz plain white flour
1 teaspoon salt
1 teaspoon sugar
1 teaspoon bicarbonate of
  soda
Cream of tartar (optional)
350g/12oz wholemeal flour
15g/½oz butter
300ml/½ pint buttermilk or
  sour milk
or
300ml/½ pint fresh milk and
  2 level teaspoons cream of
  tartar added to the flour
Beaten egg or milk

Sift the white flour, salt, sugar, bicarbonate of soda and cream of tartar (if used) into mixing bowl. Add the wholemeal flour and mix well. Rub in the butter. Mix to a soft dough with the milk, adding a little more milk if necessary. Turn on to a floured board. Knead lightly to form a smooth dough, until there are no cracks. Flatten out to a circle, approximately 17.5cm/7in diameter, and place on a floured baking sheet. Brush top with a little beaten egg, or milk, or a combination of both. Slash a cross on top. Bake at 400°F/200°C/Gas Mark 6 for 40 minutes. Cool on a wire rack. Eat very fresh.

Country Herb Soda Bread

225g/8oz strong plain flour
225g/8oz wholemeal flour
1 teaspoon salt
1 teaspoon bicarbonate of
  soda
25g/1oz butter
2 large onions
3 celery sticks
1 teaspoon mixed herbs
2 tablespoons chopped parsley
250ml/8fl.oz milk
2 teaspoons lemon juice

Topping
30ml/2 tablespoons milk
50g/2oz grated Cheddar
  cheese

Stir the flours, salt and soda together in a large mixing bowl. Rub in the butter until the mixture looks like fine breadcrumbs. Grate the onions and celery and mix with the dough. Stir in the herbs. Mix the milk and lemon juice and add to the dry ingredients to give a soft dough. Turn on to a floured surface and knead lightly. Shape into a 22.5cm/9in round and put on a lightly floured baking sheet. Score the top into 8 segments. Brush with milk and sprinkle with cheese. Bake at 400°F/200°C/Gas Mark 6 for 30 minutes. Cool on a wire rack.

Date and Walnut Loaf

Heat the oven to 350°F/180°C/Gas Mark 4 and thoroughly grease a loaf tin. Put the dates, black treacle, bicarbonate of soda and margarine cut in small pieces in a large mixing bowl and pour over the boiling water. Stir thoroughly until blended and the margarine has dissolved. Then mix in all the remaining loaf ingredients. Turn into a greased loaf tin and bake at 350°F/180°C/Gas Mark 4 for 1 hour. Cool on a wire rack.

225g/8oz chopped dates
45ml/3 tablespoons black treacle
½ teaspoon bicarbonate of soda
25g/1oz margarine
150ml/¼ pint boiling water
1 egg
50g/2oz caster sugar
50g/2oz chopped walnuts
225g/8oz self-raising flour
Pinch of salt

Seed Loaf

Sieve the flour and baking powder together. Cream the butter and sugar until light and fluffy. Work in the eggs alternately with the flour. Beat until soft and light and stir in the caraway seeds and rum or milk. Put into a greased 1kg/2lb loaf tin. Bake at 350°F/180°C/Gas Mark 4 for 1¼ hours. Cover with a piece of paper or foil if the cake begins to get too brown. Turn out and cool on a wire rack.

225g/8oz plain flour
½ teaspoon baking powder
150g/6oz butter
150g/6oz sugar
3 eggs
2 teaspoons caraway seeds
60ml/4 tablespoons rum or milk

Banana Loaf

Sift the flour, baking powder, salt and soda together. Stir in the sugar. Beat the eggs lightly and stir into the mixture with the margarine. Peel the bananas and mash the flesh so that there are no lumps. Work into the mixture with the lemon juice. Grease a 450g/1lb loaf tin and line the base. Put in the mixture and bake at 350°F/180°C/Gas Mark 4 for 1 hour. Cool in the tin for 15 minutes and then turn out on a wire rack to finish cooling. Serve sliced and buttered.

175g/6oz plain flour
1½ teaspoons baking powder
Pinch of salt
Pinch of bicarbonate of soda
50g/2oz caster sugar
2 eggs
50g/2oz melted margarine
2 large bananas
1½ teaspoons lemon juice

Baking Powder Cob

225g/8oz plain flour
4 teaspoons baking powder
1 teaspoon salt
175ml/6fl.oz milk

Mix all ingredients together in a bowl. Turn out on to floured board and knead lightly for 1 minute. Shape with hands to a round. Place on a floured baking sheet. Bake in centre of oven at 425°F/220°C/Gas Mark 7 for 25–30 minutes. For a golden brown crust, brush with milk before baking. This milk glaze can be sprinkled before baking with crushed wheat or poppy seeds, or coarse salt or grated cheese. Eat very fresh.

Baking Powder Bread (1)

450g/1lb plain flour
3 teaspoons baking powder
Pinch of salt
300ml/½ pint water (or milk and water)

Sift together the flour, baking powder and salt. Pour in cold water or milk and water, mixing quickly to a firm dough. Do not knead or overwork the dough. Shape into two small loaves to fit loaf or cake tins and bake at 425°F/220°C/Gas Mark 7 for 25 minutes. Cool on a wire rack. Eat very fresh.

Baking Powder Bread (2)

225g/8oz plain flour
1½ teaspoons baking powder
½ teaspoon salt
25g/1oz butter
150ml/¼ pint milk

Glaze
15ml/1 tablespoon golden
  syrup
15ml/1 tablespoon water

Sift together the flour, baking powder and salt. Rub in the butter and mix to a light dough with the milk. Turn on to a floured board, knead lightly and make into small rolls. Put on a greased tin and bake at 425°F/220 °C/Gas Mark 7 for 15 minutes. Dissolve golden syrup in water and brush over the rolls. Return to the oven for 45 minutes. Cool on a wire rack. Eat very fresh.

Baking Powder Crescents

350g/12oz plain flour
2 teaspoons baking powder
1 teaspoon salt
40g/1½oz butter
300ml/½ pint sour milk
Beaten egg

Sift the flour, baking powder and salt into a bowl and rub in the butter. Add enough milk to make a firm dough. Roll out thinly and divide into 12 triangular pieces. Roll up the triangles and twist into crescent shapes. Bake at 400°F/200°C/Gas Mark 6 for 15 minutes. Brush over with beaten egg and continue cooking for 5 minutes. Cool on a wire rack. Eat very fresh.

84

Dripping Rolls

Sieve the flour, baking powder and salt and rub in the dripping. Work to a soft dough with milk. Divide into 12–15 pieces and form into rolls. Bake at 425°F/220 °C/Gas Mark 7 for 15 minutes. Cool on a wire rack. Eat very fresh.

450g/1lb plain flour
2 teaspoons baking powder
Pinch of salt
50g/2oz dripping
Milk

Sweet Breakfast Rolls

Sieve the flour and baking powder together and rub in the butter until the mixture is like fine breadcrumbs. Stir in the sugar. Mix with milk to a soft dough. Form into 18 rolls and put on a floured baking sheet, not too close together. Bake at 425°F/220 °C/Gas Mark 7 for 15 minutes. Cool on a wire rack. Eat very fresh.

450g/1lb plain flour
2 teaspoons baking powder
100g/4oz butter
40g/1½oz caster sugar
300ml/½ pint milk

Baking Powder Tea Cakes

Sift the flour with the baking powder and salt. Rub in the butter and stir in the sugar, sultanas and peel. Mix with the beaten egg and enough milk to make a soft dough. Form into six flat round cakes and put on a greased and floured baking sheet. Bake at 425°F/220 °C/Gas Mark 7 for 20 minutes. Warm milk and sugar, and brush on the tea cakes. Cool on a wire rack. Eat very fresh.

350g/12oz plain flour
1½ teaspoons baking powder
Pinch of salt
75g/3oz butter
50g/2oz sugar
50g/2oz sultanas
15g/½oz chopped mixed peel
1 egg
Milk

Glaze
15ml/1 tablespoon milk
25g/1oz sugar

Hasty Muffins

Mix the flour, baking powder and salt and add enough milk to make a soft dough. Form into 5 round flat cakes and bake at 450°F/230°C/Gas Mark 8 for 10 minutes. Split, butter and eat while hot.

225g/1lb plain flour
3 teaspoons baking powder
½ teaspoon salt
Milk

Cornish Hot Cake

225g/8oz plain flour
2 teaspoons baking powder
100g/4oz dripping
75g/5oz currants
50g/2oz chopped mixed peel
50g/2oz sugar
1 teaspoon ground allspice
150ml/¼ pint milk

Sift flour and baking powder together and rub in dripping until the mixture looks like fine breadcrumbs. Add the currants, peel, sugar and spice and stir in the milk to make a firm dough. Roll to 1.25cm/½in thick on a floured board. Put on a greased baking sheet and bake at 425°F/220°C/Gas Mark 7 for 30 minutes. Cut into fingers, split open, butter and serve hot.

Malt Loaf

75g/3oz malt extract
50g/2oz soft brown sugar
25g/1oz butter
225g/8oz wholemeal flour
2 teaspoons baking powder
¼ teaspoon salt
150ml/¼ pint milk
50g/2oz currants and
  sultanas
25g/1oz chopped mixed peel

Warm the malt extract, sugar and butter together until the butter has melted. Cool a little. Sift dry ingredients into a bowl and pour in the liquid. Mix well, stir in the fruit and peel and put into a greased and floured 450g/1lb loaf tin. Bake at 325°F/170°C/Gas Mark 3 for 1½ hours. Cool on a wire rack. Serve sliced and buttered.

Ginger and Walnut Teabread

225g/8oz self-raising flour
¼ teaspoon salt
2 teaspoons ground ginger
1 teaspoon baking powder
50g/2oz butter
50g/2oz sugar
75g/3oz chopped walnuts
25g/1oz finely chopped
  crystallised ginger
1 egg
150ml/¼ pint milk
1 teaspoon Demerara sugar

Sift together flour, salt, ginger and baking powder. Rub in butter until mixture resembles fine breadcrumbs. Mix in sugar, walnuts and crystallised ginger. Mix most of the beaten egg with the milk and add to flour and butter. Beat thoroughly. This makes a very sticky dough. Turn into a greased 450g/1lb loaf tin. Brush top with remaining beaten egg and sprinkle with Demerara sugar. Bake at 350°F/180°C/Gas Mark 4 for 1 hour 5 minutes, until the teabread is golden brown and sounds hollow when tapped underneath. Serve sliced and buttered.

Kolac

Sift together flour, baking powder and salt and rub in the butter until the mixture looks like fine breadcrumbs. Stir in soft brown sugar and mix to a stiff dough with beaten egg. Roll out and use to line a greased 32.5×22.5cm/13×9in Swiss roll tin. Core and chop the apples. Chop the bananas. Spread them evenly over pastry and top with cottage cheese. Sprinkle with sugar and dot with butter. Bake at 375°F/190°C/Gas Mark 5 for 40 minutes. Cool and cut into 5cm/2in squares.

225g/8oz wholemeal flour
2 teaspoons baking powder
¼ teaspoon salt
100g/4oz butter
75g/3oz soft brown sugar
1 egg
2 eating apples
2 bananas
350g/12oz cottage cheese
50g/2oz soft brown sugar
15g/½oz butter

American Cornbread

Put the flour, cornmeal, baking powder, salt and sugar into a bowl and stir well together. Beat the egg and add the milk and melted butter. Add to the flour, stirring until well mixed. Put into a greased 20×30cm/8×12in tin. Bake at 400°F/200°C/Gas Mark 6 for 35 minutes. Serve hot. Leftover cornbread can be split and toasted.

100g/4oz plain flour
100g/4oz yellow cornmeal
1½ teaspoons baking powder
½ teaspoon salt
1 teaspoon sugar
1 egg
250ml/8fl.oz milk
*45ml/3 tablespoons melted
  butter*

Boston Brown Bread

This is best cooked in cylindrical cans which have been used for coffee or for tinned foods. The tops should be taken off neatly and the cans well cleaned before use. If these are not available, use pudding basins or stone jam jars. The bread is the traditional accompaniment to baked beans and can be made without the raisins. Sift together the three flours, soda and salt. Add the treacle and milk, and the raisins if used and beat well. Fill tins three-quarters full and cover tightly with buttered paper and foil. Put into a saucepan of boiling water which should come halfway up the cans. Cover and steam for 3 hours, topping up with hot water so the pan does not boil dry. Serve hot with butter.

100g/4oz rye flour
100g/4oz cornmeal
100g/4oz wholemeal flour
*¾ teaspoon bicarbonate of
  soda*
1 teaspoon salt
175g/6oz black treacle
450ml/¾ pint buttermilk
100g/4oz chopped raisins

8 Scones, Griddlecakes and Rusks

The oldest form of baking took place on hot stones in the fire, and this method was later adapted to using a flat plate of thick iron over the fire. This griddle or girdle was used for baking flat circles of bread and various forms of scones and cakes. These implements are still available and may be used on top of the stove; a heavy iron frying pan may be used instead. Today, most scones are cooked in the oven, but the griddle method is preferred for batter mixtures, and is very good for potato cakes and oatcakes, and many regional scones are traditionally cooked over heat rather than in the oven.

USING A GRIDDLE

A griddle should be heated while the dough or batter is being prepared, but it must not be allowed to get too hot. Sprinkle on a little flour and if it browns at once, the griddle is too hot. If the flour takes some time to colour, the heat will be correct for cooking. The general rule for preparing a griddle is 'floured for dough, greased for batter', but be careful to follow the individual instructions in recipes until you are used to this method of cooking. When a griddle has to be greased, this should be done very lightly with a piece of suet, or a little lard. Griddles should not be washed, but are best rubbed when hot with a little kitchen salt and then wiped with a piece of kitchen paper or clean dry cloth.

OVEN BAKING

When scones are to be baked in the oven, they should be placed on an ungreased baking sheet. A little flour sprinkled on the sheet will give the finished scones a floury base. Honey, syrup or cheese in the scones may cause sticking, and then the sheet should be very lightly greased. Rolled-and-cut scones should be placed close together on the baking sheet so that they will retain soft sides after baking. Scones are best wrapped in a clean cloth immediately after baking so that the steam is trapped and they remain soft.

Making scone dough is similar to making pastry, with any fat being rubbed lightly so that plenty of air is incorporated into the mixture. The liquid should be added carefully so that the dough is very light and soft but not sticky. Roll out the dough lightly and quickly and bake as soon as they are prepared. Scone dough for the oven should be about 2.5cm/1in thick, but for the griddle it should only be half as thick. A little milk brushed on top will give a slight glaze to oven scones; if an egg is used the glaze will be very shiny and brown.

POSSIBLE FAULTS

DO handle as little as possible. Measure and sieve ingredients carefully. Have oven at correct temperature.
DO NOT add too much liquid.

Not sufficiently risen – close texture. Too little raising agent. Over-handling. Too dry or too wet.

Open texture. Too much raising agent.

Tough. Too much handling. Baking temperature too low.

Too pale. Too much handling. Baking temperature too low. Top not glazed with egg or milk. Oven too slow. Baked too low in oven.

Rough surface. Inadequate mixing. Not kneaded (this should be slight but one or two turns are needed for smooth surface).

Spreading during cooking. Too much liquid. Baking tray heavily greased instead of floured.

Basic Scones

225g/8oz self-raising flour
1 teaspoon baking powder
50g/2oz butter or margarine
25g/1oz sugar
A little milk

Sieve the flour and baking powder. Rub in the fat until the mixture is like coarse breadcrumbs and stir in the sugar. Add milk to give a soft light dough which can be rolled. Roll out and cut in 5cm/2in rounds. Put close together on an ungreased baking sheet. Brush with a little milk and bake at 450°F/230°C/Gas Mark 8 for 10–12 minutes. Plain flour may be used with ½ teaspoon bicarbonate of soda and 1 teaspoon cream of tartar as raising agents. Sour milk is excellent for scones, and then the amount of cream of tartar should be halved.

Variations
50g/2oz mixed dried fruit or sultanas may be added to this scone mixture. For savoury scones omit the sugar, and add 75g/3oz grated Cheddar cheese, salt and pepper.

Oatmeal Scones

225g/8oz medium oatmeal
300ml/½ pint sour milk
225g/8oz plain flour
Pinch of salt
1 teaspoon bicarbonate of
    soda
1 teaspoon cream of tartar

Soak the oatmeal in the milk for 1 hour. Sieve the flour, salt, soda and cream of tartar together. Add to the oatmeal mixture and mix thoroughly. Turn on to a lightly floured board and knead for 2 minutes. Roll out 1.25cm/½in thick. Cut into scones and place on a floured baking sheet close together. Bake at 350°F/180°C/Gas Mark 4 for 20 minutes. Cool on a wire rack.

Yorkshire Ned Cakes

40g/1½oz lard
225g/8oz plain flour
Pinch of salt
30ml/2 tablespoons double
    cream
Milk

Rub fats into flour and salt until the mixture is like coarse bread-crumbs. Mix with cream and milk to a rather stiff dough. Roll 65mm/¼in thick and put the whole round on to a hot griddle. Cut into 4 triangles to turn, allowing 3 or 4 minutes for each side to brown. Cut in diamond shapes just before taking off the griddle. Serve hot on a very hot plate, as it spoils them to stand, and eat with butter and honey or jam.

Potato Cakes

Mash the potatoes very smoothly and work in the butter, flour and salt. Add the milk to make a stiff dough. Roll out on a floured board and cut into 6.25cm/2½in rounds or squares. Cook on a lightly greased hot griddle or thick frying pan until golden brown on both sides. Split and butter and serve hot.

225g/8oz cold potatoes
25g/1oz softened butter
50g/2oz plain flour
Pinch of salt
60ml/4 tablespoons milk

Drop Scones

Sieve flour, salt, soda and cream of tartar. Stir in the sugar. Mix to a thick batter with egg and milk, and stir in melted fat. Grease a hot griddle or thick frying pan lightly. Drop on the mixture in spoonfuls. When bubbles appear on the surface, turn quickly and cook the other side. Put in the folds of a clean cloth to keep soft while cooling.

225g/8oz plain flour
¼ teaspoon salt
½ teaspoon bicarbonate of soda
1 teaspoon cream of tartar
1 tablespoon caster sugar
1 egg
150ml/¼ pint milk
25g/1oz butter or margarine

Treacle Griddle Scones

Put the egg, sugar, treacle, milk, flour, salt and nutmeg into a bowl and beat well to a smooth batter. Grease a griddle or thick frying pan lightly. Pour spoonfuls of batter on to the surface and put five or six raisins on each one. When the batter is almost set and the scones rise, turn them with a palette knife and cook the other side until golden. Cool on a wire rack with a cloth over them so that they remain soft. Serve with butter.

1 egg
2 teaspoons caster sugar
30ml/2 tablespoons black treacle
300ml/½ pint milk
225g/8oz self-raising flour
½ teaspoon salt
½ teaspoon ground nutmeg
75g/3oz seedless raisins

Oatcakes

Stir together the flour, oatmeal and salt. Melt the lard or dripping and stir into the dry ingredients. Add just enough boiling water to give a stiff dough. Sprinkle a pastry board with oatmeal and roll out the dough very thinly. Cut into triangles or 7.5cm/3in circles. Put on a greased baking sheet and bake at 350°F/180°C/Gas Mark 4 for 30 minutes. Cool on a wire rack. They can be cooked on a lightly greased griddle over gentle heat, turning frequently.

50g/2oz plain flour
175g/6oz fine oatmeal
Pinch of salt
25g/1oz lard or dripping
Boiling water

Pikelets

225g/8oz plain flour
Pinch of salt
50g/2oz caster sugar
150ml/¼ pint milk
1 teaspoon bicarbonate of
    soda
30ml/2 tablespoons boiling
    water

Sift the flour and salt. Stir in the sugar and mix to a thick batter with the milk. Stir the soda into the boiling water and add to the batter. Grease a hot thick frying pan or griddle and drop the mixture on with a tablespoon, leaving room to spread. Cook until brown underneath with bubbles on top. Turn and cook until golden brown underneath. Eat hot with plenty of butter.

American Muffins

225g/8oz plain flour
1 heaped teaspoon baking
    powder
½ teaspoon salt
40g/1½oz sugar
1 egg
250ml/8fl.oz milk
45ml/3 tablespoons melted
    butter

Sift together flour, baking powder and salt and stir in the sugar. Beat the egg and stir in the milk and melted butter. Add to the flour and stir well until smooth. Spoon into deep individual cake tins or papers, filling them two-thirds full. Bake at 400°F/ 200°C/Gas Mark 6 for 25 minutes. Serve hot. Dried fruit, chopped nuts or whole blueberries may be added for sweet muffins. Muffins may also have the addition of a little chopped crisp bacon or grated cheese, or they can be made with a mixture of wholemeal and white flour.

American Raisin Muffins

100g/4oz seedless raisins
75g/3oz butter or margarine
100g/4oz sugar
1 egg
150ml/¼ pint sour cream
175g/6oz plain flour
1½ teaspoons baking powder
½ teaspoon salt
½ teaspoon ground cinnamon

Topping
75g/3oz butter
100g/4oz sugar
1 teaspoon ground cinnamon

Chop the raisins coarsely. Cream butter and sugar until light and fluffy, and gradually beat in the egg. Blend in the sour cream. Sieve flour, baking powder, salt and cinnamon together and fold into the creamed mixture. Stir in raisins, and fill greased patty tins two-thirds full. Bake at 375°F/190°C/Gas Mark 5 for 20 minutes. Dip hot muffins in melted butter then roll in sugar and cinnamon mixture and serve hot.

American Popovers

These are best cooked in individual ovenware pudding bowls, deep small cake tins or individual Yorkshire pudding tins, which should be hot when the mixture is put into them. Mix the flour and salt. Beat the eggs until light and add to the flour, together with the milk and melted butter. Beat well to the thickness of cream. Grease the pans and fill them one-third full with the mixture. Bake at 450°F/230°C/Gas Mark 8 for 20 minutes, then at 350°F/180°C/Gas Mark 4 for 20 minutes. Take out of the pans at once and eat hot.

100g/4oz plain flour
Pinch of salt
2 eggs
210ml/7fl.oz milk
*15ml/1 tablespoon melted
    butter*

Waffles

Sift the flour, salt and baking powder into a bowl and stir in the sugar. Make a well in the centre and drop in the egg yolks. Mix with a wooden spoon, gradually adding milk and melted butter alternately. Whisk egg whites until stiff but not dry and fold into the batter with a metal spoon. Heat a waffle iron and brush with a little melted butter. Spoon some of the batter into the waffle iron and cook for 1–2 minutes on each side until golden brown. Serve the waffles hot with clear honey or syrup. A frying pan can be used instead of a waffle iron. Grease the pan lightly and drop in a tablespoon of the mixture. Cook on each side until golden brown.

175g/6oz plain flour
Pinch of salt
3 teaspoons baking powder
25g/1oz caster sugar
2 eggs
300ml/½ pint milk
50g/2oz butter
*Melted butter to grease
    waffle pan*

Scandinavian Flatbread

Stir together the flour, sugar, soda and salt. Work in the butter until the mixture looks like fine breadcrumbs. Stir in the buttermilk with a fork until the mixture holds together. Shape into a ball and take off small pieces to make balls about 2.5cm/1in diameter. Roll out on a floured board to make rounds 10cm/4in across. Put slightly apart on greased baking sheets. Bake at 400°F/200°C/Gas Mark 6 for 5 minutes until light brown. Lift off carefully and cool on a wire rack. Store in an airtight container.

350g/12oz strong plain flour
50g/2oz sugar
*¼ teaspoon bicarbonate of
    soda*
¼ teaspoon salt
100g/4oz butter
250ml/8fl.oz buttermilk

9 Cakemaking Methods

Cakemaking is most enjoyable, but it must be undertaken with more care than many other branches of cookery. Although a beautiful cake is a work of art, it can only be achieved with some attention to scientific principles. It is possible to achieve some sort of stew for example by simply putting together random quantities of meat, vegetables, liquid and seasoning and simmering them together until the meat is tender – it may not be perfect but it will be pleasant enough to eat. Doing the same thing with a random collection of dry ingredients, liquids and sweeteners, plopped into a container and baked at any old temperature will not result in a cake which is even edible, let alone delicious, with the correct flavouring and texture. It is important therefore to follow recipes exactly, measuring ingredients meticulously, mixing in the specified way, using the correct size and shape of container, selecting the specified temperature and timing cooking exactly.

EQUIPMENT

Cakes may be most simply made with a bowl and a wooden spoon, but a rotary beater, wire whisk or electric mixer will speed up the process, although cakes must not be overbeaten. Thin wire beaters incorporate the most air. A thick-based saucepan is useful for melting ingredients such as fat and syrup which need gentle warming without risk of burning.

Cake tins come in a huge variety of sizes and shapes. For sponge cakes, 17.5cm/7in or 20cm/8in shallow round tins are most commonly used in pairs. For gâteaux, 22.5cm/9in shallow round tins are better, giving a thinner, larger cake. For plain cakes and fruit cakes, deeper tins are needed, and most recipes fit 17.5cm/7in or 20cm/8in tins. Removable bases or springform tins enable the cakes to be removed easily. Square and rectangular tins are useful for tray-baked cakes and gingerbreads, and these should be 3.75–5cm/1½–2in deep. Shallower rectangular tins are available for Swiss rolls and these may also be used for biscuits. Loaf tins and bun trays are useful if you like to do a lot of baking, and there are many fancy shaped tins for Babas, Savarins, Kugelhopf, etc.

Greaseproof paper is essential for lining tins, and non-stick parchment is invaluable for baking sheets on which slightly sticky meringue mixtures may be cooked. Rice paper is needed for one or two special cakes such as macaroons, and small paper cases are useful for individual cakes.

INGREDIENTS

If you only make cakes occasionally, buy small quantities of ingredients rather than storing them, as only fresh, high-quality ingredients will give the delicate flavour, colour and texture you want to achieve.

Flour should be plain when specified (not strong plain flour which is for breadmaking, batters and some pastries). This is very important in rich cake mixtures which need little raising agent. Self-raising flour is suggested for some cakes, and wholemeal flour is suitable for farmhouse-style cakes and some scones. Self-raising flour should not be used for pastry as it gives a spongy texture. Store flour in a bin in a cool dry place.

Raising agents are used in some mixtures to give an extra light texture. Baking powder reacts with moisture to form a gas which makes small bubbles and these expand quickly and are set by heat to give an airy lightness to the finished cake. Bicarbonate of soda is often used with honey, treacle, sour milk or acids to neutralise acids and give a soft cake.

Sweetening agents are extremely varied and give different results. Caster sugar dissolves quickly in whisked and creamed mixtures and so is best in sponge cakes. Granulated sugar is fine for many plain cakes and fruit cakes. Soft brown sugar gives a rich flavour and colour to fruit cakes and gingerbreads and comes in a number of light and dark varieties with slightly different flavours – the richest, darkest sugars are good for gingerbread and other spice cakes, but the lighter types are most suitable for light fruit cakes. Demerara sugar is grainy in texture and is usually reserved for biscuits and cake toppings. Golden syrup is sweet, light and bland, while black treacle gives a distinctive flavour, texture and colour to baking. Honey is delicious, but if substituted for sugar in a recipe, only one-third of the total should be honey, or the cake will become too brown. Dried fruit, including apricots, dates and peel are very sweet, but should not be substituted for the other sweetening agents or the texture of the cake will be affected.

Eggs should be used at room temperature, and they give volume, colour and flavour to cakes. They must be carefully separated, if this is specified, so that no yolk is left in the white or the fat from the yolk will lessen the volume of the beaten whites.

Dried fruit should be plump, fresh and clean. Nowadays, packaged fruit is generally very clean but it is a good idea to inspect it and discard any pips or stems. Large pieces of candied peel may be cut to taste, and are usually very fresh-tasting, but ready-chopped peel may be bought. Dates are best bought in a block and may be easily chopped. Glacé cherries are heavy with syrup, and it is best to wash them and then dry them very thoroughly to get rid of the surplus stickiness which makes them difficult to blend into a mixture and which may cause sinking.

METHODS

There are a number of methods used in making individual cakes, and they should always be prepared by the method specified.

Rubbing in is used for plain cakes, pastry and biscuits. This means rubbing fat into flour with the tips of the fingers so that the mixture does not become sticky. This should be done very lightly, lifting the mixture so that air is incorporated, and the mixture should look like fine breadcrumbs.

Creaming is used for many cakes. Fat should be at room temperature but not oily, and the sugar is beaten in with a wooden spoon, or on medium speed with a mixer until the texture is soft and fluffy and the mixture is pale. If the fat is melted, it will prevent air being incorporated successfully.

Whisking is used for very light cakes, and the air is incorporated by whisking whole eggs and sugar, or egg whites and sugar, until the mixture is very light and fluffy. When whole eggs are used, the mixture will be like whipped cream. If egg whites alone are used, the bowl must be fat-free or the egg whites will not whisk up well, and the mixture will form soft peaks and then stiff peaks. Generally, the 'soft peak' stage is the one to aim for in cake-making as the soft foam is more easily incorporated into the main cake mixture, but 'stiff peaks' are essential for meringue-making.

Melting is used for making gingerbreads and some other moist cakes. The fat, sugar and syrup are heated gently until the fat has melted before being mixed into the other ingredients.

Beating follows the melting of ingredients which are incorporated into dry ingredients. Some cakes such as gingerbreads need vigorous beating with a wooden spoon or electric mixer, but over-beating will spoil a rich fruit cake, and will ruin the texture of a sponge cake.

CAKEMAKING TERMS

Two specialised words are used in cakemaking methods, and it is important to understand exactly what they mean.

Folding in should be done with a knife or metal spoon. The mixture should not be overworked or patted about, but the action is sharp and clean like cutting a cake and then bringing back the spoon in a figure-of-eight shape, lifting the heavier substances from the bottom of the mixing bowl. Lighter mixtures (e.g. whisked egg whites) should be folded into heavier ones. Flour is folded into creamed mixtures so that air is not pressed out.

Consistency is important in getting the correct texture for the finished cake. A soft dropping consistency means that the mixture will drop easily from a spoon without being shaken, but it is too stiff to pour. A stiff dropping consistency means the mixture will keep its shape when shaken from a spoon, but is too soft and sticky to handle. A soft dough (such as used for scones) is one which is soft but not too sticky to handle.

BAKING AND COOLING

It is important to use the temperature specified in a recipe. Rich cakes and those which contain syrup (such as gingerbread) are generally cooked at a low-to-moderate temperature, lighter cakes from moderate-to-high, and scone-type mixtures at a high temperature. Some ovens tend to 'run hot' as the years go by, and if you find that cakes burn at the temperature specified, or rise and become crusty outside, yet retain an uncooked interior, it is most likely that your oven is at fault. The temperature can of course be checked with an oven thermometer, or the Gas or Electricity Boards will test the oven for you – a demonstrator usually does this by baking a cake as it is such a good test for the even temperature of an oven. Light the oven about 15 minutes before you want to put the cake in. Some ovens heat up more quickly nowadays, and if you have an electric oven there is an indicator light to tell you when the exact temperature has been reached.

Cakes are usually baked in the middle of the centre shelf of the oven, unless otherwise specified. The correct tin size must also be used as the depth of a cake obviously affects the time in which it will cook.

A cooked cake should be well-risen, golden, firm and springy when pressed lightly. Cakes will shrink slightly from the edges of the tin. Cakes, particularly rich fruit cakes, tend to 'sing' gently while cooking, and if a cake is still making this noise when withdrawn from the oven, it is not completely cooked. A very thin skewer or knife inserted in the centre of a cake should come out cleanly.

Leave a cake in its tin for a minute or two after baking so that it becomes firm enough to turn out. Rich fruit cakes can be left to cool for an hour in the tin until just warm, while tray-baked cakes may be cooled and iced in the tin. Cooling should be completed on a wire cake rack, and cakes must be completely cold before being stored in a tin or polythene box, or before being frozen.

POSSIBLE FAULTS

Newcomers to cooking, and sometimes the experienced too, are baffled when things go wrong. Successful cooking is more than the recipe; it is the total end-product of a careful and well-balanced combination of ingredients and correct methods of handling and baking. Use this checklist if you find your cakes are not successful.

DO measure quantities exactly. Handle mixture lightly and as little as possible. Ensure that oven is at correct temperature and that cake is in correct position in oven. Ensure lining of tin is adequate. Choose correct size of tin for the recipe.

DO NOT open oven door during baking, but, if you must, close it gently.

Badly cracked on top or 'peaked'. Too much raising agent. Too much mixture in tin. Too much or too little liquid. Oven too hot or cake too near top of oven.

Top sunk in middle. Too much raising agent. Too much liquid. Baking tin too small for quantity of mixture. Insufficient baking time. Oven too cool. Slamming door during baking.

Tunnelling in centre of cake. Over-mixing when adding flour. Mixture too dry, causing air pockets. Insufficient blending of raising agent and flour.

Fruit dropped to bottom. Mixture too wet. Fruit too wet. Glacé fruit too syrupy (washing will correct this). Fruit too large and heavy for mix. Oven too slow.

Speckling on top of cake. Baking powder and flour not well sifted together. Too much sugar. Sugar too coarse. Insufficient creaming. *Black specks*: Poor quality or inadequately ground raising agents.

Yellow spots through cake. Too much bicarbonate of soda. Soda not well dissolved in liquid. Dry ingredients not sufficiently sifted.

Texture too coarse. Fat and sugar insufficiently creamed or fat not well rubbed into flour, or (for sponge cake) not enough whisking of eggs with sugar. Inadequate final mixing of ingredients. Excess baking powder. Oven too cool.

Rubbery texture. Over-mixing. Too much egg and/or milk.

Dry and crumbly texture. Too little liquid. Fat not rubbed in sufficiently. Too much raising agent. Cooking too slowly.

Uneven texture. Fat not well rubbed in. Insufficient mixing. Air pockets caused by not putting mixture into tin all at one time.

Texture too close. Too little raising agent. Too much fat, egg or flour. Mixture too dry. Over-mixing. Inadequate creaming. Oven too slow.

Cakes forming crusty ring round sides. Sides of tin over-greased.

Cakes sticking to tin. Rich cakes – incomplete lining of tin. Other types – tin not lightly greased and dusted with flour.

Rapid staling. Mixture too dry. Incorrect storage – cake should be stored in an airtight tin in a cool place or wrapped very completely in aluminium foil. Rich cakes keep longer than plain cakes.

Insufficiently browned. Not enough sugar or egg. Mixture too liquid. Under-baking. Oven over-loaded.

Overbrowning of top. Oven too hot. Cake too near top of oven. Fruit cake taking several hours should be covered with paper or foil halfway through cooking. Too thin a layer of mixture in tin.

Bottom of cake too brown. Inadequate lining of tin for rich cake. Poor quality cake tin – thus too thin. Heat not circulating in oven due to too large a tin or baking tray.

Hard crust on top. Too much sugar. Tin too large for mixture. Oven too hot. Over-baking.

Top of small cakes not well rounded. Too wet a mixture. Not enough fat. Too much or too little raising agent. Not enough mixture in tin.

Sandwich sponge cakes insufficiently risen. Too little raising agent. Over-mixing (flour should be folded in and not vigorously stirred). Excess liquid.

10 Family Cakes

In this chapter, you will find all the cakes which suit everyday family eating, but before beginning on the recipes, be sure to look through the previous chapter on cakemaking methods. This is very important, as if the ingredients are varied, or a different tin is used, or oven temperatures are not observed, cakes may turn out badly. Be sure to collect all ingredients together and weigh them out before beginning to make the cake. Preheat the oven, allowing 15 minutes to be sure the correct temperature is reached. Grease the cake tin, and line it if necessary, before the cake mixture is prepared, so that it can go straight into the tin and be baked immediately or the precious air which has been created in the cake will be lost, and the result will be heavy. Many of these cakes used to be known as 'cut-and-come-again' because they were so tempting and the family could keep coming back for more. The following recipes are so simple that you will not mind making them over and over again.

Fatless Sponge

Whisk the eggs, sugar and salt until light, thick and creamy. Fold in the sieved flour. Put into two greased and floured 20cm/8in sandwich tins and bake at 400°F/200°C/Gas Mark 6 for 20 minutes. Cool on a wire rack and put together with jam. Sprinkle caster or icing sugar on top.

4 eggs
100g/4oz caster sugar
Pinch of salt
100g/4oz plain flour

Very Light Sponge Cake

3 eggs
150g/5oz caster sugar
75g/3oz plain flour

Separate yolks and whites of eggs and whisk whites until very stiff. Put the mixing bowl over a saucepan of hot, but not boiling, water and gradually beat in yolks and sugar. Beat for 5 minutes, then fold in sifted flour very carefully. Bake in a greased and base-lined 20cm/8in tin at 400°F/200°C/Gas Mark 6 for 45 minutes. Cool on a wire rack. Dust with a little sieved icing sugar or caster sugar.

Victoria Sandwich

100g/4oz margarine
100g/4oz caster sugar
2 eggs
100g/4oz self-raising flour

Cream the fat and sugar together until light and fluffy and almost white. Add the eggs one at a time and beat well. Fold in the sieved flour and put the mixture into two greased and floured 17.5cm/7in sandwich tins. Bake at 325°F/170°C/Gas Mark 3 for 30 minutes. Cool on a wire rack. Put together with jam and sprinkle with caster or icing sugar.

Swiss Roll

3 eggs
115g/4½oz caster sugar
75g/3oz plain flour
½ teaspoon baking powder
15ml/1 tablespoon cold water
Jam

Beat eggs and sugar until light and fluffy. Fold in flour sifted with baking powder, and the water. Spread evenly in a greased and lined Swiss roll tin. Bake at 400°F/200°C/Gas Mark 6 for 10 minutes. Turn out on a sugared paper and trim edges with a sharp knife. Spread quickly with warm jam and roll up tightly. Sprinkle with caster sugar before serving.

Genoese Sponge

4 eggs
100g/4oz caster sugar
75g/3oz plain flour
75g/3oz butter

Beat the eggs and sugar in a bowl over hot but not boiling water until light and thick. Sieve the flour. Melt the butter over low heat. Take the bowl from the heat and continue beating for 3 minutes. Fold in half the flour and the melted butter very gently. Fold in the remaining flour, stirring as little as possible. Put into a greased and floured 20cm/8in sandwich tin. Bake at 400°F/200°C/Gas Mark 6 for 30 minutes. Cool on a wire rack. Dust with icing or caster sugar or cover with butter cream or glacé icing.

Egg Yolk Sponge

Put the egg yolks and water into a bowl and whisk until well blended. Add the sugar and continue whisking until the mixture is light and foamy. Fold in the sifted flour and lemon rind. Grease a 17.5cm/7in sponge sandwich tin and line the base with greased paper. Put in the sponge mixture. Bake at 350°F/180°C/Gas Mark 4 for 25 minutes. Turn out and cool on a wire rack. Sprinkle with a little sifted icing sugar before serving. This is a useful cake to make when egg yolks are left over after making meringues.

4 egg yolks
30ml/2 tablespoons cold water
90g/3½oz caster sugar
90g/3½oz plain flour
1 teaspoon grated lemon rind
Icing sugar

One Stage Sandwich Cake

Put all the ingredients in a mixing bowl and beat for about 3 minutes until smooth. Put into a greased and base-lined 20cm/8in sandwich tin, or two 17.5cm/7in tins. Bake at 350°F/180°C/Gas Mark 4 for 35 minutes, but allow only 30 minutes for cakes in 17.5cm/7in tins. Cool on a wire rack. Split the larger cake through the centre to fill with jam or butter icing, and top with more icing or sifted icing sugar. Put the two smaller cakes together with filling between, and finish top as desired.

100g/4oz soft margarine
100g/4oz caster sugar
2 eggs
100g/4oz self-raising flour
1 teaspoon baking powder

Chocolate Sandwich Cake
Add 25g/1oz cocoa mixed with 30ml/2 tablespoons hot water to cake mixture. Fill and cover with chocolate butter cream.

Coffee Sandwich Cake
Add 15ml/1 tablespoon coffee essence and 50g/2oz chopped walnuts to cake mixture. Fill and cover with coffee butter cream and decorate with walnut halves.

Lemon or Orange Sandwich Cake
Add 2 teaspoons grated lemon or orange rind to cake mixture. Fill and cover with lemon or orange butter cream.

Cornflour Sponge

3 eggs
75g/3oz caster sugar
75g/3oz plain flour
25g/1oz cornflour
1 teaspoon baking powder
Pinch of salt
25g/1oz butter
45ml/3 tablespoons hot water

Whisk the eggs and sugar until light and fluffy. Fold in flour sifted with cornflour, baking powder and salt. Fold in the fat and water. Put into two greased 17.5cm/7in sandwich tins. Bake at 375°F/190°C/Gas Mark 5 for 20 minutes. Cool on a wire rack and fill with jam. Sprinkle the top with sieved icing sugar.

Golden Syrup Sponge

50g/2oz butter
50g/2oz sugar
60ml/4 tablespoons golden
    syrup
1 egg
30ml/2 tablespoons milk
100g/4oz self-raising flour

Melt together the butter, sugar and syrup over low heat until the butter has just melted, and cool slightly. Beat together the egg and milk. Add the egg mixture and flour alternately to the melted butter. Mix well and pour into a greased 20cm/8in sandwich tin. Bake at 350°F/180°C/Gas Mark 4 for 35 minutes. Cool on a wire rack. Spread the top with lemon glacé icing.

Coffee Sponge

3 large eggs
75g/3oz caster sugar
30ml/2 tablespoons coffee
    essence
100g/4oz self-raising flour

Whisk the eggs, sugar and coffee essence until thick and creamy. Fold in the sieved flour. Divide between two greased and lined 17.5cm/7in sponge sandwich tins. Bake at 400°F/200°C/Gas Mark 6 for 20 minutes. Cool on a wire rack. Fill with coffee or chocolate butter cream, and use butter cream or glacé icing for the topping.

Plain Cake

225g/8oz plain flour
2 teaspoons baking powder
Pinch of salt
75g/3oz butter or margarine
75g/3oz sugar
1 egg
150ml/¼ pint milk
Flavouring

Sieve together the flour, baking powder and salt. Rub in the fat until the mixture is like coarse breadcrumbs. Add the sugar, and work in the egg and milk to make a soft dropping consistency. Add any other flavourings or ingredients. Put into a greased 17.5cm/7in round cake tin. Bake at 375°F/190°C/Gas Mark 5 for 50 minutes. To flavour the cake, add spice or essence to taste; or 100g/4oz dried fruit; or 1 tablespoon cocoa.

Rich Cake

Cream the fat and sugar together until the mixture is light and fluffy. Sieve the flour and baking powder. Add a little flour to the creamed mixture, then beat in the eggs one at a time. Fold in the rest of the flour and any flavouring or additional ingredient. Put into a greased 20cm/8in round cake tin. Bake at 350°F/ 180°C/Gas Mark 4 for 1¼ hours. Add chosen spice or essence to taste when mixing; *or* add 350g/12oz mixed dried fruit.

175g/6oz butter or margarine
150g/5oz caster sugar
225g/8oz plain flour
1 teaspoon baking powder
3 eggs
Flavouring

One-Stage Rich Fruit Cake

Chop the cherries into quarters. Sieve the flour, baking powder and spices together. Put all the ingredients into a bowl and beat for about 4 minutes until completely mixed. Put into a greased and lined 22.5cm/9in round cake tin and smooth the top of the cake with a spoon. Bake at 275°F/140°C/Gas Mark 1 for 5 hours. Cover the cake with a piece of brown paper halfway through cooking if it is getting a little too brown. Leave in the tin for 15 minutes, then turn out and cool on a wire rack.

100g/4oz glacé cherries
250g/9oz plain flour
2 teaspoons baking powder
1 teaspoon ground nutmeg
1 teaspoon ground mixed
* spice*
225g/8oz soft margarine
225g/8oz light soft brown
* sugar*
5 eggs
Grated rind of 1 lemon
100g/4oz chopped mixed
* candied peel*
50g/2oz ground almonds
30ml/2 tablespoons brandy
15ml/1 tablespoon black
* treacle*
225g/8oz currants
225g/8oz sultanas
225g/8oz raisins

Wholemeal Dripping Cake

225g/8oz mixed dried fruit
75g/3oz beef dripping
150g/5oz soft brown sugar
225g/7½fl.oz water
225g/8oz wholemeal flour
1 teaspoon baking powder
Pinch of ground nutmeg
Pinch of ground cinnamon
Pinch of ground mixed spice
½ teaspoon bicarbonate of
    soda

Put the fruit into a saucepan with dripping, sugar and water. Bring to the boil and simmer for 10 minutes, stirring well. Leave to cool. Sieve together the flour, baking powder, spices and soda. Stir into the fruit mixture and mix well, but do not beat. Put into a greased 17.5cm/7in round cake tin. Bake at 350°F/180°C/Gas Mark 4 for 1½ hours. Cool on a wire rack.

Cornish Heavy Cake

225g/8oz plain flour
Pinch of salt
50g/2oz lard
50g/2oz margarine
50g/2oz sugar
75g/3oz currants
25g/1oz chopped mixed
    candied peel
45ml/3 tablespoons water

Sieve the flour and salt and rub in the fats until the mixture is like coarse breadcrumbs. Add the sugar, currants and peel and the water to make a fairly stiff dough. Knead out all the cracks gently, and shape into a round about 1.25cm/½in thick. Put on to a greased baking sheet and cross the top into eight sections with a knife. Bake at 375°F/190°C/Gas Mark 5 for 30 minutes. Cool on a wire rack.

Harvest Fruit Cake

300ml/½ pint apple purée
100g/4oz margarine
100g/4oz sugar
225g/8oz self-raising flour
1 teaspoon ground cinnamon
½ teaspoon ground ginger
½ teaspoon ground mixed spice
100g/4oz sultanas
15ml/1 tablespoon vinegar

Make the apple purée by simmering apples in just enough water to prevent burning, and sweeten very lightly, then sieve. Cream the margarine and sugar. Sieve the flour with the spices and work into the creamed mixture. Stir in the sultanas and then the vinegar and apple purée. Grease and line a 17.5cm/7in round cake tin. Pour in the mixture and bake at 350°F/180°C/Gas Mark 4 for 1½ hours. Cool on a wire rack.

Dundee Cake

Cream the butter and sugar. Beat the eggs lightly together. Sift together the flour, salt and baking powder. Add the eggs gradually to the creamed mixture alternately with a little of the flour. Stir in the ground almonds, sultanas, currants, peel and cherries. Grate the rind from the lemon and squeeze out the juice. Add to the cake mixture and finally add the remaining flour, and fold in the brandy. Grease a 20cm/8in round cake tin and line the base with non-stick baking parchment. Put in the cake mixture. Cover with foil and bake at 300°F/150°C/Gas Mark 2 for 1½ hours. Remove the foil and arrange the almonds on top of the cake. Continue baking for 1 hour. Stir together the milk and sugar and brush on the cake. Bake for 5 minutes longer. Cool in the tin for 1 hour. Finish cooling on a wire rack.

175g/6oz butter
175g/6oz sugar
3 eggs
225g/8oz plain flour
Pinch of salt
1 teaspoon baking powder
1 tablespoon ground almonds
225g/8oz sultanas
225g/8oz currants
75g/3oz chopped mixed
    candied peel
75g/3oz glacé cherries
½ lemon
15ml/1 tablespoon brandy
50g/2oz blanched split
    almonds
30ml/2 tablespoons milk
15g/½oz sugar

Guinness Cake

Cream the butter and sugar until light and fluffy and gradually beat in the eggs with a little of the flour. Sieve together the flour and spice and gradually fold into the creamed mixture. Add the dried fruit, peel and nuts and mix well together. Stir in half the Guinness to give a soft dropping consistency. Put into a greased and base-lined 17.5cm/7in round cake tin. Bake at 325°F/170°C/Gas Mark 3 for 1 hour. Reduce heat to 300°F/150°C/Gas Mark 2, and continue cooking for 1½ hours. Cool in the tin and turn on to a wire rack. Prick the base of the cake with a skewer and spoon over the remaining Guinness. Store in a tin for 1 week before eating.

225g/8oz butter
225g/8oz soft brown sugar
4 eggs
300g/10oz plain flour
2 teaspoons ground mixed
    spice
225g/8oz seedless raisins
225g/8oz sultanas
100g/4oz chopped mixed
    candied peel
100g/4oz chopped walnuts
120ml/8 tablespoons
    Guinness

Light Christmas Cake

225g/8oz butter
225g/8oz caster sugar
4 large eggs
300g/10oz plain flour
1 teaspoon baking powder
50g/2oz chopped candied
    orange peel
75g/3oz sultanas
75g/3oz currants
50g/2oz chopped glacé
    cherries
75g/3oz chopped glacé
    pineapple
Grated rind of ½ lemon
Milk

Cream butter and sugar until light and fluffy. Beat in eggs one at a time, adding a little flour each time. Gradually work in the flour sifted with baking powder, fruit and grated lemon rind. Add a little milk if necessary to make a soft consistency. Grease and line a 25cm/10in round tin and put in mixture. Bake at 350°F/180°C/Gas Mark 4 for 1½ hours. Cool on a wire rack. If liked, finish with Almond Icing and Royal Icing.

Rich Christmas Cake

225g/8oz butter
225g/8oz dark soft brown
    sugar
15ml/1 tablespoon black
    treacle
4 large eggs
60ml/4 tablespoons sherry or
    cold tea
Grated rind of 1 lemon
½ teaspoon vanilla essence
100g/4oz self-raising flour
175g/6oz plain flour
¼ teaspoon salt
1 teaspoon ground mixed
    spice
Pinch of ground cinnamon
Pinch of ground nutmeg
350g/12oz currants
350g/12oz sultanas
225g/8oz seedless raisins
50g/2oz chopped mixed
    candied peel
50g/2oz glacé cherries

Cream the butter and sugar until light and fluffy. Beat in another bowl the treacle, eggs, liquid, lemon rind and essence, but only just enough to break up the eggs. Stir a little at a time into the creamed mixture alternately with flours sifted with salt and spices. Do not beat the mixture. Add fruit, and mix just enough to distribute evenly. Put into a greased and lined 25cm/10in round cake tin. Level off the mixture and leave to stand for 1 hour. Bake at 300°F/150°C/Gas Mark 2 for 4½ hours. Leave in the tin until just warm, then cool on a wire rack. Finish with Almond Icing and Royal Icing. This cake keeps for many months in a tin, and makes an excellent wedding or christening cake.

Simnel Cake

Cream the butter and sugar until light and fluffy. Sieve the flour, baking powder, cinnamon and nutmeg. Beat the eggs into the creamed mixture, a little at a time, adding a little flour with each addition of egg. Add the remaining flour with the dried fruit and peel. The mixture should be stiff but a little milk may be added so that it becomes of a stiff consistency but will drop from a spoon. Roll out the almond paste into two 20cm/8in circles, and save the trimmings. Grease and line a 20cm/8in deep round cake tin. Put half the cake mixture into the tin and put a circle of almond paste on top. Put in the remaining cake mixture. Bake at 325°F/170°C/Gas Mark 3 for 3 hours, covering the cake with a piece of foil for the last hour if it is becoming too brown. Cool in the tin and then turn out carefully and peel off the paper. Brush the top of the cake with jam and put on the second piece of almond paste. Form the trimmings into eleven balls and put them round the edge of the cake, flattening them slightly with the hand. Brush the almond paste well with the egg white and sprinkle with caster sugar. Put under a hot grill so that the sugar becomes golden brown. Cool completely and then put a circle of glacé icing in the centre. If liked decorate with sugar eggs and fluffy chickens and tie a yellow satin ribbon round the cake. This is the traditional cake for Mothering Sunday (the fourth Sunday in Lent) which was taken home by servant girls to their mothers, as this was one of the days when they were allowed to visit them. The cake has now become more closely associated with Easter Day.

225g/8oz butter
225g/8oz sugar
350g/12oz plain flour
2 teaspoons baking powder
1 teaspoon ground cinnamon
Pinch of nutmeg
4 eggs
675g/1½lb mixed dried fruit
100g/4oz chopped mixed
   candied peel
A little milk
450g/1lb almond paste
2 tablespoons jam
1 egg white
1 tablespoon caster sugar
4 tablespoons glacé icing

Cherry Almond Cake

Wash and dry the cherries. Mix flour and salt. Cut the cherries in quarters, and toss in a little of the flour. Cream butter or margarine until soft, and add sugar, beating until light and fluffy. Beat in eggs one at a time, with a little of the flour. Stir in almonds, cherries and remaining flour. Put into greased and lined 15cm/6in tin. Bake at 350°F/180°C/Gas Mark 4 for 1 hour 20 minutes. Cool on a wire rack.

150g/6oz glacé cherries
200g/7oz self-raising flour
Pinch of salt
100g/4oz butter or margarine
100g/4oz caster sugar
3 eggs
25g/1oz ground almonds

Madeira Cake

100g/4oz butter or margarine
100g/4oz caster sugar
225g/8oz plain flour
50g/2oz ground rice
1 teaspoon cream of tartar
1 teaspoon bicarbonate of
  soda
¼ teaspoon salt
4 eggs
Juice of ½ lemon
Strip of candied citron peel

Cream the fat and sugar until light and fluffy. Stir together the flour, rice, cream of tartar, soda and salt. Beat the eggs together lightly. Add the dry ingredients alternately with the lemon juice and eggs to the creamed mixture, and beat until smooth and creamy. Put into a greased and base-lined 17.5cm/7in round cake tin. Bake at 350°F/180°C/Gas Mark 4 for 1¼ hours. After 45 minutes' baking, open the oven carefully and put the piece of candied peel on the surface of the cake (if it is put on the cake mixture at the beginning, it may sink, or become very brown and dry).

Old-fashioned Seed Cake

225g/8oz butter
225g/8oz caster sugar
4 eggs
225g/8oz plain flour
3 teaspoons caraway seeds
2 teaspoons caster sugar

Cream the butter and sugar until very light and fluffy. Add the eggs one at a time with a little flour and mix very thoroughly. Fold in the remaining flour. Reserve ½ teaspoon caraway seeds, and fold in the rest. Do not beat. Put into a greased and lined 17.5cm/7in round cake tin. Sprinkle on the remaining seeds and 2 teaspoons caster sugar. Bake at 325°F/170°C/Gas Mark 3 for 1¼ hours. Cool in the tin for 10 minutes and then continue cooling on a wire rack.

Cherry Blossom Cake

100g/4oz butter or margarine
50g/2oz caster sugar
30ml/2 tablespoons honey
2 eggs
175g/6oz self-raising flour
45ml/3 tablespoons milk

Icing
75g/3oz butter or margarine
30ml/2 tablespoons honey
75g/3oz icing sugar
A few glacé cherries
25g/1oz toasted flaked
  almonds

Cream butter and sugar together until light and fluffy. Add the honey and beat in eggs, adding a little flour. Fold in remaining flour and milk. Put into two greased 17.5cm/7in sponge sandwich tins. Bake at 350°F/180°C/Gas Mark 4 for 30 minutes. Turn out and cool on a wire rack. To make the icing, beat butter and add honey and icing sugar. Chop a few glacé cherries and add to topping. Fill cake with some of the icing and use remainder to coat top and sides. Scatter with almonds and decorate with remaining glacé cherries.

Orange Juice Cake

Separate the eggs, and beat the yolks until foamy. Add half the sugar and continue to beat until the sugar has dissolved. Sift flour, salt and baking powder and add alternately with the fruit juices. Whip egg whites until stiff, fold in remaining sugar, and fold into cake mixture. Put into a greased 20cm/8in cake tin, and bake at 350°F/180°C/Gas Mark 4 for 1 hour. Cool on a wire rack. If liked, cover with orange glacé icing, or sprinkle with sieved icing sugar.

5 eggs
200g/7oz caster sugar
225g/8oz plain flour
Pinch of salt
2 teaspoons baking powder
1 teaspoon lemon juice
Scant 150ml/¼ pint orange juice

Marble Cake

Cream the margarine and sugar until light and fluffy. Work in the eggs and vanilla essence with a little of the flour. Sieve the flour and fold it into the mixture. Put half the cake mixture into another bowl. Melt the chocolate in a bowl over hot water and add to half the mixture, beating well. Grease and line a 17.5cm/7in round cake tin. Put alternate spoonfuls of plain and chocolate mixture into the tin. Bake at 350°F/180°C/Gas Mark 4 for 45 minutes. Cool on a wire rack.

225g/8oz margarine
225g/8oz caster sugar
3 eggs
Few drops of vanilla essence
300g/10oz self-raising flour
75g/3oz plain chocolate

Date and Walnut Cake

Cream the margarine and sugar until light and fluffy. Sieve the flour and baking powder. Add the eggs to the creamed mixture alternately with a little of the flour. Beat well and then add the remaining flour, walnuts, dates and milk. Mix well to a dropping consistency. Put into a greased 17.5cm/7in round cake tin. Bake at 325°F/170°C/Gas Mark 3 for 1½ hours. Cool in the tin for 10 minutes and then finish cooling on a wire rack. To make the icing, put all the ingredients into a basin over a saucepan of hot water. Stir over simmering water until the mixture is smooth. Remove from the heat and beat well until thick. Spread on the cake and leave until cool and set.

175g/6oz margarine
175g/6oz soft brown sugar
225g/8oz plain flour
1½ teaspoons baking powder
3 eggs
50g/2oz chopped walnuts
225g/8oz chopped stoned dates
30ml/2 tablespoons milk

Icing
50g/2oz margarine
45ml/3 tablespoons milk
225g/8oz icing sugar
1 teaspoon coffee essence

Yogurt Cake

100g/4oz butter
175g/6oz caster sugar
Grated rind of 1 lemon
3 eggs
175g/6oz self-raising flour
175ml/6fl.oz natural yogurt
50g/2oz chopped mixed
   candied peel

Cream butter and sugar, add lemon rind and beat well. Separate the eggs. Add the egg yolks one at a time and beat in. Add the sifted flour alternately with the yogurt and stir in the peel. Whisk egg whites until stiff and fold into the batter. Spoon into a greased 1kg/2lb loaf tin and bake at 350°F/180°C/Gas Mark 4 for 1 hour. Turn out on to a wire tray and cool. The cake may be topped with lemon glacé icing if liked.

Raisin Shortcake

60ml/4 tablespoons orange
   juice
100g/4oz seedless raisins
175g/6oz plain flour
50g/2oz caster sugar
100g/4oz butter

Put the orange juice and raisins into a pan and bring slowly to the boil then leave until cold. Sieve flour into a basin and work in the sugar and butter until the mixture looks like fine breadcrumbs. Knead well and divide dough into two pieces. Form into equal-sized rounds. Put one on a greased baking sheet, spread on raisin mixture and top with a second round of dough, pressing together firmly and pinching edges together. Prick well. Bake at 350°F/180°C/Gas Mark 4 for 45 minutes. Mark into sections, and remove from tin when cold.

Dutch Apple Cake

450g/1lb cooking apples
45ml/3 tablespoons water
1 tablespoon sugar
75g/3oz unsalted butter
325g/11oz caster sugar
1 egg
225g/8oz plain flour
1 teaspoon baking powder
¼ teaspoon ground cinnamon
¼ teaspoon ground nutmeg
¼ teaspoon ground mixed spice
1 teaspoon salt
50g/2oz chopped walnuts
100g/4oz sultanas
1 tablespoon icing sugar

Peel, core and chop the apples. Put into a saucepan with the water and 1 tablespoon sugar and simmer, stirring occasionally until the apples form a purée. Cool. Cream the butter and sugar until light and fluffy and work in the egg, beating well. Sieve the flour, baking powder, spices and salt. Fold into the creamed mixture with the apple purée, walnuts and sultanas. Put into a greased and base-lined 22.5cm/9in round cake tin. Bake at 350°F/180°C/Gas Mark 4 for 1¼ hours. Cool on a wire rack and sprinkle sieved icing sugar on the surface.

Dark Chocolate Cake

Cream the margarine and sugar until light and fluffy. Beat in the eggs. Sieve together the flour, baking powder and soda. Fold into the creamed mixture. Mix the Guinness and cocoa to a paste, and stir into the cake mixture. Grease and base-line two 20cm/8in sponge sandwich tins. Divide the cake mixture between them. Bake at 350°F/180°C/Gas Mark 4 for 30 minutes. Cool on a wire rack.

Make the icing by melting 100g/4oz chocolate and the milk together in a bowl over a pan of hot water. Cool slightly. Cream the margarine and icing sugar and work in the melted chocolate. Beat well and spread half the icing over one cake. Top with the second cake and spread the remaining icing on top. Grate the remaining chocolate over the icing.

100g/4oz soft margarine
175g/6oz dark soft brown sugar
2 eggs
175g/6oz plain flour
1 teaspoon baking powder
½ teaspoon bicarbonate of soda
150ml/¼ pint Guinness
50g/2oz cocoa

Icing
175g/6oz plain chocolate
15ml/1 tablespoon milk
100g/4oz soft margarine
225g/8oz icing sugar

Devil's Food Cake

Sieve together the flour, baking powder, bicarbonate of soda and cocoa. Beat the butter until light and creamy and gradually beat in the sugar. Mix in the eggs, a little at a time, beating well. Fold in the flour alternately with the water. Put into two 20cm/8in greased and base-lined sandwich tins. Bake at 350°F/180°C/Gas Mark 4 for 1 hour. Turn out on a wire rack to cool. When cold, sandwich the cakes together with chocolate butter cream.

175g/6oz plain flour
1 teaspoon baking powder
1 teaspoon bicarbonate of soda
50g/2oz cocoa
100g/4oz butter
300g/10oz caster sugar
2 eggs
250ml/8fl.oz water
Chocolate butter cream

Chocolate Banana Cake

Cream butter and sugar together until light and fluffy. Beat in eggs together with 3 tablespoons of the measured amount of flour. Fold in the remaining flour and cocoa and stir in mashed bananas. Divide the mixture in two 20cm/8in greased and floured sandwich tins and bake at 350°F/180°C/Gas Mark 5 for 35 minutes. When cool, sandwich together with chocolate butter cream and coat the top of the cake with glacé icing.

175g/6oz butter
175g/6oz caster sugar
3 eggs
200g/7oz self-raising flour
25g/1oz cocoa
2 mashed bananas
Chocolate butter cream
Chocolate glacé icing

Mocha Cake

175g/6oz butter
175g/6oz caster sugar
3 eggs
175g/6oz self-raising flour
30ml/2 tablespoons coffee
    essence
50g/2oz plain chocolate
A little icing sugar

Cream the butter and sugar until light and fluffy. Gradually beat in the beaten eggs, adding a little flour with each addition. Fold in the remaining flour, essence and coarsely grated chocolate. Put into a greased and lined 20cm/8in round cake tin. Bake at 350°F/180°C/Gas Mark 4 for 1½ hours. Turn out and cool on a wire rack. Dust the top with a little sieved icing sugar when cold.

Coffee Walnut Cake

100g/4oz margarine
100g/4oz caster sugar
2 eggs
15ml/1 tablespoon coffee
    essence
100g/4oz self-raising flour
50g/2oz chopped walnuts

Icing
100g/4oz icing sugar
2 teaspoons coffee essence
A little hot water
12 walnut halves

Cream together margarine and caster sugar until light and fluffy. Gradually add lightly beaten eggs, beating well between additions. Stir in coffee essence and fold in sifted flour, together with chopped walnuts. Turn mixture into a greased deep 17.5cm/7in sandwich tin, and bake at 375°F/190°C/Gas Mark 5 for 25–30 minutes. Cool on a rack. Make the icing by sifting the sugar into a bowl. Stir in liquid coffee and sufficient hot water to give the required consistency. Decorate with icing and walnut halves.

Ginger Marmalade Sponge

100g/4oz butter
50g/2oz light soft brown
    sugar
30ml/2 tablespoons golden
    syrup
2 eggs
100g/4oz self-raising flour
¼ teaspoon baking powder
½ teaspoon ground ginger
75g/3oz orange, lemon or
    ginger marmalade
A little icing sugar

Cream the butter, sugar and syrup until light and fluffy and work in the beaten eggs. Sift the flour with baking powder and ginger, and fold into the creamed mixture. Put into two greased 17.5cm/7in sandwich tins. Bake at 400°F/200°C/Gas Mark 6 for 25 minutes. Turn out on a wire rack to cool. Sandwich together with the marmalade and sprinkle with icing sugar. Ginger marmalade or a dark coarse-cut marmalade make the best fillings.

Yorkshire Moggie Cake

Sieve flour and baking powder into a bowl and stir in the sugar. Warm the treacle, butter and milk together until just warm and melted. Stir into the dry ingredients, and beat in the egg. Put into a greased and base-lined 27.5×17.5cm/11×7in tin. Bake at 325°F/170°C/Gas Mark 3 for 1 hour. Cool and cut into squares.

450g/1lb plain flour
2 teaspoons baking powder
225g/8oz caster sugar
225g/8oz black treacle
175g/6oz butter
150ml/¼ pint milk
1 egg

Dorset Gingerbread

Grease and line a tin approximately 27.5×17.5cm/11×7in. Melt the margarine, sugar and treacle together in a thick pan. Sieve the flour, ginger and cinnamon and stir into the melted mixture with the beaten eggs. Warm the milk just to blood heat and stir in the soda. Add to the mixture, beat well and pour into the tin. Bake at 325°F/170°C/Gas Mark 3 for 1½ hours. Cool in the tin for 5 minutes and then turn out to cool on a wire rack.

225g/8oz margarine
225g/8oz soft brown sugar
225g/8oz black treacle
350g/12oz plain flour
4 teaspoons ground ginger
3 teaspoons ground cinnamon
2 eggs
250ml/½ pint milk
2 teaspoons bicarbonate of soda

Lemon Gingerbread

Put the margarine, syrup and sugar into a pan and heat gently until the fat has melted. Sieve the flour, soda and spices into a bowl. Stir in the chopped peel. Add the warm melted mixture and beat well. Beat the egg lightly and then beat into the mixture with the lemon juice. Warm the milk to lukewarm and stir into the gingerbread mixture. Grease and line a 1kg/2lb loaf tin. Pour in the mixture and bake at 350°F/180°C/Gas Mark 4 for 50 minutes. Cool in the tin for 10 minutes and then turn on to a wire rack to finish cooling.

75g/3oz margarine
45ml/3 tablespoons golden syrup
75g/3oz sugar
175g/6oz self-raising flour
1 teaspoon bicarbonate of soda
1½ teaspoons ground ginger
1 teaspoon ground mixed spice
50g/2oz chopped candied lemon peel
1 egg
15ml/1 tablespoon lemon juice
120ml/4fl.oz milk

11 Tray-Baked Cakes

Cooks who are busy particularly appreciate tray-baked cakes. The mixtures are quickly made and put into a rectangular tin for baking; icings and toppings are added while the cake is still in the tin. The tray-cakes can then be cut into squares or fingers and easily stored in a tin, and they have the advantage that the individual portions always come up looking fresh and tempting, while a cut cake never looks so appetising after its first presentation. For these cakes, use rectangular tins which are about 5cm/2in deep, as these give room for the cakes to rise, and still leave plenty of space for the icings or toppings.

Almond Slices

225g/8oz plain flour
Pinch of salt
50g/2oz caster sugar
75g/3oz margarine
2 egg yolks

Topping
100g/4oz apricot jam
2 egg whites
225g/8oz caster sugar
100g/4oz ground almonds
Few drops of almond essence

Sieve the flour and salt together in a bowl. Stir in the sugar and then rub in the margarine until the mixture is like fine breadcrumbs. Work in the egg yolks to make a stiff dough. Press into a greased Swiss roll tin. Warm the apricot jam slightly so that it spreads easily. Spread on to the dough with a palette knife. Whisk the egg whites to stiff peaks and fold in the sugar, almonds and essence. Spread on top of the jam. Bake at 375°F/190°C/Gas Mark 5 for 25 minutes. Cool in the tin and cut in slices.

Orange Squares

Rub the margarine into the flour until the mixture is like fine breadcrumbs. Press into a greased 22.5×30cm/9×12in tin. Bake at 350°F/180°C/Gas Mark 4 for 7 minutes. Meanwhile, mix together all the ingredients for the topping until well blended. Spread on the pastry base and bake for 30 minutes. While the cake is still just warm, spread on the icing. Make this by creaming together the sugar, butter and orange juice until smooth. Leave in the tin until cold and then cut into squares.

150g/5oz plain flour
75g/3oz margarine

Topping
2 eggs
50g/2oz desiccated coconut
300g/10oz demerara sugar
50g/2oz chopped walnuts
40g/1½oz plain flour
½ teaspoon baking powder
Pinch of salt

Icing
225g/8oz icing sugar
30ml/2 tablespoons melted
    butter
50g/2oz orange juice

Broonie

Stir the flour, oatmeal, ginger and soda together in a basin. Rub in the butter until the mixture is like coarse breadcrumbs. Stir in the sugar. Mix the treacle and egg together and add to the dry ingredients with enough milk to give a thick batter which will pour. Grease and flour a 15cm/6in square tin. Pour in the mixture and bake at 325°F/170°C/Gas Mark 3 for 1¼ hours. Cool on a wire rack.

100g/4oz plain flour
100g/4oz medium oatmeal
2 teaspoons ground ginger
1½ teaspoons bicarbonate of
    soda
50g/2oz butter
75g/3oz soft brown sugar
30ml/2 tablespoons black
    treacle
1 egg
Milk

Golden Flapjacks

150g/5oz margarine
75g/3oz soft brown sugar
15ml/1 tablespoon golden
  syrup
1 teaspoon lemon juice
200g/7oz porridge oats
Pinch of salt

Melt the margarine, sugar and syrup together over low heat. Remove from the heat and stir in the lemon juice, oats and salt. Spread in a greased 20cm/8in square tin and press down firmly with a fork. Bake at 350°F/180°C/Gas Mark 4 for 20 minutes. Leave in the tin for 5 minutes and mark into squares with a sharp knife while still hot. Cool in the tin, then cut into pieces before removing to a wire rack.

Walnut Meringue Bake

75g/3oz margarine
50g/2oz light soft brown
  sugar
175g/6oz self-raising flour
2 egg yolks
Few drops of vanilla essence

Topping
2 egg whites
100g/4oz caster sugar
25g/1oz chopped walnuts
25g/1oz chopped glacé
  cherries

Cream the margarine and sugar until light and fluffy. Add the flour, egg yolks and vanilla essence and work together to a firm dough. Press into a greased Swiss roll tin and flatten well with the palm of the hand. Whisk the egg whites to stiff peaks. Fold in the sugar, nuts and cherries. Spread evenly over the base and bake at 350°F/180°C/Gas Mark 4 for 30 minutes. Cool in the tin and cut into squares when cold.

Honey Bake

450g/1lb honey
175g/6oz light soft brown
  sugar
4 eggs
350g/12oz wholemeal flour
1 teaspoon baking powder
1 teaspoon ground cinnamon
¼ teaspoon ground mixed spice
50g/2oz sultanas
50g/2oz chopped mixed peel
50g/2oz chopped blanched
  almonds

Heat the honey and sugar gently until melted and well blended. Cool slightly, and then beat in the eggs. Sieve the flour, baking powder and spices. Mix the honey mixture into the flour until well blended and stir in the sultanas, peel and chopped almonds. Put into a greased and lined 22.5cm/9in square tin. Bake at 375°F/190°C/Gas Mark 5 for 1 hour. Cool in the tin and then turn out on a wire rack. Store in an airtight tin and cut into squares to serve. This cake improves with keeping.

Peppermint Cream Squares

Sieve together the flour and cocoa powder. Put the brown sugar and margarine into a bowl and cream together until light and fluffy. Beat in the flour mixture until well blended. Spread in a greased Swiss roll tin. Bake at 375°F/190°C/Gas Mark 5 for 20 minutes. Cool in the tin. Sieve the icing sugar into a bowl. Gradually add just enough hot water to make a thick paste. Flavour with a few drops of peppermint essence. Spread on the cold chocolate biscuit mixture. Put the chocolate into a bowl over hot water and heat until melted. Spread on top of the peppermint icing. Leave until cold and then cut into squares.

225g/8oz self-raising flour
2 teaspoons cocoa powder
100g/4oz light soft brown sugar
225g/8oz margarine

Icing
225g/8oz icing sugar
Hot water
Few drops of peppermint essence
175g/6oz plain chocolate

Mission Squares

Finely chop the raisins and walnuts. Sieve flour into a basin and rub in the butter until the mixture resembles fine breadcrumbs. Add sugar and stir in. Grease a 20cm/8in square cake tin, and press 225g/8oz rubbed-in mixture over base. Sieve baking powder and salt into remaining rubbed-in mixture. Add grated orange rind, raisins and walnuts and mix in thoroughly. Beat eggs, orange juice and milk together and stir into mixture. Beat well, and pour over crumbs in tin. Bake at 375°F/190°C/Gas Mark 5 for 1 hour. Cool in tin for a few minutes. Turn out and cut into 12 squares.

150g/5oz seedless raisins
40g/1½oz walnuts
365g/12½oz plain flour
150g/5oz butter or margarine
250g/9oz light soft brown sugar
3 teaspoons baking powder
Pinch of salt
1 orange
2 eggs
90ml/6 tablespoons milk

Lemon Bake

Cream the butter and sugar until light and fluffy. Work in the beaten eggs and flour to make a smooth batter. Put into a greased 25×17.5cm/10×7in tin. Bake at 350°F/180°C/Gas Mark 4 for 40 minutes. While the cake is baking, mix together the lemon juice and sugar. As soon as the cake comes from the oven, prick the top lightly with a fork. Spread on the lemon mixture to cover the cake completely. Cool in the tin and cut in squares. The lemon juice sinks through to flavour the cake and the sugar forms a crisp topping.

175g/6oz butter
175g/6oz caster sugar
2 eggs
175g/6oz self-raising flour

Topping
Juice of 1 lemon
100g/4oz caster sugar

Chocolate Banana Bars

175g/6oz plain chocolate
50g/2oz butter
100g/4oz caster sugar
3 bananas
60ml/4 tablespoons milk
1 egg
50g/2oz bran cereal
175g/6oz self-raising flour
1 teaspoon salt
½ teaspoon ground cinnamon

Velvet Icing
175g/6oz plain chocolate
25g/1oz butter
30ml/4 tablespoons milk
Pinch of salt
½ teaspoon vanilla essence
150g/5oz icing sugar

Put chocolate into a basin over a pan of hot water, and heat gently until melted. Cream together butter and sugar. Add mashed bananas, milk and egg, and mix well together. Stir in bran cereal, flour, salt and cinnamon, and beat until well blended. Spread mixture in a greased and base-lined 27.5×17.5cm/11×7in tin. Bake at 350°F/180°C/Gas Mark 4 for 30 minutes. Cool in the tin.

To make the icing, put chocolate and butter into a basin over a pan of hot water. Heat gently until melted. Remove from heat. Add milk, salt, vanilla essence and icing sugar, and beat until smooth. Spread over the cake. When the icing has set, cut the cake into bars.

Chocolate Spice Brownies

225g/8oz self-raising flour
Pinch of salt
1 teaspoon ground cinnamon
100g/4oz margarine
100g/4oz dark soft brown
    sugar
75g/3oz plain chocolate
150g/5oz golden syrup
1 teaspoon bicarbonate of
    soda
150ml/¼ pint milk

Topping
100g/4oz plain flour
1 teaspoon ground mixed
    spice
50g/2oz margarine
25g/1oz soft brown sugar
50g/2oz chopped mixed nuts

Sieve together the flour, salt and cinnamon. Rub in the margarine until the mixture is like fine breadcrumbs, and stir in the sugar. Put the chocolate and syrup together into a saucepan and heat gently. Stir in the bicarbonate of soda and add to the dry ingredients with the milk. Beat well and put into a greased and lined 27.5×17.5cm/11×7in tin. Make the topping by stirring together the flour and spice and rubbing in the margarine until the mixture is like coarse breadcrumbs. Stir in the sugar and nuts and sprinkle over the cake mixture. Bake at 375°F/190°C/Gas Mark 5 for 45 minutes. Cool in the tin and cut into squares.

Walnut Brownies

Melt 50g/2oz margarine, stir in the cocoa and set aside. Cream the remaining margarine with the sugar until lighter in colour and texture, and gradually beat in the eggs. Fold in the sieved flour; add the walnuts and cocoa mixture. Turn into a greased and base-lined 17.5cm/7in square tin and bake at 350°F/180°C/Gas Mark 4 for 45 minutes. Leave to cool in the tin, and cut in squares. If liked, sprinkle with caster sugar, or cover with melted plain chocolate.

175g/6oz margarine
2 tablespoons cocoa
175g/6oz caster sugar
2 eggs
50g/2oz plain flour
50g/2oz chopped walnuts

Coffee Frosted Brownies

Sift together flour, cocoa and baking powder. Cream butter, sugar and vanilla essence until light and fluffy then beat in eggs, one at a time. Stir in dry ingredients then transfer mixture to a well-greased 17.5×27.5cm/7×11in tin. Bake at 350°F/180°C/Gas Mark 4 for 30 minutes. Cut into squares while still warm, remove from tin and cool on a wire rack.

To make frosting, melt the butter in a pan, add coffee essence, bring slowly to the boil and then boil steadily for 2 minutes. Quickly combine with icing sugar, pour in the milk and then beat until frosting is cold and stiff enough to spread. Cover tops of cakes with frosting and then decorate each with 2 walnut halves.

75g/3oz plain flour
40g/1½oz cocoa
½ teaspoon baking powder
100g/4oz butter or margarine
225g/8oz light soft brown
  sugar
1 teaspoon vanilla essence
2 eggs

Coffee Frosting
50g/2oz butter
30ml/2 tablespoons coffee
  essence
225g/8oz icing sugar
15ml/1 tablespoon milk
75g/3oz walnut halves

Dutch Shortcake

Cream the butter and sugar until light and fluffy. Separate the eggs and beat in the yolks. Stir in the flour. Put the mixture into a greased 22.5×30cm/9×12in tin. Mix the egg whites with a fork until frothy and add the cherries, walnuts and peel. Spread over the cake mixture. Bake at 325°F/170°C/Gas Mark 3 for 55 minutes. Mark into fingers while still warm. Cool for 10 minutes and take out of tin.

175g/6oz butter
175g/6oz demerara sugar
2 eggs
175g/6oz self-raising flour
40g/1½oz chopped glacé
  cherries
40g/1½oz chopped walnuts
15g/½oz chopped mixed
  candied peel

12 Small Cakes

Small cakes always look very attractive and can range from the simple rock cake and cup cake to patisserie items which are suitable for buffet parties and receptions as well as for family tea parties.

Rock Cakes

225g/8oz self-raising flour
Pinch of salt
100g/4oz butter
100g/4oz sugar
100g/4oz sultanas
1 egg
30ml/2 tablespoons milk
1 teaspoon ground mixed
   spice
¼ teaspoon finely grated lemon
   rind

Sieve together the flour and salt. Rub in the butter until the mixture is like fine breadcrumbs. Stir in the sugar, sultanas, beaten egg, milk, spice and lemon rind. Mix well to form a stiff dough. Use a dessertspoon to put rough lumps of the mixture on a greased baking sheet. Bake at 375°F/190°C/Gas Mark 5 for 10 minutes. Cool on a wire rack.

Coffee Porcupines

150g/5oz self-raising flour
1 teaspoon baking powder
2 eggs
30ml/2 tablespoons coffee
   essence
100g/4oz soft margarine
100g/4oz caster sugar
Coffee butter icing
Toasted sliced almonds

Sieve the flour and baking powder into a bowl. Add eggs, essence, margarine and sugar and beat hard for 2 minutes until smooth. Spoon into 15 greased bun tins. Bake at 375°F/190°C/Gas Mark 5 for 10 minutes. Cool on a wire rack. Spread coffee butter icing over the cakes and stick in almond slices to look like porcupine quills.

Madeleines

These are the true French Madeleines, and not the sticky coconut castles which have adopted the name but which are so sickly to eat. They should be made in shell-shaped bun tins which are easily obtained, and this quantity of mixture will make eighteen little cakes. Cream the butter and sugar and add the eggs gradually, beating well. Sieve the flour and baking powder. Fold into the creamed mixture with the orange rind and juice. Fill the shell-shaped tins three-quarters full. Bake at 400°F/200°C/Gas Mark 6 for 8 minutes. Turn out and cool on a wire rack and dust very lightly with sieved icing sugar.

115g/4½oz unsalted butter
100g/4oz caster sugar
2 eggs
100g/4oz plain flour
1 teaspoon baking powder
1 teaspoon finely grated orange rind
15ml/1 tablespoon orange juice
A little icing sugar

Iced Fancy Cakes

Make and bake a square of Genoese sponge and cool on a wire rack. Cut out cakes with biscuit cutters, or cut squares or rectangles, or cut across diagonally to make diamond shapes. Warm apricot jam so that it can be spread easily. Use a pastry brush to cover the top and sides of each piece of cake. Roll out the almond paste very thinly on a lightly floured board so that it will not stick. Cut in shapes to fit the top of each cake. Put a piece of almond paste on each cake. Cut strips of almond paste and fit neatly around the sides of each cake. Leave in a dry place for 12 hours. Coat the cakes with fondant icing in a variety of colourings and flavourings. Pipe on decorations to taste and decorate with silver balls, crystallised flower petals, mimosa balls, glacé cherries or angelica.

Genoese sponge (page 102)
Apricot jam
Almond paste (page 180)
Fondant icing (page 186)
Decorations

Eccles Cakes

Roll out the pastry and cut into 10cm/4in circles. Mix together the currants, peel and spices. Melt the molasses sugar and butter together and stir in the fruit mixture. Cool completely. Put a spoonful into the centre of each piece of pastry. Bring the edges together over the filling and seal them firmly by pinching together. Turn them over and press lightly to flatten. Put on to a baking sheet and make a small hole in the centre of each. Brush with egg white and sprinkle with sugar. Bake at 425°F/220°C/Gas Mark 7 for 15 minutes. Lift on to a rack to cool.

450g/1lb shortcrust pastry
100g/4oz currants
25g/1oz chopped mixed peel
½ teaspoon ground allspice
½ teaspoon ground nutmeg
50g/2oz molasses sugar
25g/1oz butter
1 egg white
15g/½oz caster sugar

Chocolate Cup Cakes

100g/4oz soft margarine
100g/4oz caster sugar
2 eggs
100g/4oz self-raising flour
15g/½oz cocoa
1 teaspoon baking powder

Icing
175g/6oz plain chocolate
20g/¾oz butter
175g/6oz icing sugar
45ml/3 tablespoons warm
   water

Cream the margarine and caster sugar until light and fluffy. Work in the eggs. Sieve the flour, cocoa and baking powder together and work into the mixture. Beat well until well blended. Spoon the mixture into 24 paper cake cases on a baking sheet. Bake at 375°F/190°C/Gas Mark 5 for 20 minutes. Cool on a wire rack. Put the chocolate and butter into a bowl over hot water and heat until just melted. Take off the heat and beat in the icing sugar and water to make a thick icing. Spoon on to each cake and leave until set.

Citrus Eclairs

150ml/¼ pint water
50g/2oz butter
65g/2½oz plain flour
Pinch of salt
2 eggs

Filling
300ml/½ pint double cream
25g/1oz icing sugar
Grated rind of 1 small lemon
Grated rind of ½ orange
Icing sugar for decoration

Put the water and butter into a saucepan and heat gently until the butter melts. Bring to the boil and take off the heat. Tip in the flour and salt quickly and beat with a wooden spoon. Return to a low heat and beat the dough until it leaves the sides of the pan and forms a soft ball. Cool for a few minutes until lukewarm. Beat the eggs together and beat into the dough, a little at a time, until the mixture is smooth and shiny. Use a plain 1.25cm/½in nozzle and pipe 5cm/2in lengths on to a lightly greased baking sheet, well apart. Bake at 425°F/230°C/Gas Mark 7 for 20 minutes. Split in half and return to oven at 350°F/180°C/Gas Mark 4 for 10 minutes. Cool on a wire rack. Whisk the cream to stiff peaks and fold in the icing sugar, lemon and orange rind. Spoon the cream into the eclairs. Sprinkle sieved icing sugar on top.

Chocolate or Coffee Eclairs
Make the eclair cases in the same way. Fill with sweetened whipped cream and coat with chocolate or coffee glacé icing.

Cream Buns
Pipe buns instead of finger lengths. Fill with sweetened whipped cream and top with chocolate or coffee glacé icing, or with sieved icing sugar.

Tuiles

Cream the butter and sugar until white. Stir in the sifted flour and finely sliced almonds. (Almonds are better flaked immediately after skinning. Add two drops of almond essence for ready-flaked almonds.) Form the mixture into marble-sized balls and place 7.5cm/3in apart on a well-greased baking sheet. Flatten each ball with a fork dipped in water, and bake at 400°F/200°C/Gas Mark 6 for 8–10 minutes until they are light gold with brown edges. Remove the tray from the oven and allow the tuiles to stand for a few seconds just long enough to set. Peel the tuiles off the tin with a very sharp knife and lift them carefully on to an oiled rolling pin to form slight curve. Leave them to harden. Store *immediately* in an airtight tin. Do not attempt to bake more than 6 tuiles at a time or they will harden on the baking tray and be difficult to remove. Should this happen, return the tray to the oven for a minute or two to soften them.

65g/2½oz butter
50g/2oz caster sugar
40g/1½oz plain flour
40g/1½oz sliced almonds

Brandy Snaps

Melt the syrup, sugar and butter in a pan. Cool slightly and work in the flour and ginger. Beat until smooth and stir in the brandy. Put the mixture into small heaps on a greased baking sheet. Bake at 350°F/180°C/Gas Mark 4 for 7 minutes until spread out and golden. Cool slightly and remove with a palette knife. Roll round the greased handle of a wooden spoon. When cold, fill with whipped cream.

75g/3oz golden syrup
40g/1½oz caster sugar
75g/3oz butter
50g/2oz plain flour
1 teaspoon ground ginger
1 teaspoon brandy
150ml/¼ pint double cream

Coffee Snaps

Melt the sugar, butter and golden syrup over a gentle heat. Stir in the flour and coffee powder. Drop teaspoons of the mixture far apart on greased baking sheets. Bake at 325°F/170°C/Gas Mark 3. Allow to cool slightly, then remove from the baking sheet one at a time and roll quickly round a greased wooden spoon handle. Leave to set. Return those on the baking sheet to the warm oven at any time if they become too brittle to roll. Whip the cream and put into a piping bag fitted with a star nozzle. Pipe cream into the snaps. Dip each end in walnuts and serve at once.

40g/2½oz caster sugar
25g/1oz butter
25g/1oz golden syrup
25g/1oz plain flour
1 teaspoon coffee powder
150ml/¼ pint double cream
25g/1oz finely chopped
*   walnuts*

French Almond Meringues

3 egg whites
Pinch of salt
250g/9oz icing sugar
250g/9oz blanched almonds

Whisk the egg whites with salt to stiff peaks. Fold in the sieved icing sugar. Slice the almonds thinly and fold them into the mixture. Shape in ovals on Bakewell paper on baking sheets. Bake at 325°F/170°C/Gas Mark 3 for 30 minutes. Turn off the oven and leave in the meringues until the oven is cold. Remove from paper. Serve these meringues without cream.

Palmiers

Granulated sugar
225g/8oz puff pastry
100g/4oz raspberry or
    strawberry jam
300ml/½ pint double cream

Sprinkle a pastry board with sugar and roll out the pastry thinly into a large square. Sprinkle the pastry evenly with more sugar, and roll lightly. Fold the sides to centre, leaving a 1.25cm/½in gap down the middle. Dust again with sugar and repeat the folding. Turn one double fold directly over the other and press firmly together. Cut into 1.25cm/½in slices, and put on a damp baking sheet, leaving a large space between each. Press down with the base of a jar to flatten. Bake at 425°F/220°C/Gas Mark 7 for 8–10 minutes until golden. Turn over and bake for 3 minutes more. Lift carefully on to a wire rack to cool. Sandwich together in pairs with jam and whipped cream.

Brown Sugar Meringues

3 egg whites
Pinch of cream of tartar
175g/6oz light soft brown
    sugar
Double cream

Put the egg whites and cream of tartar into a very clean and grease-free bowl. Whisk until the egg whites stand in stiff peaks. Fold in the sugar until completely mixed. Line a baking sheet with Bakewell parchment. Put the meringue mixture on to the sheet with 2 tablespoons to form egg shapes. Bake at 250°F/120°C/Gas Mark ½ for 1 hour until completely dry. Remove meringues carefully and cool. Sandwich together with whipped cream just before serving. For a special treat, add a little finely chopped stem ginger to the cream.

Coffee Nut Meringues

Whisk the egg whites to stiff peaks. Gradually beat in the sugar and fold in the vinegar, essence, cornflour and walnuts. Line a baking sheet with non-stick parchment and place teaspoons of the mixture on the sheet. Bake at 300°F/150°C/Gas Mark 2 for 30 minutes. Serve plain or sandwich together with whipped cream.

2 egg whites
100g/4oz caster sugar
¼ teaspoon vinegar
15ml/1 tablespoon coffee essence
1 teaspoon cornflour
50g/2oz finely chopped walnuts

Chocolate Meringues

Whisk the egg whites, salt and cream of tartar until soft peaks form. Add the sugar gradually, beating until stiff peaks form and the mixture is thick and shiny. Chop the chocolate roughly (or use chocolate chips) and stir into the mixture. Cover baking sheets with baking parchment and drop on the mixture in rounded teaspoonfuls. Bake at 300°F/150°C/Gas Mark 2 for 30 minutes. Lift off the meringues and turn them over on the paper. Leave in the oven for 10 minutes more. Cool on a wire rack. Do not fill these meringues with cream.

2 egg whites
Pinch of salt
Pinch of cream of tartar
175g/6oz caster sugar
175g/6oz plain chocolate

13 Gâteaux

Many people think that there is something mysterious and complicated about gâteaux but in fact this is only the French word for 'cakes'. It has come to be accepted as the designation for rich and elaborate confections which may be eaten at tea time, but are more likely to make their appearance on a buffet table or at a dinner party. There is certainly nothing difficult about making such delicacies, for they are really simple assemblies of standard cakes or pastry bases with butter creams and whipped cream and attractive decorations. Anyone who can make a sponge cake, meringues or choux pastry can easily prepare a really superb gâteau, and once the basic assembly principles have been mastered, original combinations of ingredients can be made. The key to successful gâteau assembly is to keep it simple. Basically, most of these cakes consist of two or three layers of sponge, meringue or nut-based cake which are put together with a butter cream and/or whipped cream. A light touch is necessary in finishing the cake with whirls of butter cream or whipped cream, possibly a decoration of nuts or grated chocolate, or even just a thick dusting of sieved icing sugar. Brightly coloured fancy decorations have no place in attractive gâteaux, which depend for their success on a skilled blending of complementary flavours.

RIGHT Home-baked bread is at its best spread thickly with butter as part of a ploughman's lunch of beer, cheese and pickles

OVERLEAF, LEFT Almond stollen

OVERLEAF, RIGHT Waffles

Whisky Mocha Cake

Sift together the flour, cornflour, cocoa, coffee powder and baking powder. Cream the margarine and sugar and work in the eggs alternately with the dry ingredients. Beat well and fold in the whisky. Put into two greased and base-lined 17.5cm/7in sandwich tins. Bake at 325°F/170°C/Gas Mark 3 for 30 minutes. Cool on a wire rack.

Make the icing by creaming together the margarine, icing sugar, whisky and coffee essence. Spread one cake with half the mixture. Put on the second cake and top with the remaining icing. Sprinkle thickly with grated chocolate.

75g/3oz self-raising flour
15g/½oz cornflour
15g/½oz cocoa
15g/½oz instant coffee powder
1 teaspoon baking powder
100g/4oz soft margarine
100g/4oz caster sugar
2 eggs
1 teaspoon whisky

Icing
50g/2oz soft margarine
100g/4oz icing sugar
2 teaspoons whisky
1 teaspoon coffee essence
*50g/2oz grated plain
  chocolate*

Summer Coffee Gâteau

Cream 100g/4oz butter until it is soft but not oily. Beat in the caster sugar until the mixture is fluffy and light in colour. Add the eggs one at a time, beating well after each addition. Stir in the coffee essence and the brandy. Slice each sponge into 3 layers, making 6 in all. Put one layer at the bottom of a 17.5cm/7in cake tin with a fixed base. Spoon on a fifth of the coffee cream mixture. Continue adding layers of cake and cream, ending with a cake layer. Put the base of a 17.5cm/7in sandwich tin on the cake layers and weight it so that the cake and cream layers are pressed. Leave for 4 hours in the fridge. Turn out by dipping a knife in hot water and running it round the inside of the cake tin. Turn on to a serving plate. Cut the cake into 6 large wedges; push them together on a serving plate. Beat rest of butter until creamy. Gradually add the sifted icing sugar. Add the coffee powder. Spread round the sides of the cake and press the walnuts round the edge. Whip the cream and put in a piping bag and pipe a large swirl on each wedge. Decorate with coffee bean sweets.

*2×17.5cm/7in Victoria
  sandwich cakes*

Filling
200g/7oz butter
100g/4oz caster sugar
2 large eggs
*15ml/1 tablespoon coffee
  essence*
45ml/3 tablespoons brandy

Topping
175g/6oz icing sugar
2 teaspoons coffee powder
*50g/2oz finely chopped
  walnuts*
150ml/¼ pint double cream

LEFT   Chocolate cakes and walnut brownies

Christmas Tree

150g/5oz self-raising flour
Pinch of salt
1 teaspoon sugar
300ml/½ pint water
100g/4oz butter
2 eggs

Filling
300ml/½ pint double cream

Caramel Syrup
175g/6oz granulated sugar
150ml/¼ pint water
Pinch of cream of tartar

Decoration
Mixed coloured cherries
Christmas decorations

Sieve the flour, salt and sugar together. Put water and fat into a small saucepan, bring to the boil, then add flour mixture all at once. Stir quickly with a wooden spoon until the mixture forms a smooth ball of dough. Remove from heat, add one egg, stir, then beat very thoroughly until it has been absorbed. Repeat with the second egg to bring the mixture to a velvety consistency, so that it keeps its shape when pulled into points with the spoon. Beat thoroughly, then pipe this choux pastry out in small even balls (use a piping bag with 1.25cm/½in diameter plain tube) on greased baking sheets. Bake on a shelf near the top of the oven at 375°F/190°C/Gas Mark 5 for 20–30 minutes. When cool, either split or make a hole in the balls and fill with whipped cream.

Prepare the caramel syrup by dissolving the sugar carefully in the water. Add a small pinch of cream of tartar, then boil rapidly to a pale gold. Stop the boiling by putting the bottom of the saucepan into a bowl of cold water then tilt the pan by raising it on a cloth on one side.

To assemble the tree, take a ball of choux pastry, dip one side into the syrup and stick on to the cake board. Then take another and repeat the process, sticking it so that the edge of the ball slightly overlaps the other. Continue until a complete ring is formed around the board. Proceed building up another ring on top of the first one making it slightly smaller than the first. Continue in this way until the top ring is closed completely. Decorate with cherries and little Christmas decorations. Take a fork and pull threads from the caramel to wrap around the tree. If the syrup becomes too set, warm it slightly to soften.

Praline Cream Gâteau

225g/8oz butter
225g/8oz caster sugar
4 eggs
25g/1oz ground almonds
350g/10oz plain flour
2 teaspoons baking powder
30ml/2 tablespoons water

Cream the butter and sugar until light and fluffy. Add the eggs one at a time, beating between each addition. Stir in dry ingredients gradually, adding the water between each addition. Put into a greased and lined 25cm/10in round cake tin and bake at 350°F/180°C/Gas Mark 4 for 1¼ hours until firm. Turn out and cool on a wire rack. The cake may be made in advance and stored in an airtight tin for several days before completion.

To make the Praline Cream, spread the ground almonds on to a clean baking tray and heat in a moderate oven until golden brown, with a roasted smell and appearance. Leave to cool. Heat

100g/4oz sugar with 150ml/¼ pint water in a small saucepan until the temperature reaches 247°F/102°C, or when a little dropped into a cup of cold water forms a large firm ball when rolled between the thumb and forefinger. Pour over the egg yolks, whisking continuously and add the roasted ground almonds. Put the remaining sugar and water into a small pan and heat until it becomes a deep golden caramel. Whisk into the egg yolk mixture until it thickens and cools. Leave until cold and then fold in the whipped cream.

Split the cake in half and spread the lower half with apricot jam. Spread on a thick layer of Praline Cream and put on the top layer of cake. Coat the sides of the cake with apricot jam and then with Praline Cream. Chop 50g/2oz almonds and split the remaining almonds. Roast in a medium oven until golden. The almonds may be placed on a lightly oiled tin and grilled to the required colour if the oven is not in use. Sprinkle the chopped almonds on to a piece of greaseproof paper and holding the cake by the base and top, roll the side in the nuts until lightly coated. Put the cake on to a serving dish. Coat the top with apricot jam and Praline Cream. Whip the cream and decorate the cake with it, using any remaining Praline Cream in piped decorations. Arrange the halved roasted almonds on the top and keep in a cool place until served.

Praline Cream
25g/1oz ground almonds
125g/5oz granulated sugar
165ml/5½ fl.oz water
3 egg yolks
125ml/¼ pint double cream

Decoration
2 tablespoons apricot jam
65g/2½oz blanched almonds
250ml/½ pint double cream

Linzertorte

Put the margarine, sugar, ground nuts, lemon rind, egg and 25g/1oz flour into a bowl. Cream with a fork until well mixed. Work in the remaining flour and cinnamon to make a soft dough. Turn on to a lightly floured board and work with the fingertips until smooth. This dough is very delicate, so be sure to handle it with care. Roll out two-thirds of the dough to line a 20cm/8in fluted flan ring placed on a baking sheet. Chill for 30 minutes. Fill this pastry case with raspberry jam, or with the raspberries which have been lightly cooked in their own juice and sweetened to taste. Roll out the remaining dough and cut into 1.25cm/½in strips. Arrange in a lattice over the top. Bake at 375°F/190°C/Gas Mark 5 for 35 minutes. Cool and then brush the lattice and edge of the pastry with redcurrant jelly. Dust lightly with sieved icing sugar.

175g/6oz soft margarine
50g/2oz caster sugar
50g/2oz ground hazelnuts or
walnuts
Grated rind of 1 lemon
1 egg
225g/8oz plain flour
½ teaspoon ground cinnamon
450g/1lb raspberries or
raspberry jam
2 tablespoons redcurrant jelly
1 tablespoon icing sugar

Praline Ring

100g/4oz unsalted butter
175g/6oz caster sugar
3 eggs
Grated rind of 1 lemon
175g/6oz self-raising flour
50g/2oz cornflour
Pinch of salt
30ml/2 tablespoons whisky

Filling
100g/4oz granulated sugar
50g/2oz custard powder
300ml/½ pint milk
225g/8oz unsalted butter
45ml/3 tablespoons whisky

Praline
25g/1oz unsalted butter
100g/4oz granulated sugar
225g/8oz blanched chopped
  almonds

Cream the butter and sugar until light and fluffy. Work in the eggs one at a time, beating well, and stir in the lemon rind. Sieve together the flour, cornflour and salt. Fold into the creamed mixture and finally fold in the whisky. Put into a greased and floured ring cake tin and bake at 375°F/190°C/Gas Mark 5 for 1 hour. Cool on a wire rack.

To make the filling, mix the sugar and custard powder with a little milk. Bring the rest of the milk to the boil, take off the heat and stir in the custard powder mixture. Stir well and return to the heat and simmer gently until thick and creamy. Cool, stirring occasionally. Cream the butter until very light and work in the cooled custard and whisky, whisking until smooth. Split the cake across to make three layers, and put together again with the filling. Spread the remaining filling over the surface of the cake. To make the praline, melt the butter and sugar over low heat and stir until light brown. Stir in the almonds until they are golden. Spoon on to a buttered baking sheet and leave until cold and hard. Crush with a rolling pin or an electric blender. Sprinkle the praline over the cake.

Bûche de Noël

Swiss Roll
2 eggs.
65g/2½oz caster sugar
50g/2oz self-raising flour
Pinch of salt

Filling
75g/3oz chestnut purée (tube
  or canned)

Chocolate butter cream
65g/2½oz butter
50g/2oz caster sugar
30ml/2 tablespoons water
Pinch of cream of tartar
1 egg yolk
40g/1½oz plain chocolate

Grease and line a Swiss roll tin. Whisk together the eggs and sugar until thick and creamy. The mixture is ready when the whisk is lifted from the mixture and leaves an impression. Lightly fold in the flour and salt using a metal spoon. Spread the mixture evenly into the tin. Bake at 425°F/220°C/Gas Mark 7 for 10 minutes. The sponge should be golden brown and springy to the touch. Turn out on to a sheet of greaseproof paper dusted with caster sugar. Peel off the lining paper and trim the edges of the sponge with a sharp knife. Roll up with a sheet of greaseproof inside and cool on a wire tray. Unroll carefully when cold. Spread with chestnut purée filling and re-roll.

To make chocolate coating, cream the butter and sugar together until pale and fluffy. Add remaining ingredients, mix well together. Melt the chocolate in a bowl over hot water. Coat the roll and mark with a fork to give a log effect. If possible chill before serving. Dust lightly with icing sugar and decorate with a sprig of holly.

Rum Babas

In a large bowl, mix together all the yeast batter ingredients until smooth. Leave to stand until frothy, about 20 minutes for fresh yeast or 30 minutes for dried yeast. Add all other ingredients and beat thoroughly for 3–4 minutes. Grease 12 dariole or castle pudding moulds and half-fill with dough. Stand moulds on a baking sheet and cover with lightly oiled polythene. Leave to rise until the dough is almost to top of mould (about 30–40 minutes in a warm place). Bake at 400°F/200°C/Gas Mark 6 for 15–20 minutes, until a deep golden brown. Leave to cool in moulds for 5 minutes. Turn out and trim tops if unevenly risen so that Babas stand up. Place on a plate, cut end down and prick well with a skewer. Pour over prepared warm rum syrup to soak Babas completely. Leave to cool.

Prepare the rum syrup while the Babas are cooking. Place sugar and water in a heavy-based pan and dissolve sugar over a gentle heat. When sugar is completely dissolved bring to the boil and boil for 1 minute. Remove from heat and stir in the rum.

Warm the apricot jam and water and sieve. Brush surfaces of the cooled Babas with the warm glaze.

Whip the cream until just stiff and pipe, or spoon, on top of Babas. Place a piece of cherry in the centre of each.

Batter
25g/1oz fresh yeast or
15g/½oz dried yeast
90ml/6 tablespoons warm milk
50g/2oz strong plain flour

Other ingredients
175g/6oz strong plain flour
½ teaspoon salt
25g/1oz caster sugar
4 eggs
100g/4oz soft (not melted) butter
100g/4oz currants

Rum Syrup
450g/1lb granulated sugar
450ml/¾ pint water
45–60ml/3–4 tablespoons rum

Glaze
5 tablespoons apricot jam
15ml/1 tablespoon water

Topping
150ml/¼ pint double cream
Glacé cherries

Mocha Torte

Mark two 20cm/8in circles on greaseproof paper. Oil thickly and sprinkle with flour. Grind the walnuts in a blender keeping a few for decoration. Mix with sieved icing sugar. Beat the egg whites to stiff peaks. Fold in the walnut mixture, and divide in two halves. Bake at 350°F/180°C/Gas Mark 4 for 35 minutes until circles feel firm and crisp. Cool and loosen from the paper. Cream the butter and icing sugar and work in coffee essence. Beat in egg yolks one at a time. Just before eating, assemble the cakes and icing, and decorate the top with reserved walnuts.

225g/8oz walnut halves
175g/6oz icing sugar
3 egg whites

Icing
100g/4oz unsalted butter
175g/6oz icing sugar
30ml/2 tablespoons coffee essence
2 egg yolks

Savarin

Batter
50g/2oz strong plain flour
25g/1oz fresh yeast or
  15g/½oz dried yeast
90ml/6 tablespoons warm
  milk

Other ingredients
175g/6oz strong plain flour
½ teaspoon salt
25g/1oz caster sugar
4 eggs
100g/4oz soft (not melted)
  butter

Rum Syrup
550g/1¼lb granulated sugar
600ml/1 pint water
90–150ml/6–10 tablespoons
  rum

Glaze
5 tablespoons apricot jam
15ml/1 tablespoon water

Filling
225g/8oz halved strawberries
100g/4oz green grapes
2–3 slices fresh pineapple cut
  1.25cm/½in thick

In a large bowl, mix together all the yeast batter ingredients until smooth. Leave to stand until frothy, about 20 minutes for fresh yeast or 30 minutes for dried yeast. Add all remaining ingredients and beat thoroughly for 3–4 minutes. Grease one 20–22.5cm/8–9in ring mould and half-fill with the dough. Place mould inside a large oiled polythene bag and leave to rise until almost to top of mould (about 30–40 minutes in a warm place). Bake at 400°F/200°C/Gas Mark 6 for 20–25 minutes until deep golden brown. Leave the Savarin to cool in tin for 5 minutes, then turn out on to a wire rack and leave to cool. Put a large plate or tray under the rack. Using a very fine skewer, make holes all over the top of the Savarin.

To prepare the syrup, place sugar and water in a heavy-based pan and dissolve sugar over a gentle heat. When sugar has completely dissolved, bring syrup to the boil and boil for 1 minute. Remove from the heat and stir in the rum. Spoon the hot syrup over the Savarin. Pour any syrup which has drained into the plate or tray back into pan and spoon over Savarin again. Continue until about 150ml/¼ pint syrup is left. Reserve this for the fruit. Place the Savarin on a serving plate. Warm the apricot jam and water and sieve. Brush surface of the Savarin with the glaze.

If the strawberries are large, cut them in half. Cut the grapes in half and remove pips. Cut the pineapple into approximately 2.5cm/1in pieces. Mix the fruit with the remaining syrup. Pile into the centre of the Savarin and serve with cream.

Economical Orange and Banana Savarin

Batter
25g/1oz strong plain flour
15g/½oz fresh yeast or
  18g/¾oz dried yeast
150ml/¼ pint warm milk

Other ingredients
100g/4oz strong plain flour
¼ teaspoon salt

In a large bowl, mix together all yeast batter ingredients until smooth. Leave to stand until frothy, about 20 minutes for fresh yeast or 30 minutes for dried yeast. Add remaining ingredients and beat thoroughly for 3–4 minutes. Turn mixture into a greased 17.5cm/7in ring mould and place in a large, oiled polythene bag and leave to rise until almost to the top of the mould (about 30 minutes in a warm place). Bake at 400°F/200°C/Gas Mark 6 for 20–25 minutes until firm and golden brown. Leave the Savarin to cool in tin for 5 minutes, then turn out on to a wire rack.

To prepare the syrup, place all ingredients in a heavy saucepan and heat gently until the sugar dissolves. Bring syrup to boil and boil for 1 minute. Strain off the orange rind. Reserve 60ml/4 tablespoons of syrup for the fruit. Place Savarin on serving plate and spoon over the remaining hot syrup. Leave to cool. Warm honey for glaze and brush over surface of the Savarin. Divide oranges into segments, slice bananas and cut grapes in half, removing the pips. Mix the fruit with remaining syrup and pile into centre and arrange around the edge of the Savarin.

15g/½oz caster sugar
1 egg
25g/1oz soft (but not melted) butter

Orange Syrup
225g/8oz granulated sugar
300ml/½ pint water
Grated rind and juice of 1 orange
60ml/4 tablespoons clear honey

Glaze
45ml/3 tablespoons melted clear honey

Filling
3 oranges
3 bananas
100g/4oz grapes

Coffee Fruit Log

Grease a 32.5×22.5cm/13×9in Swiss roll tin. Line the base with greased greaseproof paper. Sift together flour, baking powder and salt. Add eggs and margarine. Mix ingredients together then beat well for 2–3 minutes. Mix in remaining ingredients. Spread mixture evenly in tin. Bake at 350°F/180°C/Gas Mark 4 for 25–30 minutes until firm to touch. Cool in tin for 1 minute. Loosen sides of cake with a knife. Turn out on to a large sheet of greaseproof paper, oiled on both sides, and place on a wire cooling rack. Roll up with the paper and leave until completely cold.

To make the butter cream, cream butter until soft, gradually beat in icing sugar until light and fluffy and then beat in coffee essence.

Unroll the cake very carefully (it may crack slightly). Use a little butter cream to spread over the inside of the cake. Roll up tightly like a Swiss roll. Spread the outside of the cake with remaining butter cream and mark in lines with a round ended knife. Stick flaked browned almonds along the top. This cake is best made at least one day in advance.

100g/4oz self-raising flour
1 teaspoon baking powder
½ teaspoon salt
2 eggs
100g/4oz soft margarine
175g/6oz mixed dried fruit
25g/1oz chopped mixed candied peel
25g/1oz glacé cherries

Butter cream
100g/4oz butter
225g/8oz icing sugar
30ml/2 tablespoons coffee essence
15g/½oz flaked browned almonds

Cider Syrup Cake

6 eggs
175g/6oz caster sugar
175g/6oz plain flour

Syrup
150ml/¼ pint sweet cider
100g/4oz caster sugar

Filling
600ml/1 pint double cream
25g/1oz icing sugar
1 teaspoon rum
10 marrons glacé

Separate eggs. Whisk egg whites until stiff. Whisk in egg yolks and sugar alternately. Sieve flour over the mixture and fold in with a metal spoon. Divide mixture between two greased and base-lined 20cm/8in sandwich tins. Bake at 400°F/200°C/Gas Mark 6 for 20 minutes. Turn on to a wire rack. To make syrup, put cider and sugar into a saucepan and stir over a low heat until sugar has dissolved. Boil until reduced by half. Allow to cool. Pour syrup over the two sponges. Put cream into a basin and whisk until stiff. Stir in icing sugar and rum. Remove a quarter of the cream and to this add four chopped marrons glacé. Spread this mixture over one sponge cake. Carefully lift the other sponge and place on top. Spread remaining cream over the cake, and pipe rosettes around the top edge. Decorate with marrons glacé.

Cider Apple and Raisin Gâteau

450ml/¾ pint sweet cider
150g/5oz sugar
100g/4oz seedless raisins
3 eggs
75g/3oz caster sugar
65g/2½oz plain flour
1 cooking apple
125ml/¼ pint double cream

Put 250ml/½ pint cider, 100g/4oz granulated sugar and the raisins into a saucepan. Bring to the boil and reduce the liquid by half. Cool, cover and allow to stand overnight. Whisk the eggs and caster sugar in a large bowl over hot but not boiling water until thick. Remove from the bowl and continue to whisk until cold. Fold in the sifted flour, a third at a time. Turn into two greased 17.5cm/7in sandwich tins and bake at 375°F/190°C/Gas Mark 5 for 15 minutes. Allow to cool in the tins for 5 minutes before turning on to a wire rack. Drain the raisins, reserving the syrup. Peel, core and slice the apple. Poach very gently in the remaining cider and sugar until just tender. Drain and cool. Whip the cream stiffly. Put one of the cake layers on a serving dish, brush with the reserved syrup. Spread half the whipped cream over the cake and cover with the raisins. Put the other cake layer on top, brush again with the reserved syrup (reserving 30ml/2 tablespoons). Arrange the poached apple slices on top. Brush with the remaining syrup and decorate with the remaining whipped cream.

14 Biscuits and Cookies

We call them 'biscuits' and the Americans call them 'cookies', but basically they are those nice small crisp flat cakes which are so good to nibble with a cup of tea or coffee, or to serve with an ice cream or light mousse or fruit pudding. They are extremely easy to make and do not need the baking skills required by cakes, and they are far cheaper than commercially made biscuits. Many people feel that biscuits are complicated because they need to be rolled out like pastry and then cut into shapes which takes time and a dextrous hand. However, biscuits may be made much more easily by being pressed into cake tins; piped; cut from a roll of dough; rolled in balls with the hands, or dropped in spoonfuls on to baking sheets.

Use large baking sheets for biscuits, or Swiss roll tins, or square or rectangular cake tins and make sure the baking sheets are well greased unless a recipe indicates otherwise. For *rolled biscuits*, make the dough firm and roll it out thinly before cutting with a biscuit or scone cutter, or with the floured rim of a drinking glass. *Piped biscuits* must be made from a firm dough which can be piped easily, and this may be done with an icing bag and tube, or with a metal canister biscuit-piper.

Shortbread and flapjack mixtures are very easily prepared in greased cake tins, and the mixture should be pressed down firmly with a fork before baking. When the mixture is taken from the oven, squares or fingers should be marked out with a sharp knife, but the biscuits should be cooled in the tin and then cut through into shapes.

Many biscuit mixtures may be rolled into small balls with the hands, or spoonfuls can be placed on the baking sheet. Always leave room for these biscuits to expand, and flatten them slightly with a fork or palette knife dipped in water as they will then form a neater shape when baked. The same type of soft biscuit dough may be formed into a sausage-shape and then chilled in the refrigerator or frozen before being cut into slices for baking. Biscuits are usually cooked at a moderate temperature for a short time (about 10–15 minutes) and care must be taken that they do not become too brown, as they are very thin in comparison with a cake mixture. Do not judge whether biscuits are cooked by their crispness, as they will be soft when they come from the oven. It is best to leave them on the baking sheet for a minute or two to become firmer before lifting carefully on a wire rack to become crisp. As soon as they are cool, biscuits should be packed carefully in an airtight tin to retain their crispness.

Wholemeal Cheese Biscuits

100g/4oz wholemeal flour
¼ teaspoon salt
1 teaspoon mustard powder
25g/1oz margarine
225g/8oz grated Cheddar
   cheese
30ml/2 tablespoons water

Sieve the flour, salt and mustard together and rub in the margarine. Add the finely grated cheese and mix to a dough with cold water. Knead gently and roll out thinly. Cut 5cm/2in rounds with a plain cutter. Put on a greased baking sheet and prick the biscuits with a fork. Bake at 450°F/230°C/Gas Mark 8 for 7 minutes until puffed up and lightly browned. Lift off carefully and cool on a wire rack.

Wholemeal Biscuits

100g/4oz plain flour
225g/8oz wholemeal flour
½ teaspoon salt
75g/3oz margarine
50g/2oz lard
50g/2oz light soft brown
   sugar
1 egg
60ml/4 tablespoons water

Sieve together the flours and salt. Rub in the fat until the mixture is like fine breadcrumbs. Mix in the sugar, beaten egg and water to give a soft dough. Roll out and cut into 5cm/2in rounds with a plain cutter. Put on to a greased baking sheet and prick with a fork. Bake at 350°F/180°C/Gas Mark 4 for 25 minutes. Lift off carefully and cool on a wire rack. If liked, the backs of the biscuits may be coated with melted chocolate.

Oatmeal Tea Biscuits

Stir together the oatmeal, flour and salt and rub in the fat until the mixture is like fine breadcrumbs. Add the sugar, cinnamon, cream of tartar and soda, and mix to a paste with the egg and milk. Knead until smooth and roll out thinly. Cut into 5cm/2in rounds with a biscuit cutter and prick with a fork. Put on a greased baking sheet and bake at 350°F/180°C/Gas Mark 4 for 15 minutes. Lift off sheet carefully and cool on a wire rack. These biscuits are good as a sweet biscuit, but are also excellent with cheese.

225g/8oz fine oatmeal
225g/8oz wholemeal flour
Pinch of salt
100g/4oz butter
100g/4oz light soft brown sugar
½ teaspoon ground cinnamon
1 teaspoon cream of tartar
¼ teaspoon bicarbonate of soda
1 egg
A little milk

Sugar Biscuits

Stir the flour and sugar together in a bowl and rub in the fat until the mixture is like fine breadcrumbs. Mix to a stiff dough with the beaten egg, grated rind and juice of the lemon. Roll out thinly and cut into 5cm/2in rounds with a cutter. Put on a greased baking sheet. Bake at 350°F/180°C/Gas Mark 4 for 15 minutes. Lift off carefully and cool on a wire rack. These biscuits may be cut in fancy shapes and iced, or they may be put together in pairs with jam or icing.

225g/8oz self-raising flour
100g/4oz caster sugar
100g/4oz margarine or butter
1 egg
½ lemon

Butter Shorties

Place all ingredients in a basin. Rub butter into the dry ingredients, press and knead until a pliable paste is formed. Roll paste out. Using a 6.25cm/2½in fluted cutter, cut about 18 biscuits, re-rolling paste when necessary. Place on a baking tray and bake at 350°F/180°C/Gas Mark 4 for 15 minutes. Cool on a wire rack.

100g/4oz butter (softened)
50g/2oz caster sugar
40g/1½oz bran cereal
175g/6oz self-raising flour

Orange Crescents

150g/5oz plain flour
50g/2oz fine semolina
75g/3oz butter
50g/2oz caster sugar
1 teaspoon finely grated
    orange rind
1 egg yolk
2 teaspoons cold water
1 egg white
2 teaspoons caster sugar

Stir the flour and semolina together in a bowl and rub in the fat until the mixture is like fine breadcrumbs. Add the sugar and orange rind and mix to a stiff paste with the egg yolk beaten with the water. Knead on a lightly floured board until smooth and then roll out thinly. Cut into crescent shapes and put on a greased baking sheet. Beat the egg white lightly, coat biscuits and sprinkle with caster sugar. Bake at 350°F/180°C/Gas Mark 4 for 10 minutes. Cool on a wire rack.

Swedish Cookies

225g/8oz plain flour
100g/4oz butter
2 hard-boiled egg yolks
45ml/3 tablespoons cold
    water
75g/3oz plain chocolate
75g/3oz chopped dates
1 egg white
1 tablespoon sugar

Sieve the flour and rub in the butter until the mixture is like fine breadcrumbs. Sieve the egg yolks and work into the flour with the water to make a firm dough. Roll pastry 65mm/$\frac{1}{4}$in thick and cut into two rectangles. Chop the chocolate and mix with the dates, and arrange on one piece of dough. Cover with the second piece of dough and roll very lightly so that the chocolate and dates push through the dough. Cut the mixture into 7.5cm/3in squares and cut the squares in half to form triangles. Put on a lightly greased baking sheet. Beat the egg white lightly and brush the top of each triangle with it. Sprinkle on sugar. Bake at 375°F/190°C/Gas Mark 5 for 20 minutes. Cool on a wire rack.

Spiced Feather Biscuits

100g/4oz butter
75g/3oz sugar
1 egg
100g/4oz plain flour
$\frac{1}{2}$ teaspoon ground cardamom

Icing
175g/6oz icing sugar
2 teaspoons coffee essence
15–30ml/1–2 teaspoons
    water

Cream butter and sugar, until light and fluffy. Add egg yolk, flour and ground cardamom and knead to a soft dough. Roll out to 1.25cm/$\frac{1}{2}$in thickness and cut out rounds with a 6.25cm/2$\frac{1}{2}$in fluted biscuit cutter. Re-roll trimmings and cut out remaining rounds. Place on a greased baking sheet and bake at 350°F/180°C/Gas Mark 4 for 15 minutes. Cool on a wire rack. Whisk egg white until fluffy, stir in 150g/5oz icing sugar and beat thoroughly. To half of this add coffee essence and the extra 25g/1oz icing sugar. Place in piping bag fitted with a fine writing pipe. Spread white icing over tops of biscuits. Pipe lines of coffee icing over this at 1.25cm/$\frac{1}{2}$in intervals. Using a fine skewer, draw out coffee lines to make an attractive feathered appearance. Leave to set.

Dutch Speculaas

Cream the butter and sugar together until light and fluffy. Work in the sieved ingredients, lemon rind, almonds and biscuit crumbs. Knead well. Roll out the mixture to 3mm/⅛in thickness and cut into heart, animal or Christmas shapes. Place on a greased baking sheet and bake at 350°F/180°C/Gas Mark 4 for 10–15 minutes. Cool on a wire rack and lightly sprinkle with icing sugar before serving.

75g/3oz butter
65g/2½oz light soft brown
 sugar
115g/4½oz self-raising flour
Pinch of salt
¼ teaspoon ground mixed spice
½ teaspoon ground cinnamon
Grated rind of ½ lemon
50g/2oz chopped almonds
15g/½oz crushed digestive
 biscuits
A little icing sugar

Dutch Kerstkransjes

Sieve the flour, icing sugar and salt together. Cream the butter with the vanilla essence. Work in the flour mixture, knead very well, then add sufficient egg to bind. Chill the mixture for 1 hour.

Roll out to about 3mm/⅛in thickness. Cut into circles about 6.5cm/2½in diameter and remove the centres with a 2.5cm/1in cutter. Gather up left-over dough, knead lightly and roll out again. Brush rings with beaten egg and sprinkle almonds and sugar on top. Lift on to ungreased baking sheets and bake at 350°F/180°C/Gas Mark 4 for 10–15 minutes until golden brown.

150g/5oz plain flour
50g/2oz icing sugar
Pinch of salt
100g/4oz butter
½–1 teaspoon vanilla essence.
Egg to bind

Glaze
1 egg
25g/1oz finely chopped
 blanched almonds
25g/1oz sugar

Giant Currant Cookies

Sift flour and fine semolina. Rub in butter until the mixture is like fine crumbs. Add sugar, orange rind and currants. Stir in beaten eggs and milk, mixing to a stiff light dough. Turn on to a well-floured board and knead lightly. Roll to a thin sheet and cut into rounds, using a 7.5cm/3in biscuit cutter. Place on a greased baking sheet and bake at 375°F/190°C/Gas Mark 5 for 12 minutes.

100g/4oz self-raising flour
100g/4oz fine semolina
100g/4oz butter
100g/4oz caster sugar
Grated rind of 1 orange
100g/4oz currants
2 eggs
15ml/1 tablespoon milk

Easter Biscuits

350g/12oz plain flour
Pinch of salt
Pinch of ground mixed spice
175g/6oz butter
175g/6oz sugar
1 egg
75g/3oz currants
25g/1oz chopped mixed
  candied peel
White of egg
Caster sugar

Sieve the flour, salt and spice together. Cream the butter and sugar and work in the egg. Add the currants and peel and the flour mixture and work together to a fairly soft dough, which is stiff enough to roll out. Roll out thinly and cut into rounds with a 7.5cm/3in biscuit cutter. Put on to a greased baking sheet and bake at 350°F/180°C/Gas Mark 4 for 10 minutes. Beat the egg white lightly and brush over the biscuits. Sprinkle with caster sugar. Return to the oven for 3 minutes. Lift off carefully and cool on a wire rack.

Raisin Spice Cookies

100g/4oz self-raising flour
½ teaspoon ground cinnamon
¼ teaspoon ground nutmeg
100g/4oz fine semolina
100g/4oz butter
100g/4oz caster sugar
2 eggs
15ml/1 tablespoon milk
75g/3oz seedless raisins

Sift flour, spices and fine semolina. Rub in butter. Stir in sugar, beaten eggs and milk, and finally raisins to make a stiff, light dough. Knead lightly on a well-floured board. Roll out thinly and cut into rounds, using a biscuit cutter or the floured rim of a glass tumbler. Place on a greased baking sheet and bake at 375°F/190°C/Gas Mark 5 for 12 minutes until crisp and golden. Cool on a wire rack.

Lemon Peel Biscuits

100g/4oz butter
75g/3oz caster sugar
1 egg
1 teaspoon lemon juice
225g/8oz plain flour

Icing
100g/4oz icing sugar
2 teaspoons lemon juice
Strips of candied lemon peel

Cream the butter and sugar and work in the egg, lemon juice and flour. Work into a soft dough and chill for 30 minutes. Roll out thinly and cut into shapes with biscuit cutters. Put on to a greased baking sheet and bake at 375°F/190°C/Gas Mark 5 for 10 minutes. Lift on to a wire rack to cool. Mix the icing sugar with the lemon juice and if necessary a little water to make a smooth icing. Put a spoonful on top of each biscuit and top with a strip of candied lemon peel.

Ginger Snaps

Stir together the flour, sugar, salt, bicarbonate of soda and ginger. Put the lard, butter and golden syrup into a thick pan and melt together over low heat. Cool and work into the dry ingredients with the beaten egg. Chill for 1 hour. Roll out the mixture thinly, cut into shapes and put on a greased baking tray. Bake at 350°F/180°C/Gas Mark 4 for 10 minutes. Lift off carefully and cool on a wire rack.

225g/8oz plain flour
100g/4oz dark soft brown sugar
Pinch of salt
½ teaspoon bicarbonate of soda
1 teaspoon ground ginger
40g/1½oz lard
25g/1oz butter
100g/4oz golden syrup
1 small egg

Fairings

Stir together the semolina, flour and caster sugar. Rub in the fat and mix to a firm paste with the spices and egg. Roll out thinly and cut into rounds. Put on to greased baking sheets, sprinkle with caster sugar and bake at 350°F/180°C/Gas Mark 4 for 15 minutes. Cool on a wire rack.

100g/4oz fine semolina
150g/5oz self-raising flour
100g/4oz caster sugar
100g/4oz margarine
¼ teaspoon ground cinnamon
¼ teaspoon ground ginger
1 egg
1 tablespoon caster sugar

Nut Shortbread Fingers

Stir the flour and sugar together and rub in the butter until the mixture is like large breadcrumbs. Add vanilla essence and finely chopped nuts and angelica. Knead the ingredients together to form a dough. Roll out 65mm/¼in thick and cut into fingers 7.5×2.5cm/3×1in. Put on to a baking sheet and chill for 10 minutes. Bake at 375°F/190°C/Gas Mark 5 for 10 minutes. Lift on to a wire rack to cool.

300g/10oz plain flour
75g/3oz caster sugar
225g/8oz butter
Few drops of vanilla essence
50g/2oz finely chopped walnuts or hazelnuts
25g/1oz angelica

Nut Biscuits

1 small tin condensed milk
50g/2oz butter
25g/1oz chopped walnuts
25g/1oz sultanas
50g/2oz cornflakes
Rice paper

Heat milk and butter until butter has melted but do not let them get too hot. Mix in other ingredients. Put small spoonfuls on rice paper on a baking sheet and bake at 350°F/180°C/Gas Mark 4 for 10 minutes. Leave on tin for 5 minutes, then finish cooling on a wire rack. Trim the rice paper neatly around the biscuits.

Nut Drop Cookies

75g/3oz self-raising flour
25g/1oz fine semolina
50g/2oz butter
40g/1½oz caster sugar
50g/2oz chopped dates
25g/1oz chopped walnuts
1 egg
½ teaspoon vanilla essence

Stir the flour and semolina in a bowl and rub in the butter until the mixture is like fine breadcrumbs. Stir in the sugar, dates and walnuts. Mix with the egg and essence to a stiff mixture. Arrange in 12 heaps on a greased baking sheet and bake at 400°F/200°C/Gas Mark 6 for 12 minutes. Cool on a wire rack.

Coffee Almond Shortcakes

100g/4oz butter
75g/3oz caster sugar
30ml/2 tablespoons coffee
   essence
150g/5oz plain flour
40g/1½oz finely chopped
   blanched almonds

Cream together the butter and sugar until light and fluffy and beat in the coffee essence. Work in the flour to make a smooth dough. Divide the mixture into 15 small pieces and roll into balls with the hands. Roll in chopped almonds and put on a greased baking sheet well apart. Flatten slightly with a palette knife. Bake at 375°F/190°C/Gas Mark 5 for 25 minutes. Cool on a wire rack.

Coffee Nut Wafers

100g/4oz margarine
100g/4oz sugar
1 tablespoon coffee powder
2 eggs
100g/4oz plain flour
Pinch of salt
Vanilla essence
50g/2oz chopped mixed nuts

Cream the margarine, sugar and coffee powder until light and fluffy. Stir in the beaten eggs and then add the sieved flour and salt. Mix well and flavour with a little essence. Stir in the nuts. Divide into 24 small pieces about the size of a walnut. Put on to greased baking sheets, leaving room to spread. Bake at 350°F/180°C/Gas Mark 4 for 10 minutes. Cool on a wire rack.

Coffee Kisses

Sieve flour and salt into a basin. Rub in butter. Stir in sugar and cornflakes. Add yolk and coffee essence, and mix to a stiff paste with a little milk. Divide mixture into 24 balls. Place a little apart on a baking sheet. Flatten mixture slightly with a palette knife. Bake at 375°F/190°C/Gas Mark 5 for about 15 minutes. Allow to cool on a wire rack. To make butter cream, beat butter, sugar and coffee essence together. Sandwich biscuits in pairs.

175g/6oz self-raising flour
Pinch of salt
75g/3oz butter
50g/2oz caster sugar
50g/2oz cornflakes
1 egg yolk
1 teaspoon coffee essence
A little milk

Coffee Butter Cream
25g/1oz butter
50g/2oz icing sugar
1 teaspoon coffee essence

Hungarian Chocolate Biscuits

Cream the butter and sugar and work in the flour, cocoa and essence to make a soft dough. Divide into walnut-sized pieces, roll into balls and put on a greased baking sheet. Flatten with a fork dipped in water. Bake at 350°F/180°C/Gas Mark 4 for 12 minutes. Lift off carefully and cool on a wire rack. To make the filling, put the cocoa and coffee into a small thick pan and heat together to make a thick cream. Take off the heat and beat in the butter and then sugar to make a thick creamy icing. Leave until cold. Sandwich together pairs of biscuits with this filling.

225g/8oz butter
100g/4oz caster sugar
225g/8oz self-raising flour
50g/2oz cocoa
1 teaspoon vanilla essence

Filling
50g/2oz cocoa
45ml/3 tablespoons strong
  black coffee
50g/2oz butter
50g/2oz caster sugar

Chocolate Gingers

Melt the fat and syrup in a heavy pan and leave to stand for 30 minutes. Stir in the flour, sugar and ground ginger. Put in teaspoonfuls on a greased baking sheet. Bake at 350°F/180°C/Gas Mark 4 for 10 minutes. Lift off very carefully and cool on a wire rack. Put the cube sugar in a thick pan and heat until it turns pale brown. Add the chopped almonds and peel, stir well and spread quickly on the biscuits. Leave until set. Melt the chocolate in a bowl over hot water. Turn the biscuits over and coat the flat sides with melted chocolate, and mark in lines with a fork.

75g/3oz margarine or butter
75g/3oz golden syrup
50g/2oz plain flour
50g/2oz sugar
½ teaspoon ground ginger
100g/4oz cube sugar
25g/1oz blanched almonds
25g/1oz chopped mixed
  candied peel
175g/6oz plain chocolate

Ginger Muesli Biscuits

225g/8oz muesli cereal
½ teaspoon ground ginger
100g/4oz margarine
30ml/2 tablespoons honey
1 egg
25g/1oz plain flour

Mix the muesli and ginger. Melt the margarine and honey in a thick pan and add to the dry ingredients. Add the beaten egg and flour and mix well. Press into a greased 17.5cm/7in square shallow tin. Bake at 300°F/150°C/Gas Mark 2 for 45 minutes. Cool slightly and mark into squares with a sharp knife. Leave in the tin until cold before cutting up.

Chocolate Fruit Flapjacks

75g/3oz margarine
30ml/2 tablespoons golden
    syrup
100g/4oz porridge oats
25g/1oz demerara sugar
25g/1oz chopped candied peel
25g/1oz glacé cherries
25g/1oz chopped walnuts
50g/2oz plain chocolate
15g/½oz butter

Melt the margarine and golden syrup together in a pan over low heat. Stir in the oats, sugar, peel, chopped cherries and walnuts. Grease a 17.5cm/7in square tin and line with a piece of greased greaseproof paper. Put in the mixture and press down with a fork. Bake at 350°F/180°C/Gas Mark 4 for 25 minutes. Leave to cool in the tin and then turn out on a wire rack to cool completely. Melt the chocolate and butter together in a bowl over hot water. Spread on the biscuits and cut into squares or fingers.

Coconut Flapjacks

100g/4oz margarine
150g/5oz self-raising flour
150g/5oz sugar
25g/1oz cornflakes
65g/2½oz desiccated coconut

Melt the margarine in a large saucepan, and stir in all the other ingredients until thoroughly mixed. Press into a greased 22.5×30cm/9×12in tin. Bake at 350°F/180°C/Gas Mark 4 for 30 minutes. Cool for 5 minutes in the tin, and mark into squares. Finish cooling in the tin and cut into squares.

Melting Shortbread

225g/8oz butter
100g/4oz icing sugar
225g/8oz plain flour
100g/4oz cornflour
Pinch of salt
Caster sugar

Cream the butter and sugar until light and fluffy. Work in the flour, cornflour and salt to make a smooth dough. Press into a 17.5×27.5cm/7×11in tin. Bake at 325°F/170°C/Gas Mark 3 for 40 minutes. Sprinkle with caster sugar while hot. Leave in the tin until cold and cut into squares.

Chocolate Shortbread

Cream the butter and sugar and work in the flour and cocoa until the mixture is smooth and evenly coloured. Put into a greased 17.5×27.5cm/7×11in tin and press down with a fork. Sprinkle the almonds evenly on top and press lightly into the dough. Bake at 325°F/170°C/Gas Mark 3 for 40 minutes. Cool in the tin and cut into fingers.

225g/8oz butter or margarine
75g/3oz icing sugar
250g/9oz plain flour
25g/1oz cocoa
50g/2oz flaked almonds

Ginger Shortcake

Sift the flour, salt and ginger together and rub in the butter until the mixture is like fine breadcrumbs. Stir in the sugar and knead into a smooth dough. Roll into a round 1.25cm/½in thick which will fit a greased sponge sandwich tin lined with greaseproof paper. Lift the shortcake into the tin very carefully and crimp the edges by pinching with the fingers. Prick lightly with a fork. Bake at 300°F/150°C/Gas Mark 2 for 45 minutes until golden. Turn on to a wire rack. Put the icing ingredients into a small saucepan and heat gently until melted and blended. Beat together and pour over the shortcake while it is just warm. Cool completely and cut into triangles.

175g/6oz plain flour
Pinch of salt
½ teaspoon ground ginger
100g/4oz butter
50g/2oz caster sugar

Icing
50g/2oz butter
25g/1oz icing sugar
1 teaspoon ground ginger
3 teaspoons golden syrup

Almond Shortbread

Sift the flour and rice into a bowl. Add the almonds, sugar and peel, and mix together. Have the butter soft but not oily, and put it into the centre of the flour mixture. Knead together until thoroughly mixed. Press into a greased Swiss roll tin and prick all over. Bake at 275°F/140°C/Gas Mark 1 for 1 hour. Mark into squares and cool in the tin. Cut into squares and remove from the tin.

200g/7oz plain flour
25g/1oz ground rice
25g/1oz chopped blanched almonds
75g/3oz caster sugar
25g/1oz chopped mixed candied peel
175g/6oz butter

Melting Orange Fingers

1 large orange
225g/8oz butter
50g/2oz icing sugar
225g/8oz plain flour

Icing
225g/8oz icing sugar

Grate the orange rind finely and squeeze out the juice. Reserve the juice for making the icing. Cream the butter and icing sugar until light and fluffy and work in the orange rind and flour. Put into a piping bag with a large star nozzle, and pipe 7.5cm/3in lengths on to a baking sheet. Chill for 20 minutes. Bake at 325°F/170°C/Gas Mark 3 for 20 minutes until the biscuits are pale gold at the edges. Cool on a wire rack. Sieve the icing sugar and add orange juice. Mix well and add a little water if necessary to make a fairly thin icing. Spread a little icing on each biscuit.

Danish Vanilla Wreaths

250g/9oz plain flour
¼ teaspoon baking powder
190g/6½oz butter
115g/4½oz sugar
50g/2oz ground almonds
1–2 drops vanilla essence
Egg to bind

Work all the ingredients together and let the mixture stand for 20 minutes, in a cool place. Put the mixture into a piping bag fitted with a medium star vegetable nozzle and pipe small rings on to a well-greased baking sheet. If mixture is too stiff to pipe, beat in a few drops of milk until the correct consistency is obtained. Bake at 400°F/200°C/Gas Mark 6 for 10 minutes until light brown. Cool on a wire rack.

Viennese Biscuits

175g/6oz margarine
40g/1½oz icing sugar
Vanilla essence
115g/4½oz plain flour
40g/1½oz cornflour
A few glacé cherries

Cream the margarine and icing sugar together until light and fluffy. Add 2 or 3 drops of vanilla essence. Sieve the flour and cornflour together and fold into the creamed mixture. Using a star pipe, pipe the mixture on to a greased baking sheet. Decorate with pieces of glacé cherry. Cook at 350°F/180°C/Gas Mark 4 for 15–20 minutes. Remove the biscuits and cool on a wire rack.

Coffee Ovals

Cream butter and sugar together. Stir in coffee essence then blend in flour. Roll into two long sausage shapes, and roll each in chopped nuts. Wrap in foil or greaseproof paper and place in refrigerator for 1 hour. Slice at an angle to make oval-shaped biscuits. Place on greased baking sheets and bake at 350°F/ 180°C/Gas Mark 4 for 15 minutes.

175g/6oz butter
100g/4oz sugar
30ml/2 tablespoons coffee essence
250g/9oz plain flour
25g/1oz chopped nuts

Caraway Biscuits

Cream the butter and sugar until light and fluffy and work in the egg. Add the sieved flour and salt, lemon rind and juice, soda and caraway seeds. Mix to a firm dough and shape into a sausage-shape about 5cm/2in diameter. Cut in 1.5cm/½in slices. Put on a greased baking sheet. Bake at 400°F/200°C/Gas Mark 6 for 10 minutes. Lift off carefully and cool on a wire rack.

100g/4oz butter
200g/7oz sugar
1 egg
350g/12oz plain flour
¼ teaspoon salt
Grated rind of 1 lemon
30ml/2 tablespoons lemon juice
¼ teaspoon bicarbonate of soda
1½ teaspoons caraway seeds

Bosworth Jumbles

Cream the butter and sugar together and work in the egg, flour, lemon rind and almonds. Form the mixture into a long sausage shape and break off small pieces. Form into 'S' shapes. Put on a greased baking sheet and bake at 350°F/180°C/Gas Mark 4 for 10 minutes. Lift off carefully and cool on a wire rack. The legend is that the recipe was found on Bosworth field, scene of the battle in the Wars of the Roses where Richard III was killed.

150g/5oz butter
150g/5oz caster sugar
1 egg
300g/10oz plain flour
1 teaspoon grated lemon rind
50g/2oz ground almonds

15 Pastry

It isn't difficult to make good pastry, but a little extra care in preparation will produce delicious results. Even if you have little time, and want to use frozen pastry or a mix, don't forget the importance of an attractive finish to your dish, and spare a minute to make a special glaze or fancy trimming.

PROPORTIONS OF INGREDIENTS

The type of pastry depends on the proportion of fat to flour. Whether pastry is short or flaky depends on the gluten in the flour and the way its action is controlled during the pastry-making process.

For *short* pastry the gluten must be broken up by rubbing the fat into the flour so that each grain is covered and the fat keeps the grains separate when the water is added.

For *flaky, rough puff* and *puff* pastes the pastry must rise in layers of flakes. Instead of rubbing in the fat, add it in pieces, so that by repeated folding and rolling, layers of dough are covered by layers of fat.

Flour

Most recipes stipulate plain flour for short pastry. Some cooks use self-raising flour with good results, although the texture is different. For flaky, rough puff and puff pastry, strong plain flour (such as is used in breadmaking) is recommended. The best way to store flour is in its own bag on a cool, dry, airy shelf, not in a bin. Never mix fresh flour with old stock.

Fats

Always use the proportion of fat to flour stated in the recipe. Too little can make pastry hard and too much makes pastry unmanageable and very short. For shortcrust, the proportion is usually half as much fat as flour. Equal quantities of margarine and lard make a very good dough. The fat should be soft enough – but not too soft – to rub in easily, using the tips of the fingers and thumbs, until the mixture looks like fine breadcrumbs. Don't over-rub – this makes the pastry break when rolled out. If the pieces get bigger again instead of smaller, the mixture is being over-rubbed. The amount of water required varies a little, but is usually about 30ml/2 tablespoons for 225g/8oz flour. It is best to add the water all at once by sprinkling. The dough should be firm but not sticky. If it is too dry, the pastry will crack.

PREPARING PASTRY

Except for hot water and choux pastry, the cooler everything is the better – your hands, the mixing bowl, the kitchen. The best surface for rolling out pastry is a marble slab. The less you handle the pastry the better. Shape the pastry into a round, square or oblong according to your requirements before rolling out. Right-handed workers should press more heavily with the left hand until even rolling with hands becomes a habit. Never try to stretch it on to a pie – it will only shrink away from the edge during cooking. It is better to roll it out a little larger than the required size and trim it. The trimmings can be re-rolled and used for decoration. Cut thin strips and use them plain or twisted for a lattice trimming on a fruit or jam tart, or make pastry leaves as the traditional decoration for a meat pie. To lift rolled pastry, roll loosely round rolling pin.

Before attaching strips to the rim of a dish or to the pastry itself, moisten them with water. Brush over the pastry lid with milk or beaten egg to glaze it, and if it's a sweet pie, you can dredge it with caster sugar. Glaze evenly as pools of liquid make the pastry soggy. Cut a little hole or slit in the shape of a cross in the centre of the lid to allow steam to escape, but omit this if the pie is to be frozen before baking.

The Fork-Mix Method

Since the advent of vegetable cooking fats and soft margarines, it has been possible to abandon the traditional rubbing-in method for shortcrust pastry. All the ingredients, including carefully measured water, are put into the mixing bowl and mixed to a dough with a fork. An electric mixer will of course do the same thing in even less time. Avoid over-mixing.

Baking

Always pre-heat the oven for about 15 minutes to the correct temperature as stated in the recipe. Use a baking sheet under a pie plate to help spread the heat evenly. As a general rule, bake pies and tarts near the top of the oven. If the pastry browns too quickly, cover it with a sheet of foil or greaseproof paper. Some people like their pastry to be very pale, others prefer a deeper golden colour, but it should never be really brown. When lining a flan ring, pie plate etc. press the pastry firmly against the base to expel the air; otherwise the air will expand in the heat of the oven and push the pastry up through the filling. Cool such things as tartlets, flan cases and vol-au-vents on a wire tray to allow steam to escape and pastry to keep crisp.

PASTRY COOKERY TERMS

Rubbing in is the term used for mixing fat into flour. Flour and the small lumps of fat are passed through the fingertips only until the mixture resembles fine breadcrumbs. Temperature of the fat is important. Very hard or very soft fat does not rub evenly. For good results use fat at room temperature when the consistency is firm but just spreadable.

Knocking up is the term used for sealing together the edges of pies, tarts, sausage rolls. Dampen one edge of pastry with water, lightly press other edge on top then seal edges together by sharply tapping with the back of a knife. The edges can be decorated in different ways. See Decorations.

Baking blind is the term used for cooking a pastry case without any filling. The uncooked pastry case must be lined with kitchen foil or greaseproof paper and filled with baking beans, crusts of bread or rice to prevent the bottom rising during cooking. Alternatively the base can be pricked with a fork before lining with only tin foil; beans and crusts are not then required. Remove lining 5 minutes before the end of cooking time to allow the base to become firm.

LINING A FLAN RING

Place flan ring on a baking sheet. Roll out pastry into a circle about 5cm/2in larger than flan ring. To lift pastry, loosely roll round rolling pin or fold in half and then fold again. Place pastry in flan ring and unroll or unfold. Ease carefully into shape without pulling or stretching. Start in the middle and work to sides of flan ring to push out air under base. Press into sides with forefinger or a small ball of pastry, being careful not to crack pastry. Roll across top with rolling pin to cut off surplus pastry. A plain flan ring is used for savoury recipes and a fluted flan ring for sweet recipes.

EDGES FOR PIES

Damp edge of pie dish with water. Line edge with pastry strip and brush with egg wash. Cover with pastry lid. Press edges lightly together. Trim edges with a sharp knife held at a slight angle away from dish and cut in short clean strokes. 'Knock up' edges to seal and give a neat edge.

To flute edges, press thumb on top outer edge and, with back of a knife, draw edge towards centre of pie for 1.5cm/½in. Repeat round pie edge. For savoury pies leave about 1.75cm/¾in between cuts.
   For sweet pies leave about 65mm/¼in between cuts.

To fork edges, press back of a fork, prongs to centre of pies, into edges.

To crimp edges, pinch edges between thumb and first finger of both hands, then slightly twist in opposite directions.

TOP DECORATIONS

Make a hole in centre for steam to escape then decorate if the pie is savoury.

For savoury pies, decorate with pastry leaves and a tassel or rose.

Make leaves from a strip of pastry about 2.5–3cm/1–1½in wide. Cut into diamond-shaped pieces. Make veins on leaf with back of a knife. Pinch in one end.

Make a tassel from a strip of pastry 2.5cm/1in wide by 15cm/6in long. Make 1.25–1.75cm/½–¾in cuts every 65mm/¼in along strip. Roll up and place in centre of pie, and spread ends out.

Make a rose from a small ball and 2 small pastry circles. Cover ball with circles and press edges together under ball to seal. Cut a cross into top of ball with a sharp knife. Open out and turn back segments to form rose.

For sweet pies, dust with icing or caster sugar when baked.

BAKING GLAZES

For savoury pies, brush top evenly with egg wash, and also use it to fix decorations. Make egg wash from equal quantities of egg and water and a pinch of salt. Use whole egg or only egg yolks. Milk can be used instead of water.

For sweet pies, brush top with milk or water and sprinkle with caster sugar before baking. Egg white can be used and sprinkled with caster sugar 7–10 minutes before the end of baking.

JAM GLAZES FOR FRUIT TARTS

Open tarts or flans made with fresh, canned or frozen fruit should be finished with a jam glaze brushed on after baking. A yellow glaze made from apricot jam should be used for white, orange and green fruit. A red glaze made from raspberry jam or redcurrant jelly should be used for red, purple and pink fruit.

Apricot Glaze

Add 60ml/4 tablespoons water and the juice of $\frac{1}{2}$ lemon to 450g/1lb apricot jam. Bring slowly to the boil, simmer for 5 minutes and sieve. Return to the pan and boil for 5 minutes, and brush on the fruit while warm. The glaze may be stored in a jam jar.

Raspberry Glaze

Prepare in the same way as Apricot Glaze.

Redcurrant Glaze

Beat some redcurrant jelly until well broken up. Strain into a pan and heat gently without stirring until clear, but do not boil. Use while still warm.

FLANS

Flans made with sweet or fruit fillings are always useful since they can be eaten hot after a cold meal, or can be made in advance to eat cold. They are delicious served with pouring cream, or with whipped cream which can be flavoured with a liqueur to enhance a fruit filling.

Plain shortcrust pastry or sweet shortcrust pastry can be used. A sweet shortcrust is particularly good with fruit, but may be too sweet for many people if used with a syrup, jam or mincemeat filling. Puff and flaky pastry can also be used with fruit, and are traditional with old-fashioned cheesecake fillings.

The finish of sweet flans is very important to tempt the appetite, and well-presented flans look good on a buffet table. Fruit flans are usually glazed with sieved apricot or raspberry jam, or with redcurrant jelly. Custard-type flans should be well-coloured, and meringue toppings golden and crisp. Spare pastry can be used to make a decorative lattice, or small rings or crescents. Pastry decoration should be glazed with milk, or with beaten egg and milk, and sprinkled with caster sugar immediately after baking.

Pastry should be baked to a golden brown. A removable flan ring will enable the outer edge of a flan to colour if removed about ten minutes before the end of cooking. Fluted ovenware dishes are often used for sweet flans, and they look pretty and help to keep a flan firm if it has a rather deep, soft filling. If such a container is used, it is wise to allow 5 minutes' extra cooking time, as the china does not conduct the heat to the pastry as efficiently as metal. Sometimes sweet flans become a little soggy. The problem can be overcome by brushing the pastry base with egg white before putting in the filling (particularly worthwhile if a fruit flan is to be frozen, since the filling may 'leak' a little when thawed). French chefs ensure a crisp bottom for their fruit flans by putting the metal baking sheet holding the pastry case on the hot ring of a cooker for a minute or two before the flan goes into the oven. At home, this is not always easy, and the trick needs practice. To achieve the same effect, pre-heat a metal baking sheet on the shelf in the oven, and put the prepared flan on another baking sheet. As soon as the oven is opened, put the flan sheet on top of the hot baking sheet, which will heat the bottom pastry quickly.

MERINGUE TOPPINGS

Fruit tarts and those with a creamy filling can be topped with meringue. The egg whites should be beaten stiff but not dry, and the sugar beaten into them gradually until well blended. The filling is best cooled before topping with the meringue mixture. Spread it on evenly, peaking slightly in the centre, or pipe on with a decorative tube. Make sure that the meringue covers the filling completely and reaches right up to the pastry. Bake at 325 °F/170 °C/Gas Mark 3 for 15 minutes, so that the outside is crisp and the inside still soft. If too much sugar is used, or it is too coarse, the meringue will 'weep'. The topping will shrink and be tough if the oven is too low.

BAKING TEMPERATURES

The temperatures given in the following recipes are the ideal ones to use when preparing everyday dishes. In some recipes temperatures may vary slightly according to the fillings being used.

PLAIN PASTRY

These basic recipes are useful as guides to the correct ingredients and methods to use for the majority of recipes. For a quick calculation of the quantity of made pastry which will result, simply add the total flour and fats and any other weighed ingredients such as sugar e.g. 225g/8oz flour makes approximately 350g/12oz shortcrust pastry; with the additional cheese, it will make approximately 450g/1lb cheese pastry. A few ounces of pastry left over from a piecrust or flan need never be wasted as it can easily be converted into a secondary dish such as jam tarts or cheese straws.

Shortcrust Pastry

Sift together flour and salt. Rub in fat until mixture resembles fine breadcrumbs. Add water and mix to a stiff dough. Turn out on to a floured board and lightly knead until smooth. Roll out to required shape and thickness. Bake in a hot oven, 425°F/220°C/Gas Mark 7 for 20–25 minutes. Small tarts and thin pastry cases are cooked at 400°F/200°C/Gas Mark 6 for 10–15 minutes.

225g/8oz plain flour
½ teaspoon salt
50g/2oz margarine
50g/2oz lard
30–45ml/2–3 tablespoons cold water

Sweet Shortcrust Pastry

Sift together flour and salt. Rub in butter until mixture resembles fine breadcrumbs, then stir in sugar. Blend egg yolk and water together, add all at once to rubbed-in mixture, and mix to a firm dough. Knead lightly on a floured board. Roll out to required shape. Bake in a fairly hot oven, 400°F/200°C/Gas Mark 6 for 20–25 minutes. Small tarts and thin cases take about 10–15 minutes.

175g/6oz plain flour
¼ teaspoon salt
75g/3oz butter
25g/1oz caster sugar
1 egg yolk
15ml/1 tablespoon cold water

Cheese Pastry

225g/8oz plain flour
½ teaspoon salt
Pinch of Cayenne pepper
100g/4oz margarine or butter
100g/4oz finely grated hard
   cheese
1 egg
2 teaspoons cold water

Cheese must be dry and finely grated. A soft sticky cheese does not mix in evenly and makes pastry difficult to handle, as does coarsely grated cheese. Use a strong-flavoured cheese for a good flavour, e.g. half Cheddar, half Parmesan.

Sift together flour, salt and Cayenne. Rub in fat until mixture resembles fine breadcrumbs. Add grated cheese. Blend egg yolk and water together. Add to rubbed-in mixture and mix to a firm dough. Knead gently on lightly floured board until dough is smooth. Roll out to required thickness.

FAULTS IN SHORTCRUST, SWEET SHORTCRUST AND CHEESE PASTRIES

Hard and/or tough pastry. Insufficient fat. Too much liquid. Over-handling. Cooking too slowly.

Pastry crumbly and hard to handle. Too much fat. Over-mixing. Not enough liquid to bind fat and flour.

Pastry too short. Too much fat. Too little water.

Pastry soggy. Excess of liquid. Insufficient cooking. Oven too cool.

Pastry shrinks when cooked. Fat insufficiently rubbed in. Water unevenly mixed in.

Flan case base risen during cooking. Self-raising flour used. Pastry not carefully pressed into tin to exclude air underneath. Pastry not well enough pricked to prevent air pockets, or not weighted down with baking beans or foil during baking.

Pastry rising in bottom of custard tart. Bottom pastry not sufficiently pressed to pie plate to exclude all air. Placed in too cool an oven.

Cooked flan case breaks too easily after removal from tin. Too short a pastry. Over-cooking. Careless handling.

Soggy bottom pastry of a plate pie. Filling too wet. Under-cooked. Pie plate too thick. Oven not hot enough. Placed too high in oven.

Cooked rich shortcrust pastry has speckled appearance. Sugar too coarse-grained. Too much sugar. Baked in too hot an oven.

Cooked cheese pastry tough and rubbery with a rough appearance. Cheese grated too coarsely. Cheese too fresh, causing it to stick together, and not dispersed properly in mixing. Cooked in too hot an oven causing cheese to melt and bubble.

RICH PASTRY

Use a firm fat, in the proportion given in the recipe, and knead the pastry until it is elastic. Roll out evenly, keeping the pastry straight at the sides and ends. If the fat breaks through the pastry, put in a cold place to harden. To use the pastry, roll it fairly thinly so that it will expand well and cook through. Trim off rounded edges before use. Refrigerate for at least 30 minutes – or an hour if it is very warm – before baking. While cooling, it is essential to cover the pastry to prevent the surface drying. Place pastry on a floured plate and place this in a polythene bag or cover with foil.

Bake in a hot oven at first to expand the air in the pastry, then cover and reduce the heat until the filling is cooked. To use the trimmings, keep them flat and place one on top of the other. Press with a lightly floured rolling pin, fold and roll out lightly as before.

Puff Pastry

450g/1lb plain flour
1 teaspoon salt
450g/1lb hard margarine
2 teaspoons lemon juice
285ml/9½ fl.oz cold water

Sift together flour and salt. Divide margarine into four. Rub one quarter into flour then mix to a pliable dough with lemon juice and water. Turn out on to a floured board and knead well until smooth. Rest 15 minutes in a cool place. With 2 knives, form remaining margarine into a slab 12.5cm/5in square on a floured board. Roll dough into an oblong 27.5×15cm/11×6in. Place slab of fat on top end of dough leaving a margin of about 1.25cm/½in along sides and top. Fold rest of dough over, placing upper edges of dough together. Brush off surplus flour.

When *first rolling*, turn pastry round so that folded edge is on left-hand side. Press three open edges together with rolling pin to seal. Press dough across about 5 times with rolling pin to flatten. Roll out into an oblong about 30×15cm/12×6in keeping edges straight.

When *second rolling*, fold pastry in three by folding bottom third upwards and top third downwards and over to cover it. Turn so that folded edge is again on the left. Seal edges and roll out as before. Fold, turn and seal edges as before. Place pastry on floured plate in a polythene bag and rest in a cold place for 20 minutes.

When *third to sixth rollings*, roll out 4 more times, always turning and sealing dough as before. Rest 20 minutes between each rolling. If any patches of fat still show, give dough another rolling. Rest dough before rolling out to required thickness. Trim edges. Glaze with egg or milk before baking.

Rough Puff Pastry

225g/8oz plain flour
½ teaspoon salt
75g/3oz lard
75g/3oz hard margarine
90–120ml/6–8 tablespoons
   water

Sift flour and salt into a basin. Cut up fat roughly into small pieces, about 65mm/¼in. Add to flour and mix to a soft dough with water. Roll out on a floured board to an oblong, approximately 30×15cm/12×6in and fold bottom third upwards and top third downwards and over it. Turn dough so that folded edge is on left-hand side and seal edges. Roll, fold and seal edges twice more keeping folded edge always to the left. If pastry becomes too soft, chill between rollings. Roll out to required size. Trim edges. Glaze with egg or milk before baking.

Flaky Pastry

Make dough as for puff pastry, rubbing in one quarter of margarine. Cut remaining margarine into 3 portions.

When *first rolling*, roll out dough into an oblong about 30×15cm/12×6in keeping edges straight. Cut one portion of fat into small pieces and place in lines over top two-thirds of dough leaving margin of 1.25cm/½in round edges. Fold bottom uncovered third upwards and top third downwards and over to cover it.

When *second rolling*, turn dough so that folded edge is on left-hand side. Press edges together with rolling pin to seal. Roll out into an oblong and place on second portion of fat as above. Fold, turn and seal edges. Place on a floured plate in a polythene bag and rest for 20 minutes in a cool place.

When *third rolling*, as above using last portion of fat but there is no need to rest the dough.

When *fourth rolling*, roll out as before without adding fat. Rest dough as above. Finally roll out to required thickness. Trim edges. Glaze with egg or milk before baking.

450g/1lb plain flour
350g/12oz hard margarine
2 teaspoons lemon juice
285ml/9½fl.oz cold water

FAULTS IN PUFF, ROUGH PUFF AND FLAKY PASTRIES

Pastry hard and tough: too much water added to flour dough. Insufficient fat. Flour dough badly kneaded. Too much flour used during rolling and not brushed off before folding. Over-handling. Pastry not kept cool during rolling. Oven too cool so pastry does not set and fat runs out.

Pastry badly risen. Flour dough too stiff and badly kneaded. Lemon juice omitted. Fat unevenly distributed. Fat too warm and blends with flour instead of remaining in layers. Insufficient resting time between rollings. Not rested in cool place. Too cool an oven.

Pastry unevenly risen. Unevenly rolled. Unevenly folded. Fat unevenly distributed. Sides not kept straight and corners not kept square. Edges not cut off before using pastry. Insufficient resting between rollings or before baking. Uneven oven temperature – pastry rises more quickly on hottest side of oven.

Pastry soggy in middle when cold. Insufficient fat rolled in. Underbaking. Cooked too high in oven. Too hot an oven.

Pastry 'leaking' fat. Too soft a dough. Fat too soft during rolling and folding. Uneven rolling and folding. Oven too cool.

WHOLEMEAL PASTRY

Pastry made from brown flour is good for savoury dishes such as meat pies and sausage rolls, and many people like to use it for all pastry dishes. The pastry is best made with 81% flour, or a mixture of 81% and 100% wholemeal flour. 100% wholemeal flour on its own has a high proportion of coarse bran and is therefore not so good for pastry. Use the same proportion of fat and flour as for white pastry, but add water carefully as the wholemeal flour can take up a good deal of moisture and too much will make the pastry very hard and crisp like a biscuit.

Mixer Shortcrust Pastry

450g/1lb plain flour
Pinch of salt
225g/8oz lard, butter, or
*   lard/margarine*
45ml/3 tablespoons cold
*   water*

Put sifted flour, salt and fat in the mixer bowl and mix on the lowest speed, gradually increasing speed until the mixture is like coarse breadcrumbs. Sprinkle water on the mixture and continue mixing until pastry just binds together. Form into a ball, and roll out on lightly floured board to use as required.

Mixer Sweet Shortcrust Pastry

175g/6oz plain flour
100g/4oz butter
1 teaspoon caster sugar
1 egg yolk
2 teaspoons cold water

Put flour, butter and sugar in the mixer bowl and mix on the lowest speed, gradually increasing speed until mixture is like coarse breadcrumbs. Add egg yolk and water and switch off the mixer as soon as they are incorporated in pastry. Roll on a lightly floured board and use for sweet tarts and flans. This pastry is rather delicate and needs careful handling when rolling.

Mixer Rough Puff Pastry

Sift flour and salt into bowl, and add butter cut into 2.5cm/1in pieces. Mix on minimum speed for 30 seconds. Sprinkle water over and turn off as soon as incorporated in dough. Chill in refrigerator for 10 minutes. Roll out on a lightly floured board into a rectangle 15cm/6in wide and 1.75cm/¾in thick. Fold in three, give pastry one half turn and roll out again. Fold and leave in refrigerator for 15 minutes. Repeat rolling and resting process twice more, then roll out to use as required.

In the following recipes, quantities are given for made pastry so that frozen pastry or pastry made with a packet mix may be substituted.

175g/6oz plain flour
Pinch of salt
150g/5oz butter
45ml/3 tablespoons iced water

Almond Tartlets

Roll out the pastry and cut into 18 rounds to fit small tartlet tins. Put a little jam in the bottom of each pastry case. Whisk the egg whites until stiff and fold in the sugar and almonds. Put on top of the jam in each pastry case. Bake at 350°F/180°C/Gas Mark 4 for 15 minutes.

225g/8oz made shortcrust pastry
2 tablespoons jam
2 egg whites
150g/5oz sugar
100g/4oz ground almonds

Almond Boats

Roll out the pastry thinly and use to line 24 small boat tins. Prick the bottoms of the pastry cases and trim the edges. Beat together the butter and sugar, then mix in the remaining ingredients except icing sugar, water and cherries. Spoon into the prepared tins, set on a baking tray and bake at 400°F/200°C/Gas Mark 6 for 15 minutes until golden brown. Remove the baked boats from their tins carefully with the tip of a sharp knife and cool on a wire rack. Make a thin icing with the icing sugar and water and spoon over the cooled boats. Decorate each with a piece of cherry.

350g/12oz made sweet shortcrust pastry
100g/4oz butter
100g/4oz caster sugar
100g/4oz ground almonds
25g/1oz plain flour
2 eggs
75g/3oz sieved icing sugar
Water to mix
Glacé cherries for decoration

Nineteenth-Century Cheesecakes

225g/8oz made puff pastry
225g/8oz cottage cheese
175g/6oz sugar
6 egg yolks
50g/2oz butter
Pinch of ground nutmeg
Pinch of salt
Grated rind of 2 lemons
Candied peel, currants and
    sultanas

Line 18 small tart tins with the pastry. Sieve the cheese and mix with all the other ingredients except the dried fruit, and put into tart cases. Sprinkle top of each with a mixture of chopped candied peel, currants and sultanas. Bake at 375°F/190°C/Gas Mark 5 until pastry is golden, about 20 minutes.

Apple Strudel

Strudel paste
225g/8oz plain flour
Pinch of salt
1 egg
15ml/1 tablespoon oil
Tepid water

Filling
450g/1lb apples
50g/2oz walnuts
50g/2oz currants or sultanas
2 teaspoons mixed spice
50g/2oz soft brown sugar
2 tablespoons breadcrumbs
65g/2½oz butter

Sieve the flour and salt into a basin and drop the egg into the centre. Mix the oil with 90ml/6 tablespoons tepid water and use the liquid to mix the flour and egg to a smooth dough. Work the dough on a pastry board until smooth and elastic. Cover with a cloth and rest the dough for an hour while preparing the filling. Peel and core the apples and slice very thinly. Add the chopped nuts and fruit, spice and sugar. Fry the breadcrumbs in 25g/1oz melted butter until golden brown.

Put a clean teacloth on the table and flour this lightly. Roll out the dough on the teacloth, then pull and stretch the dough over the backs of the hands until thin and transparent. Trim off the thicker edges. Brush over the entire thin paste with the remaining melted butter and sprinkle the breadcrumbs over, then evenly spread with the apple and fruit mixture. Lifting the cloth by the two nearside corners roll up the dough into a long thin sausage, then bend into a horseshoe shape and place on a baking sheet. Brush over the top of the strudel with any remaining fat and bake at 425°F/220°C/Gas Mark 7 for 30 minutes until crisp and golden brown. Sprinkle thickly with icing sugar and serve in slices.

Apple Crisps

Roll out the pastry to line a tin about 25×20cm/10×8in. Sprinkle with half the breadcrumbs. Warm the jam slightly and spread half of it over the crumbs. Peel the apples and cut them in neat slices in lines on the pastry. Brush with the remaining jam and scatter on the remaining crumbs. Bake at 425°F/220°C/Gas Mark 7 for 20 minutes, and then at 350°F/180°C/Gas Mark 4 for 10 minutes.

350g/12oz made shortcrust pastry
5 tablespoons soft white breadcrumbs
6 tablespoons apricot jam
450g/1lb crisp eating apples

Treacle Apple Squares

Divide the pastry into halves and roll out both pieces to fit a rectangular tin about 17.5×27.5cm/7×11in. Line the tin with half the pastry and prick the bottom well. Peel and core the apples and cut them in thin slices. Mix together the apples, treacle, sugar and cinnamon, and spread the mixture over the pastry. Moisten the edges with water, top with the second piece of pastry and press gently to seal the edges. Bake at 425°F/220°C/Gas Mark 7 for 15 minutes, and then at 350°F/180°C/Gas Mark 4 for 30 minutes. Cool slightly, cut into squares and dust with a little icing sugar.

350g/12oz made shortcrust pastry
675g/1½lb cooking apples
30ml/2 tablespoons black treacle
25g/1oz brown sugar
1 teaspoon ground cinnamon

Pineapple Honey Pie

Cut the pastry in two and roll out each piece to fit a 20cm/8in pie plate. Line the plate with pastry, and arrange the pineapple rings on top. Pour the honey and lemon juice over the pineapple and sprinkle with lemon rind. Damp the edge and cover the pie, sealing the edges firmly. If liked, roll out the trimmings and cut into fancy shapes with a small biscuit cutter. Arrange on the pie and brush with milk. Bake at 375°F/190°C/Gas Mark 5 for 25 minutes. Dust with a little caster sugar before serving.

350g/12oz made shortcrust pastry
550g/20oz tin pineapple rings
15ml/1 tablespoon clear honey
Grated rind and juice of ½ lemon
Milk for glazing

Maple Apple Pie

4 large eating apples
45ml/3 tablespoons maple
   syrup
1 tablespoon plain flour
350g/12oz made shortcrust
   pastry
25g/1oz butter

Peel and core the apples and cut into slices. Toss them with the syrup and flour. Roll out the pastry into two circles and use one to line a 22.5cm/9in pie plate. Fill with apple slices, dot with butter, and cover with the top crust. Flute the edges of the crusts and cut 6 slits in the top. Bake at 400°F/200°C/Gas Mark 6 for 10 minutes. Lower and heat to 375°F/190°C/Gas Mark 5 and bake for 30 minutes.

Four Fruit Pie

225g/8oz cooking apples
225g/8oz dessert pears
350g/12oz plums
225g/8oz blackberries
350g/12oz made flaky pastry
Caster sugar to taste
Milk for glazing

Peel the apples and pears. Slice the apples, cube the pears, and stone the plums. Put the fruit into a large saucepan with very little water. Cover and simmer gently until fruit is almost tender. Drain, reserving the juice and allow the fruit to cool. Divide the pastry in half. Roll one half of the pastry out and use to line a 20cm/8in deep pie plate. Place fruit in the dish with a little of the reserved juice, and add caster sugar to taste. Roll out the remaining pastry, damp edges and use to cover pie. Trim, seal edges well, and pinch decoratively. Use pastry trimmings to make leaves to decorate pie. Brush with a little milk, and sprinkle lightly with caster sugar. Bake at 425°F/220°C/Gas Mark 7 for 20 minutes, then reduce to 350°F/180°C/Gas Mark 4 for 25 minutes.

Norfolk Apple Pie

450g/1lb made shortcrust
   pastry
1kg/2lb cooking apples
25g/1oz butter
1 tablespoon granulated sugar
2 tablespoons orange
   marmalade
1 tablespoon currants
Caster sugar

Line a 22.5cm/9in pie plate with half the pastry. Peel, core and slice the apples and cook them without any water, adding the small knob of butter to prevent them burning. When they are soft, stir in the sugar and beat them to a pulp. Pour half of this into the pastry case, spread over the marmalade, and sprinkle on the currants. Put the remaining apple pulp on the top. Make a lid from the other piece of pastry and put on top. Trim and decorate the edges. Bake at 400°F/200°C/Gas Mark 6 for 15 minutes, then reduce heat to 350°F/180°C/Gas Mark 4 for 20 minutes. Dredge the top with caster sugar and serve hot.

Raisin Pie

Roll out the pastry thinly and use half to line a 20cm/8in plate. Cover with the oatmeal and pour on the treacle. Sprinkle the raisins evenly over the tart. Moisten the edges of the tart with water and cover with the rest of the pastry. Press edges together to seal, and trim off surplus pastry. Flute the edges. Bake at 425°F/220°C/Gas Mark 7 for 30 minutes. Serve hot or cold.

350g/12oz made shortcrust pastry
2 tablespoons oatmeal
30ml/2 tablespoons black treacle
75g/3oz seedless raisins

Special Mince Pie

Line a 20cm/8in pie plate with three-quarters of the pastry. Roll out the remainder into a circle and cut the centre with a drinking-glass. Mix the mincemeat with the apple, ginger, breadcrumbs and rinds and put into the prepared pie plate. Put the top on, seal the edges, brush over with water and dust with sugar. Bake at 400°F/200°C/Gas Mark 6 for 30 minutes. Serve hot or cold.

350g/12oz made sweet shortcrust pastry
450g/1lb fruit mincemeat
225g/8oz finely chopped apple
50g/2oz chopped stem ginger
2 tablespoons breadcrumbs
Grated rind of 1 orange
Grated rind of 1 lemon
Caster sugar

Raspberry and Apple Pie

Peel the apples and slice them thinly. Mix together the apple slices, raspberries, lemon juice, sugar, tapioca flakes and salt. Line a 22.5cm/9in pie plate with half the pastry. Put in the filling and cover with the remaining pastry. Make a slit in the lid and bake at 400°F/200°C/Gas Mark 6 for 20 minutes, and then at 350°F/180°C/Gas Mark 4 for 20 minutes. The tapioca flakes help to make a firm filling which cuts easily.

225g/8oz cooking apples
450g/1lb raspberries
15ml/1 tablespoon lemon juice
225g/8oz sugar
2 tablespoons tapioca flakes
Pinch of salt
350g/12oz made shortcrust pastry

Duke of Cambridge Tart

225g/8oz made shortcrust
    pastry
75g/3oz chunky orange
    marmalade
2 egg yolks
75g/3oz butter
75g/3oz sugar

Line a 20cm/8in flan ring with pastry and bake blind at 400°F/200°C/Gas Mark 6 for 15 minutes. Spread marmalade on the bottom of the pastry. Mix the egg yolks, butter and sugar and cook gently over heat until the mixture bubbles. Pour over the marmalade and bake at 325°F/170°C/Gas Mark 3 for 15 minutes. Serve cold with whipped cream spread on top.

Thame Tart

225g/8oz made shortcrust
    pastry
175g/6oz raspberry jam
175g/6oz lemon curd
300ml/½ pint double cream

Line a 20cm/8in flan ring with pastry and bake blind at 425°F/220°C/Gas Mark 7 for 15 minutes. Remove flan ring and bake for 5 minutes until pastry is lightly golden. Cool the pastry case. Spread in a layer of raspberry jam. Top this with lemon curd, and then with whipped cream.

This was a famous dish in the three inns of John Fothergill about thirty years ago, and was named after his inn 'The Spread Eagle' at Thame. It is very quick and easy to prepare, particularly if ready-baked flan cases are kept in a tin or the freezer, and it is most delicious.

Suffolk Tart

225g/8oz made shortcrust
    pastry
2 egg yolks
25g/1oz sugar
250ml/8fl.oz milk
25g/1oz breadcrumbs
50g/2oz ground almonds
25g/1oz butter
Almond or vanilla essence
1 egg white
1 tablespoon raspberry jam

Line a 20cm/8in flan ring with pastry. Make a custard by blending the egg yolks with the sugar and pouring the warm milk over, mixing well. Return to the pan and cook over gentle heat, stirring all the time, until the custard just coats the back of the spoon. Do not allow it to boil. Stir in the crumbs, almonds, butter and flavouring, then fold in the stiffly whisked egg white. Spread the jam over the pastry case, pour in the filling and bake at 350°F/180°C/Gas Mark 4 for 40 minutes.

Treacle Cream Tart

Line a 20cm/8in flan ring with the pastry. Warm the syrup with the butter, then pour on to the egg and cream beaten together and add the lemon rind. Pour into pastry case, leaving plenty of room for the mixture to rise, and bake at 400°F/200°C/Gas Mark 6 for 30 minutes.

225g/8oz made shortcrust pastry
225g/8oz golden syrup
50g/2oz butter
1 egg
75ml/2½ fl.oz single cream
½ teaspoon grated lemon rind

Coconut Tart

Thoroughly blend the egg yolks with the sugar and flour. Slowly add the boiled milk. Return to the saucepan over a low heat, stirring constantly until the mixture thickens. Do not allow to boil. Leave to cool. Meanwhile, line a 20cm/8in pie plate with the pastry. Prepare the topping by melting the sugar with the water in a saucepan over a low flame. Stir until it begins to thicken. Add the strained coconut and boil until transparent. Pour the filling into the pastry case and cover with the coconut topping. Bake at 375°F/190°C/Gas Mark 5 for 35 minutes.

3 egg yolks
50g/2oz sugar
1 tablespoon plain flour
300ml/½ pint milk
225g/8oz made flaky pastry

Topping
300g/10oz caster sugar
75ml/5 tablespoons water
150g/6oz soaked desiccated coconut

Lemon Meringue Pie

Line a deep 22.5cm/9in pie plate with the pastry and bake blind at 400°F/200°C/Gas Mark 6 for 15 minutes. Remove paper and beans and continue baking for 10 minutes.

Mix sugar, boiling water, cornflour, flour and salt, stirring well over heat until the mixture boils. Cover and cook for 20 minutes in a double saucepan. Add the butter. Lightly beat the egg yolks in a basin and pour on the hot mixture. Return to a double saucepan and cook for 2 minutes. Cool and stir in lemon rind and juice. Fill the pastry case. Whisk the egg whites until very stiff, and fold in the sugar. Pile on top of the lemon filling, and bake at 325°F/170°C/Gas Mark 3 for 15 minutes.

350g/12oz made shortcrust pastry
350g/12oz sugar
360ml/12fl.oz boiling water
4 tablespoons cornflour
4 tablespoons plain flour
Pinch of salt
1 teaspoon butter
4 egg yolks
Grated rind of 2 lemons
150ml/¼ pint lemon juice

Meringue topping
3 egg whites
175g/6oz caster sugar

Honey Cheesecake

100g/4oz cottage cheese
50g/2oz honey
50g/2oz caster sugar
½ teaspoon ground cinnamon
2 eggs
225g/8oz made shortcrust
  pastry

Blend together sieved cottage cheese, honey, sugar, cinnamon and eggs. Line a 20cm/8in pie plate with pastry and fill with the cheese mixture. Sprinkle thickly with a mixture of extra cinnamon and extra caster sugar, and bake at 375°F/190°C/Gas Mark 5 for 35 minutes.

Fresh Fruit Flan

225g/8oz made sweet
  shortcrust pastry
1 tablespoon redcurrant jelly
100g/4oz green grapes
100g/4oz black cherries
1 orange
100g/4oz strawberries

Roll out pastry thinly and use to line a 20cm/8in flan ring. Prick the bottom of the pastry and press a piece of aluminium foil over the surface. Bake at 400°F/200°C/Gas Mark 6 for 25 minutes until light golden. Cool before use. Make a glaze by melting the jelly with a few drops of water in a saucepan. Leave to cool. Cut the grapes in half and remove pips. Stone the cherries and divide the orange in segments. Cut the strawberries in half. About 30 minutes before serving, arrange the fruits over the bottom of the pastry and spoon the glaze over. Serve with whipped cream flavoured with Kirsch.

Apple and Honey Tart

1kg/2lb cooking apples
75ml/5 tablespoons honey
Grated rind of 1 small lemon
25g/1oz butter
1 teaspoon ground cinnamon
1 teaspoon brandy or sherry
225g/12oz made sweet
  shortcrust pastry
3 eating apples
Juice of ½ lemon

Peel and core the cooking apples. Slice and cook gently with 45ml/3 tablespoons water in a covered pan until soft. Add 45ml/3 tablespoons honey, the grated lemon rind, butter and cinnamon and simmer uncovered until reduced to a thick purée. Allow the apple purée to cool and stir in brandy or sherry.

Roll out the pastry and line a 20cm/8in flan ring. Pour on the apple purée. Core the eating apples but do not peel. Halve them and slice very thinly. Arrange on top of the purée. Bake for 30 minutes at 400°F/200°C/Gas Mark 6. Place 30ml/2 tablespoons honey in a pan with the lemon juice and heat gently until the honey dissolves. Brush or spoon over the surface of the tart to give a shiny glaze.

Gooseberry Amber Tart

Line a 20cm/8in flan ring with pastry. Prepare the fruit by topping and tailing. Put in a saucepan with a little water and cook until softened a little, then add sugar and let it dissolve. Continue simmering gently until fruit is pulped. Remove from stove and sieve. When fruit has cooled a little, beat in butter and egg yolks. Bake at 375°F/190°C/Gas Mark 5 for 40 minutes until filling is firm to the touch. Beat whites of egg until stiff and fold in caster sugar. Spread over the pie and return to oven to colour and crisp for 10 minutes.

225g/8oz made shortcrust pastry
675g/1½lb gooseberries
100g/4oz sugar
25g/1oz butter
2 eggs
100g/4oz caster sugar

Cinnamon Plum Tart

Line a 22.5cm/9in pie plate or sandwich tin with pastry fluting the edges. Halve and stone plums and arrange in a pattern, cut side up, all over the pastry. Mix together sugar and cinnamon and sprinkle half on plums. Squeeze over lemon juice and dot with butter. Bake at 350°F/180°C/Gas Mark 4 for 40 minutes, then sprinkle with remaining cinnamon sugar.

225g/12oz made sweet shortcrust pastry
675g/1½lb plums
200g/7oz caster sugar
1 teaspoon ground cinnamon
Squeeze of lemon juice
25g/1oz butter

Peach Pie

Line a 20cm/8in flan ring with pastry. Skin the peaches, halve and remove stones. Arrange peach halves, cut side down. Add almonds and icing sugar to well-beaten eggs and pour over the peaches. Bake at 375°F/190°C/Gas Mark 5 for 40 minutes.

225g/8oz made flaky pastry
450g/1lb fresh peaches
100g/4oz ground almonds
100g/4oz icing sugar
3 eggs

Custard Tart

Line a 20cm/8in flan ring with the pastry and bake blind at 400°F/200°C/Gas Mark 6 for 20 minutes. Remove the paper and beans and cool the pastry slightly. Beat the eggs and sugar together. Heat the milk just to boiling point and pour on to the eggs, stirring continuously. Cool slightly and strain into a jug. Pour carefully into the pastry case and sprinkle with nutmeg. Continue baking for 25 minutes.

350g/12oz made shortcrust pastry
2 eggs
2 tablespoons caster sugar
300ml/½ pint milk
Pinch of ground nutmeg

16 Icings

Many cakes benefit from some kind of icing or decorative topping, but it is very important to choose a suitable finish for individual cakes. A light glacé icing is perfect for sponge cakes for instance, but does not look or taste right with a rich fruit cake; on the other hand the solid royal icing which traditionally tops a Christmas cake would be totally unsuitable for a sponge cake. There are a number of basic icings which may be varied by flavouring and colouring, and also some easy finishes for cakes which do not involve an icing at all.

Decorative Finishes

Whipped cream which has been lightly sweetened may be used for sponge cakes. Swirl it with a fork or the back of a spoon. Sprinkle with coarsely grated chocolate or chopped nuts.

Icing sugar may be sieved over the top of a sponge cake or plain cake to coat the surface with a light dusting of sugar. For a more elaborate design, place a paper doily on top of the cake and shake on the sieved icing sugar. Lift the doily off carefully and the design remains on the cake. Cakes which have been coated with butter cream may be further decorated with icing sugar – do this by placing narrow strips of greaseproof paper on the icing, then dusting with sieved icing sugar. Remove the strips to give a pattern of alternate butter cream and sugar stripes. Chopped nuts may be sprinkled on the alternate stripes. If chopped nuts have been sprinkled thickly on the top and/or sides of a butter cream-iced cake, they can be coated with sifted icing sugar to give a most attractive finish.

Jam may be warmed and brushed thickly on the top and sides of a sponge or plain cake, then sprinkled liberally with coconut or finely chopped blanched or toasted nuts.

Nuts, chocolate vermicelli or grated chocolate may be specified to coat the sides of a cake. To do this professionally, sprinkle the nuts or chocolate thickly on a piece of greaseproof paper. Spread butter cream over the sides of the cake, then hold it by the top and bottom and run the buttercreamed edge like a wheel across the paper so that it picks up the trimmings. Replace on a cake board or serving dish and complete the decoration of the top of the cake.

Icing Equipment

Little equipment is needed for the most simple forms of icing. A nylon sieve is necessary, as wire sieves will spoil the colour of icing sugar. Otherwise only a spoon and bowl are needed for mixing, and a palette knife for applying the icing. A turntable is useful if you do a lot of icing, as the cake can be placed on this and turned slowly so that icing does not become smudged or uneven. If this is not available, a cake board may be placed on an upturned bowl and may easily be rotated. For simple piping, a nylon bag and some basic pipes are useful. A 30cm/12in bag is the most useful size, and the nylon variety may be boiled. A writing tube is useful, and large and small star pipes will give a sufficient variety of patterns for the beginner.

BASIC ICINGS

The recipes in this chapter are for simply made basic icings. Professional bakers make more elaborate versions of these, most of which involve boiling sugar syrups, and if you become very interested in the subject of making icings and decorating cakes, it is worth attending evening classes or buying a special book on the subject.

Glacé Icing is often known as water icing, and is a blend of icing sugar and water or other liquid which spreads very easily and dries quickly. It is suitable for small cakes and light sponges and biscuits. The icing cracks when kept for a few days, so it is best used on cakes which are going to be eaten quickly. This icing also makes biscuits soft, so is best spread on them just before serving. This icing does not hold its shape, and is not used for piping, although it may be thickened and used for writing.

Butter Cream is a mixture of butter, icing sugar and flavouring.

Soft margarine may be used instead and gives a good texture, but is best when combined with strong flavouring such as chocolate or coffee. A higher proportion of icing sugar gives a harder texture, but the icing is never hard enough to use as a substitute for Royal Icing on Christmas cakes, for instance. Butter cream keeps well, and can be frozen, and it is the icing to use for piping on sponges and gâteaux.

Fondant Icing is a boiled icing which can be used to coat light cakes or fruit cakes, with or without almond paste underneath. This icing can be rolled out to coat a cake, or can be moulded into flowers and other shapes. A sugar syrup is necessary for the boiling process, but it is worth making a quantity of this icing at one time as it can be stored. This icing is not suitable for piping.

Uncooked Fondant Icing is sometimes known as Plastic Icing, as it can be moulded and rolled out to coat a cake and to make decorative shapes. It does not become as hard as Royal Icing and is very easy to make.

American Frosting is another boiled icing which needs a sugar thermometer for success. It sets firmly but has a soft texture and may be used on sponges and such things as walnut cakes and chocolate cakes. It may be used instead of Royal Icing for fruit cakes without almond paste underneath, and keeps well. This icing must be handled quickly as it sets fast, and it is not suitable for piping.

Fudge Icing is a combination of a boiled sugar mixture with additional icing sugar. It has a soft spreading consistency and sets well, but hardens with keeping. It is particularly good with chocolate, coffee and spice cakes.

Chocolate may be melted over hot water and used as a simple coating for cakes but tends to be hard and difficult to cut. A little butter beaten into the melted chocolate gives a softer icing which is easier to slice – liquid should not be added to melted chocolate or it will become grey and poorly textured.

Almond Paste or marzipan is a mixture of ground almonds, sugar and egg. It can be mixed with a sugar syrup, but this professional method is rarely used at home. Almond paste is used under other icings or may be used alone to ice a cake, but it is always put on over a thin coating of jam so that cake crumbs do not become mixed with the icing. Almond paste must not be over-handled or it will become oily and spoil the appearance of the top icing.

Royal Icing is for rich fruit cakes for weddings, Christmas etc., as it is firm and will hold decorations, and can also be used for intricate piping. It is not suitable for light textured cakes.

Glacé Icing

a) Mix sieved icing sugar and just enough cold water to give the necessary consistency. 22–30ml/1½–2 tablespoons water will give a soft flowing consistency; 15ml/1 tablespoon will give a firmer consistency.

b) Put the icing sugar and water into a saucepan and stir over very low heat until well blended, which will give a good shine to the icing.

225g/8oz icing sugar
Water

Using Glacé Icing

Make either method a) or b) and add any flavouring required. Fruit juice may be substituted for water, or a few drops of essence, or cocoa powder. Colouring may also be added at this stage, allowing drops to fall from a fine skewer so that the icing is not highly coloured. Beat the icing well and pour on the cake. If necessary, spread quickly with a palette knife, using long sweeping movements. To add decorations, dip them in a little spare icing and place on the half-set icing so that they will not slip. The above recipe will coat the top of a 20cm/8in cake; use 175g/6oz sugar for a 17.5cm/7in cake and 350g/12oz sugar for a 25cm/10in cake. If a cake is more than 5cm/2in deep, double the quantities to coat top and sides.

Butter Cream

Put the butter into a basin. It should be soft but not oily or hot. Sieve in the icing sugar and beat with a wooden spoon until light and fluffy. A little hot water will help to give the icing a soft creamy lightness. Add flavouring and colouring to taste. Additional icing sugar may be added to give a firmer icing but this will be difficult to spread. Margarine may be used instead of butter, but is better when strong flavouring such as cocoa or coffee is used.

100g/4oz unsalted butter
225g/8oz icing sugar

Using Butter Cream

This icing may be used inside cakes as well as on top. To coat the top of a cake, put on all the icing and then spread with long sweeping movements with a palette knife – the icing will never be completely smooth. If liked, the icing may be swirled with the back of a spoon. If the sides of the cake are to be iced, this should be done first and any additional decoration such as chopped nuts applied (see page 177). The above recipe will coat the top of a

20cm/8in cake; use 75g/3oz butter for a 17.5cm/7in cake, or 175g/6oz butter for a 25cm/10in cake, varying the other ingredients in proportion. Allow double icing for top and filling one layer; but treble icing for top, filling and sides.

Simple Almond Paste

100g/4oz icing sugar
100g/4oz caster sugar
225g/8oz ground almonds
1 teaspoon lemon juice
Few drops of almond essence
Beaten egg to mix

Stir the sugars together and add the almonds, lemon juice and almond essence. Add enough egg to bind the mixture and give a firm paste. Knead lightly on a board sprinkled with icing sugar. Egg yolk may be used instead of whole egg for mixing the almond paste, and the egg whites can then be used in the Royal or American icing used on top.

Using Almond Paste
Do not overhandle almond paste as the almond oil will come out and discolour icing placed on top. Roll out the almond paste on a lightly floured board which will prevent sticking. Brush the top of the cake with a little warm jam and coat with almond paste. Leave to dry out for 48 hours without any covering. If you are anxious to finish icing the cake quickly, brush the almond paste with egg white and leave to dry for 15 minutes before putting on the icing – the cake will not need 48 hours' drying time, and the almond paste remains soft but will not spoil the top icing.

To calculate the amount of almond paste necessary for a cake, the above recipe will coat the top of a 20cm/8in round or 17.5cm/7in square cake generously. Double the amount if you wish to coat the sides as well. For the top of a 22.5cm/9in round or 20cm/8in square cake, use 175g/6oz almonds and increase the other ingredients in proportion. For the top of a 25cm/10in round or 22.5cm/9in square cake, use 225g/8oz almonds and other ingredients in proportion.

RIGHT   Coffee eclairs

OVERLEAF   Cake decorations and iced tea cakes

Rich Almond Paste

Stir the almonds and icing sugar together until well mixed and even coloured. Add the vanilla essence, brandy, lemon juice, orange flower water and eggs and work together to make a stiff paste. Knead very thoroughly until the icing is smooth and shiny.

450g/1lb ground almonds
450g/1lb icing sugar
1 teaspoon vanilla essence
1 teaspoon brandy
Juice of 1 lemon
½ teaspoon orange flower water
2 eggs

Royal Icing

Whisk the egg whites lightly, but do not over-beat them. Sieve the icing sugar and add very gradually to the egg whites. Add the lemon juice and continue beating until the icing stands up in peaks and is very white. For coating a cake, the icing should not stand in sharp points, but should be like softly whipped cream. For piping the icing must be capable of standing in stiff upright peaks which is achieved by beating, but not by adding more sugar. Over-beating causes air bubbles which cannot be removed, so take extra care if using an electric mixer. If you do not want very hard icing, add 1 teaspoon glycerine. A softer icing may be obtained by substituting 30ml/2 tablespoons warm water for 1 egg white.

2 egg whites
450g/1lb icing sugar
15ml/1 tablespoon lemon juice

Using Royal Icing

This icing must be applied over a base of almond paste. If the icing is made before it is needed, cover the bowl with a damp cloth so that it does not harden. Put all the icing on top of the cake and gradually work it from the centre over the top and down the sides. Spread the icing over the sides of the cake evenly and then neaten the top of the cake with long sweeping movements of a straight-edged knife or ruler. Neaten the sides with vertical movements of the knife or ruler. Special occasion cakes should have two thinner coats of Royal Icing, rather than one thick one, and the first coat must be thoroughly dried before the second one is applied. This recipe will give one coat for the top and sides of a 17.5cm/7in cake, and leave a little for piping. Double quantities will be needed for two coats of icing.

LEFT   S-shaped biscuits

Fondant Icing

150ml/¼ pint water
450g/1lb granulated sugar
Large pinch of cream of
   tartar

Put the water and sugar into a large heavy saucepan and dissolve the sugar slowly over low heat without stirring. When the sugar has dissolved, bring to the boil, add cream of tartar, and boil to 240°F/120°C. Put into a bowl and leave to cool until a skin forms on the top. Beat until the icing thickens, then turn the fondant on to a cold surface and work with a knife until it is thick and smooth. Knead with the hands to a thick creamy consistency. To use the icing, put it in a bowl over hot water and heat until it looks like thick cream. Pour on to the cake, or dip small cakes into the icing. Fondant icing is best used on top of almond paste. Flavouring and colouring may be added to taste.

Uncooked Fondant Icing

60ml/2fl.oz liquid glucose
1 egg white
450g/1lb icing sugar

Soften the glucose by putting into a cup and standing the cup in hot water. Add the egg white and glucose to sieved icing sugar to make a stiff paste. Turn on to a board and knead well. Roll out like pastry on a little cornflour, which will make the icing shiny. Make the icing the size of the top of the cake and halfway down the sides. Lift on to the cake, and mould down the sides with the hands. This is an easy icing which gives a firm smooth finish to a cake. Flavouring and colouring may be added to taste.

American Frosting

225g/8oz sugar
60ml/4 tablespoons water
1 egg white

Put the sugar and water into a thick saucepan and heat gently, stirring until the sugar has dissolved. Beat to 240°F/120°C without further stirring. Beat the egg white to stiff peaks in a large bowl. Take the hot sugar syrup from the heat and wait until the bubbles die down. Pour it into the bowl while continuing to whisk (an electric mixer is useful for this operation). The mixture will thicken and start to look opaque when it is nearly cold. Pour quickly on to the cake, swirling the frosting into peaks with a palette knife. Add flavouring and colouring to taste.

Seven Minute Frosting

Put all the ingredients into the top of a double saucepan, or into a bowl over a pan of hot water. Have the hot water boiling fast, and beat the mixture hard with an egg beater until stiff enough to stand in peaks, which will take 7 minutes. During cooking, scrape the sides of the bowl from time to time with a spatula. Pour over the cake and swirl the frosting into peaks with a palette knife.

1 egg white
175g/6oz sugar
30ml/2 tablespoons cold water
¼ teaspoon cream of tartar
Pinch of salt

Coconut Frosting

This icing should be made while the cake is cooking. Blend together the sugar, coconut, butter and cream and spread on top of the warm cake. Put under a medium-hot grill until golden brown. This is very good on plain cakes.

175g/6oz dark soft brown sugar
50g/2oz desiccated coconut
30ml/2 tablespoons melted butter
45ml/3 tablespoons double cream

Honey Frosting

Put the honey into a thick saucepan and heat to 240°F/120°C. Whisk the egg white to stiff peaks. Pour on the hot honey while continuing to beat. Beat until the mixture is thick enough to hold its shape. This tastes delicious on spice cakes and gingerbreads.

175g/6oz honey
1 egg white

Brown Sugar Frosting

Put the butter and sugar into a thick saucepan and bring to the boil. Boil and stir for 2 minutes. Add the milk and bring back to the boil, stirring all the time. Pour on to the icing sugar, beating well, until smooth, and put on to the cake.

100g/4oz butter
175g/6oz brown sugar
60ml/4 tablespoons milk
250g/9oz icing sugar

Fluffy Lemon Icing

1 tablespoon grated orange
   rind
40g/1½oz unsalted butter
450g/1lb icing sugar
30ml/2 tablespoons lemon
   juice
15ml/1 tablespoon water

Add the rind to the butter and cream until the butter is very soft. Cream in half the sugar. Add the lemon juice and water alternately with the remaining icing sugar, beating well until soft and smooth.

Coffee Fudge Frosting

50g/2oz butter
350g/12oz icing sugar
30ml/2 tablespoons coffee
   essence
30ml/2 tablespoons single
   cream

Melt the butter very gently. When just melted, take off the heat and add half the icing sugar and the essence. Beat until smooth. Add the remaining icing sugar and then beat in the cream to give a spreading consistency.

Chocolate Glaze

65g/2½oz plain chocolate
65g/2½oz icing sugar
2 tablespoons caster sugar
90ml/6 tablespoons boiling
   water

Put the chocolate into a bowl over hot water and let it melt. Stir in the icing sugar. Put the caster sugar and water into a pan and boil together for 5 minutes. Pour the syrup on to the chocolate mixture and beat hard until the icing is of coating consistency. Pour on the cake while the glaze is still hot.

17 Gluten-Free Recipes

These recipes are suitable for children and adults who are unable to eat ordinary bread and other products which contain wheat, rye or oatmeal flour. None of the ingredients used contains gluten and all are easy to obtain from chemists and health food stores.

The loaves made from these recipes are small, because gluten-free bread stales rapidly. They can best be stored for short periods at normal room temperature in a polythene bag with the end loosely folded underneath the loaf to allow air to circulate.

Long term storage of gluten-free bread, cakes and pastry in a domestic food freezer is most satisfactory. Freeze the products immediately after baking and cooling so that they are at their freshest.

TO FREEZE BREAD

Pack the loaves carefully in polythene bags or freezer foil and seal with as much air as possible excluded. Label packages with contents and date and keep a record of bread in storage so that it may be used within a reasonable period and at its best condition. The high quality storage life of gluten-free bread in a freezer is 4–6 weeks.

Gluten-free bread toasts satisfactorily and toasting is a good way of using slightly stale loaves.

The raising agents used are yeast or gluten-free baking powder.

Gluten-free baking powder may be made at home. All the ingredients are available from the chemist.

Gluten-free Baking Powder

75g/3oz wheat starch
90g/3½oz bicarbonate of soda
50g/2oz cream of tartar
50g/2oz tartaric acid

Mix all ingredients together and rub through a fine sieve. Repeat sieving twice more. Store in an airtight container.

Gluten-free Bread

1 teaspoon sugar
150ml/¼ pint warm water
1 teaspoon dried yeast or
    15g/½oz fresh yeast
175g/6oz gluten-free flour
50g/2oz instant milk powder
½ teaspoon salt
8g/¼oz lard

Grease a 450g/1lb loaf tin. Add the sugar to the water and sprinkle in the dried yeast. Leave until frothy (about 10 minutes) or mix the fresh yeast and water together. Place the dry ingredients in a bowl and rub in the fat. Add the yeast liquid and beat to a smooth batter. Pour into tin. Place the tin in a lightly greased polythene bag and leave until the mixture reaches the top of the tin. Bake at 375°F/190°C/Gas Mark 5 for 30 minutes.

Cheese Loaf
Add 75g/3oz finely grated cheese, seasoned with freshly ground pepper, to the dry ingredients.

Gluten-free Victoria Sandwich Cake

75g/3oz gluten-free flour
1 teaspoon gluten-free baking
    powder
50g/2oz caster sugar
50g/2oz margarine
2 egg yolks
2 teaspoons cold water
2 teaspoons milk
½ teaspoon vanilla essence

Grease and line a 15cm/6in sandwich tin. Sift together the flour and baking powder. Cream together the sugar and margarine. Beat the egg yolks and water together. Add the creamed mixture. Beat well. Fold in the flour carefully. Stir in the milk and vanilla essence. The mixture should be of a dropping consistency. Place in the prepared tin. Bake on the middle shelf of the oven at 350°F/180°C/Gas Mark 4 for 25–30 minutes until lightly brown. Turn out and cool on a wire rack.

Gluten-free Fruit Cake

Line and grease a 15cm/6in round cake tin. Cream together the fat and sugar until light and fluffy. Lightly beat the egg and flavouring. Add gradually to the creamed mixture, beating well. Sift in the wheat starch, gluten-free flour and baking powder. Fold carefully and thoroughly into the creamed mixture. Stir in the dried fruit. Turn into the prepared tin and bake at 350°F/180°C/Gas Mark 4 for 1–1¼ hours until firm and golden. Cool for 10 minutes and remove from tin. Cool on a wire rack.

100g/4oz butter or margarine
100g/4oz caster sugar
2 eggs
75g/3oz wheat starch
75g/3oz gluten-free flour
Pinch of baking powder
175g/6oz sultanas
Lemon juice or vanilla essence

Cinnamon Buns

Sift together the cornflour, cinnamon and baking powder. Cream together the butter and sugar. Beat the eggs and add a little at a time to the creamed mixture, beating well after each addition. Stir in the dry ingredients. Add a little milk if necessary to make a soft mixture. Place spoonfuls into paper cases. Bake at 400°F/200°C/Gas Mark 6 for 15 minutes. When cool, ice and decorate.

225g/8oz cornflour
½ teaspoon ground cinnamon
2 teaspoons gluten-free baking powder
175g/6oz butter or margarine
75g/3oz sugar
2 eggs

Shortbread Biscuits

Grease two baking sheets. Place the butter and flour in a mixing bowl. Rub the fat into the flour until it resembles breadcrumbs. Add the sugar and salt and continue rubbing in until the mixture sticks together. Knead thoroughly. Roll out to 1.25cm/½in thick and cut with a biscuit cutter. Prick well and bake at 350°F/180°C/Gas Mark 4 for 20 minutes until just lightly coloured.

100g/4oz butter
175g/6oz gluten-free flour
50g/2oz caster sugar
Pinch of salt

Gluten-free Sponge Cake

Grease two 17.5cm/7in sandwich tins. Sift together the cornflour, gluten-free flour and baking powder. Separate the eggs, whisk the whites stiffly, then add and beat in the yolks. Gradually add the sugar. Beat until sugar has dissolved. Add the sifted dry ingredients and fold in carefully. Divide into the two tins. Bake on top shelf of oven at 375°F/190°C/Gas Mark 5 for 15 minutes. Cool on a wire rack.

40g/1½oz cornflour
40g/1½oz gluten-free flour
1 teaspoon gluten-free baking powder
3 eggs
100g/4oz sugar

Shortcrust Pastry

75g/3oz margarine
200g/7oz wheat starch
Pinch of salt
1 egg
30–45ml/2–3 tablespoons
  water

Rub fat into the wheat starch and salt. Beat the egg and water together and add to the dry ingredients. Mix in, knead well and turn out on to a board. Roll out and use as required. This recipe makes enough for one 17.5cm/7in flan case or 18 tartlets.

Further information may be obtained from the following:

The Secretary
The Coeliac Society
PO Box 181
London NW2 2QY

This society was inaugurated in 1968 solely to aid coeliac patients. Meetings through the country are held frequently and there is an extensive mailing list to keep members up to date with the latest information regarding foods and recipes for coeliacs. A list of gluten-free products is available from this source, as is a very informative booklet.

An additional list of gluten-free baby foods is available from:
Gerber Baby Council, Claygate House, Esher, Surrey
Telephone: Esher 62181

Other sources of gluten-free information are:
1) Welfare Foods (Stockport) Ltd.,
63–65 Higher Hillgate, Stockport, Cheshire
Telephone 061–480–9408
(Particularly concerned with Rite Diet Flour)

2) Energen Special Wheat Starch and Recipes
Energen Foods Co Ltd., Energen Works, Ashford, Kent
Telephone: Ashford 1180

3) Gluten-free products and recipes for using cornflour:
Brown and Polson Ltd., Claygate House, Esher, Surrey
Telephone: Esher 62181

18 Freezing Bread, Cakes and Pastry

The freezer is a boon to anyone who bakes, for batch baking is practical, saves fuel, and the results can be stored most successfully. Use only good quality packaging materials made especially for use in freezers, e.g. heavy duty foil, polythene bags and sealed polythene containers, and exclude as much air as possible before sealing tightly. Pack fragile foods in polythene or rigid containers after sealing in foil or polythene bags. Be sure to label each package with contents and date. The storage times given should be used as an indication of the length of time goods will keep in perfect condition. Food kept over the suggested time is still quite safe to use but the appearance, flavour and texture may begin to deteriorate.

YEAST

Contrary to popular belief yeast cells are not killed by low temperatures and fresh yeast freezes well.

To freeze, weigh out yeast into 8g/¼oz, 15g/½oz, or 25g/1oz cubes, whichever quantity is normally used. Wrap cubes individually in polythene, label quantities and pack in a freezer container. Label with date. High Quality Storage Life: six months.

To thaw for immediate use, grate yeast coarsely or thaw at room temperature for about 30 minutes.

BREAD

All baked bread freezes well provided it is freshly baked when frozen, but length of storage time varies with the type of bread. To freeze, wrap in heavy duty aluminium foil or polythene bags. If bread is likely to be required quickly, always wrap in foil so that it can be placed frozen in a hot oven to thaw and refreshen. High Quality Storage Life: white and brown bread keep well for up to 4 weeks. Enriched bread and rolls (milk, fruit, malt loaves and soft rolls) keep up to 6 weeks. Crisp crusted loaves and rolls have a limited storage time as the crusts begin to 'shell off' after 1 week. Vienna-type loaves and rolls keep for 3 days only.

To thaw loaves, leave in packaging at room temperature for 3–6 hours depending on the size of loaf or leave overnight in refrigerator or place frozen loaf wrapped in foil in a hot oven, 400°F/200°C/Gas Mark 6 for 45 minutes. Toast: sliced bread can be toasted while frozen. Separate slices carefully with a knife before toasting.

Rolls: leave in packaging at room temperature for 1½ hours or place frozen rolls wrapped in foil in a hot oven, 450°F/230°C/Gas Mark 8 for 15 minutes. Crusty loaves and rolls thawed at room temperature should be refreshed before serving. Place unwrapped loaves or rolls in a hot oven, 400°F/200°C/Gas Mark 6 for 5–10 minutes until crust is crisp.

BREAD DOUGHS

All doughs can be frozen but the storage times vary with the type of dough, plain or enriched, and also whether it is frozen risen or unrisen. All standard bread recipes can be frozen, but the best results are obtained from doughs made with 50% more yeast than is given in the standard recipes, ie. 15g/½oz yeast should be increased to 20g/¾oz.

Freeze dough in quantities you are most likely to use – i.e. 500g/1lb 2oz dough for a 450g/1lb loaf tin. Heavy duty polythene bags, lightly greased, are best. They must be tightly sealed as any air left inside causes skinning on the dough surface which will crack during handling and gives the baked dough crumb a streaky appearance. If there is a chance of the dough rising a little before freezing, leave 2.5cm/1in space above the dough.

Unrisen Dough

To freeze, form dough into a ball after kneading. Place in a large lightly greased polythene bag, seal tightly and freeze immediately. High Quality Storage Life: plain white and brown doughs keep up to 8 weeks. Enriched dough keeps up to 5 weeks.

To thaw, unseal polythene bag and then tie loosely at the top to allow space for rising. Leave for 5–6 hours at room temperature or overnight in the refrigerator. Complete rise in warm place, then knock back, shape, rise and bake.

Risen Dough

To freeze, place dough in a large lightly greased polythene bag, loosely tied at the top and put to rise. Turn risen dough on to a lightly floured surface, flatten firmly with knuckles to knock out air bubbles, then knead until firm. Replace in polythene bag, tightly seal and freeze immediately. High Quality Storage Life: plain and enriched white and brown doughs keep up to 3 weeks. Dough kept longer than these times gives poor results.

To thaw see unrisen dough instructions. After thawing, knock back if required, shape, rise and bake.

Part-Baked Rolls and Loaves

Both home-baked white and wheatmeal rolls can be frozen partly baked. This is a very successful way of freezing rolls as the frozen rolls can be put straight from the freezer into the oven to finish baking. It is the best method of freezing rolls to serve for breakfast. Loaves are not so successful as rolls, because during part-baking the crust becomes well-formed and coloured before the centre of the loaf is set.

To part-bake rolls, place shaped and risen rolls in a slow oven, 300°F/150°C/Gas Mark 2 for about 20 minutes. The rolls must be set, but still pale in colour. Cool on a wire rack.

To freeze, pack cooled rolls in usable quantities in heavy duty foil or polythene bags. Seal and freeze. As the sides of the rolls are still slightly soft, care must be taken when packing not to squash them. High Quality Storage Life: up to four months.

To thaw and finish baking, unwrap and place frozen rolls in oven to thaw and complete baking. Bake white rolls at 400°F/200°C/Gas Mark 6; brown rolls at 450°F/230°C/Gas Mark 8 for 20 minutes.

OTHER BREADS – CROISSANTS AND DANISH PASTRIES

Both baked croissants and Danish pastries freeze well. The unbaked dough can also be frozen in bulk.

Unbaked Dough

Prepare to stage when all fat has been added, but do not give final rolling. *To freeze*, wrap in polythene and seal tightly, label and freeze immediately. High Quality Storage Life: up to 6 weeks.

To thaw, leave in polythene bag, unseal and re-tie loosely, allowing space for dough to rise. If possible thaw overnight in a refrigerator, or leave 5 hours at room temperature. Complete final rolling, shaping and baking.

Baked Croissants

To freeze, pack in a single layer in a polythene bag or heavy duty foil, or place in a foil tray sealed with foil. High Quality Storage Life: up to 8 weeks.

To thaw, leave in packaging at room temperature for 1½–2 hours then refresh, wrapped in foil, in a hot oven, 425°F/220°C/Gas Mark 7 for 5 minutes; or place frozen, wrapped in foil, in a moderate oven, 350°F/180°C/Gas Mark 4 for 15 minutes.

Baked Danish Pastries

It is preferable to freeze the pastries without icing so that they can be refreshed in the oven, but they can be frozen when iced. *To freeze*, pack cooled pastries in a sealed polythene container or in heavy duty foil. High Quality Storage Life: up to 4 weeks.

To thaw iced pastries, leave in loosened packaging at room temperature for 1½ hours. Plain pastries: treat as iced pastries, then refresh in a moderate oven, 350°F/180°C/Gas Mark 4 for 5 minutes. Frozen pastries may be put straight into the oven at a temperature of 350°F/180°C/Gas Mark 4 and heated for 10 minutes.

SAVARINS, BABAS, BRIOCHES AND TEABREADS

For best results, bake then freeze. *To freeze*, wrap in heavy duty foil or polythene bags, then if decorated, in boxes. High Quality Storage Life: Savarins and Babas – up to 3 months; Brioches – up to 4 weeks; Teabreads – up to 6 weeks.

To thaw Savarins – leave in packaging at room temperature for 2–3 hours. Complete and serve. Babas: place frozen, wrapped in foil, in a hot oven, 400°F/200°C/Gas Mark 6 for 10–15 minutes or leave in packaging for 45 minutes at room temperature. Complete and serve. Brioches – place frozen, wrapped in foil, on baking tray in a hot oven, 450°F/230°C/Gas Mark 8 for 10 minutes. Teabreads: leave in packaging at room temperature for 2–3 hours or, if undecorated, place foil-wrapped loaf in moderate oven, 350°F/180°C/Gas Mark 4 for 15–20 minutes.

PIZZA

Freeze either unbaked or baked. *To freeze unbaked*, prepare to baking stage. Wrap in heavy duty foil or polythene. High Quality Storage Life: up to 3 months.

To thaw, remove packaging and place frozen in cold oven set at 450°F/230°C/Gas Mark 8. Turn on oven and bake for 30–35 minutes.

To freeze baked, wrap cooled pizza in heavy duty foil or polythene. High Quality Storage Life: up to 2 months.

To thaw, remove packaging and place frozen in a hot oven, 400°F/200°C/Gas Mark 6 for 20 minutes, or leave in packaging at room temperature for 2 hours before baking for 10–15 minutes.

BAKED CAKES AND SCONES

Scones and all types of baked cakes, plain or rich, freeze well. Swiss rolls, sponge cakes and flan cases, which do not keep long after baking, freeze extremely well. Cakes can be frozen undecorated or decorated. As rich fruit cakes keep satisfactorily in airtight tins there is little point in freezing them.

Scones and Undecorated Cakes

To freeze, wrap cooled scones and cakes well in foil or polythene bags. High Quality Storage Life: undecorated cakes – up to 6 months.

To thaw scones – leave in packaging at room temperature for 1–1½ hours or place frozen, wrapped in foil, in a fairly hot oven, 400°F/200°C/Gas Mark 6 for 10 minutes.

Undecorated cakes – leave in packaging at room temperature. Small cakes take 1 hour, larger cakes 2–3 hours, sponge cakes and flans 1½–2 hours, Swiss roll 2–2½ hours.

Decorated Cakes

Freeze unwrapped to prevent damage to decoration. When frozen wrap well in foil and place in boxes for protection. High Quality Storage Life: decorated cakes – up to 3 months.

To thaw, unwrap to prevent wrapping sticking to cake during thawing and leave at room temperature for 2–4 hours depending on size.

UNBAKED CAKE MIXTURES

Rich creamed mixtures e.g. for a Victoria sandwich, freeze satisfactorily. Whisked sponge cake mixtures do not freeze well.

To freeze, place creamed mixtures in sealed polythene containers or cartons in usable quantities *or* line cake tin with greased foil, add cake mixture and freeze uncovered. When frozen remove from tin, wrap in heavy duty foil and seal tightly. High Quality Storage Life: up to 2 months.

To thaw, leave mixture in cartons at room temperature for 2–3 hours, then fill tins and bake. Return mixture frozen in tin shape to original tin and place frozen and uncovered in a pre-heated oven. Bake as usual allowing about 5 minutes extra for a sandwich cake, longer for deeper cakes.

Icings and fillings which freeze well are: butter cream, fresh whipped cream, glacé icing, almond paste, jam glazes. Boiled icing, e.g. American frosting, soft meringue icing and custard cream filling do not freeze satisfactorily.

UNBAKED BISCUIT MIXTURES

Any biscuit mixture containing over 100g/4oz fat to 450g/1lb flour freezes satisfactorily. Biscuits which are cut out are difficult to store without damage and the easiest way to freeze the mixture is in rolls of the same diameter as the required biscuit. Several different flavours can be made from one large batch of mixture. Soft mixture can be piped before freezing. *To freeze*, wrap each roll individually in heavy duty foil and seal. Pipe or spoon soft biscuit mixtures on to a baking sheet and freeze uncovered on the tray. When frozen, lift off with a palette knife and pack in polythene bags or containers and seal. High Quality Storage Life: up to 6 months.

To thaw, leave rolls of mixture in packaging at room temperature until sufficiently soft to cut into slices. Bake as normal. Place frozen piped or spooned biscuits on a baking tray and bake at usual temperature, allowing about 5 minutes longer than normal.

PASTRY

Many people like to make a large batch of pastry and prepare a lot of recipes at the same time for freezing. Bulk pastry can be stored, or prepared pastry cases, or complete pies. Foil and polythene are excellent freezer wrappings for these items, but delicate baked goods are best packed in boxes to avoid crushing. Unbaked pastry will store for 3 months; baked pastry for 6 months, although there is little point in keeping food for so long. Pies of all kinds are at their best if kept no longer than 1–2 months.

Shortcrust Pastry

Shortcrust pastry frozen in bulk takes 3 hours at room temperature to thaw before it can be rolled and there is little advantage in freezing it this way. Shape into pies, flan cases, tartlets or pie lids before freezing, unbaked or baked.

Unbaked Pastry High Quality Storage Life: 3 months.

Pies, large and small: make large pies in foil dishes or plates. Make small pies in patty tins or foil dishes. Do not make a steam vent in lid. Freeze uncovered. When frozen, leave large and small pies in foil dishes, and seal with foil. Remove small pies from patty tins and pack in heavy duty foil or polythene bags.

Flan cases: freeze in flan ring or foil case until hard. Remove ring or case, wrap in a polythene bag or heavy duty foil, then in a box for protection. Tartlet cases: freeze uncovered in patty tins. When frozen remove from tins, pack in polythene or heavy duty foil and pack in a box.

Pie lids: prepare in quantity and cut into shape to fit pie dish. Freeze uncovered. Pack several together separated by foil or polythene sheets and then in a box.

To thaw unbaked pastry Pies: unwrap and place in a pre-heated oven and bake as usual allowing extra time for thawing. Cut a vent in the pastry when it begins to thaw. Flan cases: unpack and place frozen case into flan ring on a baking sheet. Bake blind at 400°F/200°C/Gas Mark 6 for 20–25 minutes.

Tartlet cases: unpack and place frozen into patty tins and bake at 400°F/200°C/Gas Mark 6 for 20–25 minutes, reduce oven to 300°F/150°C/Gas Mark 2 and bake for a further 10–15 minutes.

Baked Pastry High Quality Storage Life: meat pies 3–4 months; fruit pies up to 6 months; unfilled pastry cases up to 6 months.

Pies, large and small: bake in foil dishes or plates. Cool quickly, leave in the dish and pack in heavy duty foil. Freeze immediately.

Flan and tartlet cases: pack cooled cases in sealed polythene containers, polythene bags or heavy duty foil and then into a box.

To thaw Pies: leave at room temperature for 2–4 hours depending on size of pie. Reheat in oven if required hot. Flan and tartlet cases: leave at room temperature for about 1 hour.

Flaky and Puff Pastry

Unbaked Pastry High Quality Storage Life: 3 months.
Bulk pastry: prepare up to last rolling. Pack in polythene bags or heavy duty foil.

Pies: freeze as for shortcrust pastry pies.

Pie lids: freeze as for shortcrust pastry.

Vol-au-vent cases: prepare in quantity, freeze uncovered on a baking sheet or tray. When frozen, pack in sealed polythene containers, or wrap in polythene bags or heavy duty foil and pack in box.

To thaw unbaked pastry Bulk pastry: leave 3–4 hours at room temperature or overnight in the refrigerator.

Pies: unwrap and place frozen in oven. Bake flaky pastry at 425°F/220°C/Gas Mark 7 for 25 minutes. Bake puff pastry at 450°F/230°C/Gas Mark 8 for 15–20 minutes. Reduce both oven temperatures to 375°F/190°C/Gas Mark 5 if filling requires longer.

Pie lids: dampen edge of filled pie dish and place frozen lid on top. Bake as above for pies.

Vol-au-vent cases: place frozen on a baking sheet in a hot oven, at 450°F/230°C/Gas Mark 8 for 15 minutes.

Baked pastry Pies and vol-au-vent cases can be frozen baked but are fragile to store and take up more room than when frozen unbaked. Pack carefully in sealed polythene containers. High Quality Storage Life: up to 6 months.

To thaw baked pastry Pies: leave at room temperature for 2–4 hours depending on size. Reheat if required.

Vol-au-vent cases: leave at room temperature for 1 hour or place frozen cases uncovered in a hot oven at 450°F/230°C/Gas Mark 8 for 5–10 minutes.

Pies

Complete pies can be frozen cooked or uncooked depending on the filling. A baked pie usually keeps longer (depending on the filling), but an unbaked pie has a better flavour and smell, and the pastry is crisper and flakier if freshly baked before serving.

Baked Pies Pies should be cooled quickly before freezing, and they are most easily stored if prepared and frozen in foil. The container can be covered with foil or put into a polythene bag for freezing.

Unbaked Pies Pies with or without bottom crusts can be frozen. To prevent sogginess, freeze unbaked pies on a metal or plastic tray before wrapping. Don't cut air vents in pies before freezing, but do this just before baking. Bake without thawing, and allow ten minutes longer than normal cooking time.

Meat Fillings Meat pies, pasties and turnovers can be cooked completely, so that they can be served cold after thawing, or reheated. Preparation time is saved if the filling is cooked, then topped with uncooked pastry for freezing. The time taken to cook the pastry after freezing takes little longer than heating the whole pie. To stop a bottom crust of a plate pie becoming soggy, brush the surface with melted lard before putting in the filling.

Fruit fillings Fruit pies may be frozen with cooked or uncooked fillings, but apples tend to turn brown if stored in a pie for more than four weeks, even if dipped in lemon juice. It is better to combine frozen pastry and frozen apples to make a pie if necessary.

Surplus fruit can be made into pie fillings for freezing, ready to pair with fresh or frozen pastry when needed. Freeze the fruit mixture in a pie plate lined with foil, then remove from the container and wrap in the foil for storage. Use the same container for making up the pie later. A little arrowroot, cornflour or flaked tapioca mixed with fruit will give a firm pie filling which cuts well and does not seep into bottom pastry. If the surface of the bottom crust of fruit pies is brushed with egg whites, they will not become soggy after thawing.

Open Tarts and Quiches These can be completely cooked before freezing. It is best to open-freeze these on metal or plastic trays before wrapping, to avoid damaging the surface of the filling. If they are prepared in foil pie plates for freezing, the filling is often rather shallow. For a deep filling, make in a flan ring, but after open-freezing, pack into a box to avoid breaking the sides.

Index